Broadcasting Propaganda

Recent titles in the PRAEGER SERIES
IN POLITICAL COMMUNICATION
Robert E. Denton, Jr., *General Editor*

BROADCASTING PROPAGANDA

International Radio Broadcasting
and the Construction of
Political Reality

PHILO C. WASBURN

Praeger Series in Political Communication

PRAEGER

Westport, Connecticut
London

Library of Congress Cataloging-in-Publication Data

Wasburn, Philo C.
    Broadcasting propaganda : international radio broadcasting and the
construction of political reality / Philo C. Wasburn.
        p.   cm. — (Praeger series in political communication)
    Includes bibliographical references and index.
    ISBN 0–275–93841–7 (alk. paper)
    1. International broadcasting—Political aspects.   2. Radio in
propaganda.   3. Radio in politics.   I. Title.   II. Series.
HE8697.8.W37   1992
327.1′4—dc20   92–15783

British Library Cataloguing in Publication Data is available.

Library of Congress Catalog Card Number: 92–15783
ISBN: 0–275–93841–7

First published in 1992

Praeger Publishers, 88 Post Road West, Westport, CT 06881
An imprint of Greenwood Publishing Group, Inc.

Printed in the United States of America

The paper used in this book complies with the
Permanent Paper Standard issued by the National
Information Standards Organization (Z39.48–1984).

10 9 8 7 6 5 4 3 2 1

The person who imagines that he could not be the victim of propaganda because he could distinguish truth from falsehood is exceedingly susceptible to propaganda, because when propaganda does tell the "truth," he is convinced that it is no longer propaganda.

Jacques Ellul

Credibility in the mind of the audience is the *sine qua non* of news. All else is either propaganda or entertainment.

Anthony Smith

To Mara, Aaron, Leah, and Hope

Contents

Tables

Series Foreword

In several other forums I have argued that the essence of politics is "talk" or human interaction.[1] Such interaction may be formal or informal, verbal or nonverbal, public or private but it is always persuasive, forcing us consciously or subconsciously to interpret, to evaluate, and to act. Communication is the vehicle for human action.

From this perspective, it is not surprising that Aristotle recognized the natural kinship of politics and communication in his writings *Politics* and *Rhetoric*. In the former, he establishes that humans are "political beings [who] alone of the animals [are] furnished with the faculty of language."[2] And in the latter, he begins his systematic analysis of discourse by proclaiming that "rhetorical study, in its strict sense, is concerned with the modes of persuasion."[3] Thus, it was recognized over twenty-three hundred years ago that politics and communication go hand in hand because they are essential parts of human nature.

Back in 1981, Dan Nimmo and Keith Sanders proclaimed that political communication was an emerging field.[4] Although its origin, as noted, dates back centuries, a "self-consciously cross-disciplinary" focus began in the late 1950s. Thousands of books and articles later, colleges and universities offer a variety of graduate and undergraduate coursework in the area in such diverse departments as communication, mass communication, journalism, political science, and sociology.[5] In Nimmo and Sanders's early assessment, the "key areas of inquiry" included rhetorical analysis, propaganda analysis, attitude change studies, voting studies, government and the news media, functional and systems analyses, technological changes, media technologies, campaign techniques, and research techniques.[6] In a survey of the state of field in 1983, the same authors and Lynda Kaid, found additional, more specific areas of concern such as the presidency, political polls, public opinion, debates, and advertising to name a few.[7] Since the first study, they also noted a shift away from the rather strict behavioral approach.

Today, Dan Nimmo and David Swanson assert that "political communication has developed some identity as a more or less distinct domain of scholarly work."[8] The scope and concerns of the area have further expanded to include critical theories and cultural studies. While there is no precise definition, method, or disciplinary home for the area of inquiry, its primary domain is the role, processes, and effects of communication within the context of politics broadly defined.

In 1985, the editors of *Political Communication Yearbook: 1984* noted that "more things are happening in the study, teaching, and practice of political communication than can be captured within the space limitations of the relatively few publications available."[9] In addition, they argued that the backgrounds of "those involved in the field [are] so varied and pluralist in outlook and approach, . . . it [is] a mistake to adhere slavishly to any set format in shaping the content."[10] And more recently, Swanson and Nimmo called for "ways of overcoming the unhappy consequences of fragmentation within a framework that respects, encourages, and benefits from diverse scholarly commitments, agendas, and approaches."[11]

In agreement with these assessments of the area and with gentle encouragement, in 1988 Praeger established the series entitled "Praeger Series in Political Communication." The series is open to all qualitative and quantitative methodologies as well as contemporary and historical studies. The key to characterizing the studies in the series is the focus on communication variables or activities within a political context or dimension. Scholars from the disciplines of communication, history, political science, and sociology have participated in the series. To date, there are nearly fifty titles in the series.

In this volume, Philo Wasburn, a political sociologist, identifies the social structures and processes that have shaped and continue to influence international radio broadcasting. Drawing on the social construction of reality perspective, on media system dependency theory, and on empirical studies of the politics of the mass media, he analyzes the political functions performed by international broadcasting organizations such as the British Broadcasting Corporation, the Voice of America, and Radio Moscow for their sponsoring nations.

For most Americans, where television is the primary source of political information, it may be surprising to learn that international radio broadcasting is a primary source of political information for hundreds of millions of people throughout the world. For many nations, international broadcasts provide the only source for comprehensive and relatively unbiased news of national and international politics. Today, more than eighty nations actively support international radio broadcasts targeted to listeners outside their national borders. Thus, since Guglielmo Marconi produced the first transatlantic wireless signal in 1901, radio has served as an important tool for political propaganda and the symbolic construction of political reality.

Wasburn provides another important contribution to the study of political communication that deserves wide attention from both students and scholars. It is a unique study of the role and importance of the medium of radio. As a medium, radio has largely been ignored, while focus upon television and newspapers has steadily increased. Second, this study provides an international perspective on political communication. Too many of our studies are limited to American politics and campaigns. As an area of scholarship, we need more studies of the role of communication in politics beyond the American experience. Third, the author contributes to the research and literature on political propaganda with excellent contemporary and historical examples and case studies. Finally, this work provides genuine insight and clarity as well as demonstrates the importance of the theoretical perspectives of symbolic interactionism and the social construction of reality.

I am, without shame or modesty, a fan of the series. The joy of serving as its editor is in participating in the dialogue of the field of political communication and in reading the contributors' works. I invite you to join me.

Robert E. Denton, Jr.

NOTES

1. See Robert E. Denton, Jr., *The Symbolic Dimensions of the American Presidency* (Prospect Heights, IL: Waveland Press, 1982); Robert E. Denton, Jr. and Gary Woodward, *Political Communication in America* (New York: Praeger, 1985, Second Edition, 1990); Robert E. Denton, Jr., and Dan Hahn, *Presidential Communication* (New York: Praeger, 1986); and Robert E. Denton, Jr., *The Primetime Presidency of Ronald Reagan* (New York: Praeger, 1988).

2. Aristotle, *The Politics of Aristotle*, trans. Ernest Barker (New York: Oxford University Press, 1970), p. 5.

3. Aristotle, *Rhetoric*, trans. Rhys Roberts (New York: The Modern Library, 1954), p. 22.

4. Dan Nimmo and Keith Sanders, "Introduction: The Emergence of Political Communication as a Field," in *Handbook of Political Communication*, Dan Nimmo and Keith Sanders, eds. (Beverly Hills, CA: Sage, 1981), pp. 11–36.

5. Ibid., p. 15.

6. Ibid., pp. 17–27.

7. Keith Sanders, Lynda Kaid, and Dan Nimmo, eds. *Political Communication Yearbook: 1984* (Carbondale, IL: Southern Illinois University, 1985), pp. 283–308.

8. Dan Nimmo and David Swanson, "The Field of Political Communication: Beyond the Voter Persuasion Paradigm," in *New Directions in Political Communication*, David Swanson and Dan Nimmo, eds. (Beverly Hills, CA: Sage, 1990), p. 8.

9. Sanders, Kaid, and Nimmo, p. xiv.

10. Ibid., p. xiv.

11. Nimmo and Swanson, p. 11.

Introduction

Guglielmo Marconi realized some of the implications of his successful production of the first transatlantic wireless signal on December 12, 1901. Wireless across the sea meant the very shrinkage of the earth. It meant new and revolutionary communication among all the nations on the face of the globe. He later reflected:

It is difficult to estimate the enormous influences broadcasting is going to exert on humanity in a hundred different directions. For the first time in the history of the world, man is now able to appeal by means of direct speech to millions of his fellows, and there is nothing to prevent an appeal being made to fifty millions of men and women at the same time. (Dunlap 1937: 137)

Marconi underestimated the importance of his invention. Today, hundreds of millions of people throughout the world depend on international radio broadcasting (IRB) for their understanding of the political world. In Western industrial nations, IRB serves some listeners as a source of political information, ideas, and perspectives that receive little attention in their domestic media. This is true despite the common assumption that the numerous, competitive domestic media in these nations make available to all citizens the expression of a wide range of political viewpoints and relatively comprehensive, presumably unbiased accounts of national and international politics. Censorship in other parts of the globe makes international broadcasts the only alternative to total reliance on a media directly controlled by the government. Illiteracy in most of the poorer nations makes international broadcasting one of the few alternatives that millions of people can find to ignorance of political affairs.

Marconi's invention would provide nations that were far distant from one another socially, culturally and politically as well as geographically with a new means for immediate, direct, and extensive communication. It could be used to reduce misperception of one nation by another and thereby reduce the likelihood of international conflict. Marconi saw himself as a man who dealt in cold, scientific facts and practicalities, not utopian fantasies (Dunlap 1937: 333). However, his dream was to have produced a device the use of which might encourage mutual understanding, trust, and peace among nations (Briggs 1961: 309).

Marconi's initial thoughts about his discovery, however, were considerably less idealistic. When first asked about its utility, Marconi replied, without hesitation, simply that it might be used for military purposes, in place of the field telegraph. It was only later that he pondered its potential contribution to world harmony (Dunlap 1937: 64).

From the very beginning, others, as well, focused on the military, economic, and political significance of long distance wireless communication. In 1916, Russia transmitted Morse bulletins encouraging German troops to mutiny (Radio Nederland Wereldomroep 1982). A year later, on the morning of the Bolshevik seizure of power, Vladimir Lenin broadcasted from the cruiser *Aurora*, proclaiming what had been accomplished by the revolution and elaborating his vision of the future. The broadcast was heard not only in Russia but also in Germany, France, and Austria (Paulu 1974: 33). During the late 1920s and early 1930s, the Netherlands, France, and Great Britain initiated international radio services to help maintain and strengthen their lucrative ties with overseas possessions.

With the outbreak of World War II, IRB entered its most notorious period. In France, Britain, and the United States, extensive government use of the means of mass communication to motivate citizens to act in support of the state, such as occurred in the Soviet Union, Italy, and Germany, was seen as a threat to the very existence of democracy. Furthermore, the use of information manipulation as an international tool of diplomacy was considered unnecessary and contrary to the received rules of foreign relations (Short 1983: 1). However, Germany's aggressive use of the radio, which commenced almost immediately after Hitler was named chancellor in 1933, eventually modified these views. Within the United States, during World War II, the radio industry ultimately made all its resources available to the federal government. War information messages, programming supporting the war effort, the selling of war bonds, campaigns to reduce civilian usage of important materials, and other services were performed (DeFleur and Ball-Rokeach 1989: 108). Internationally, radio counterattacks against Germany were waged by the British, who soon were joined by the Free French and Norwegians and later by the Americans. Prompted by the war, short-wave covered the world by 1941, with broadcasts in forty languages transmitted from fifty-five countries (Abshire 1976: 21).

The experience of World War II made it clear that no country can afford to ignore the effects its foreign policy will have on world opinion generally as well as on states directly affected by it. In that sense at least, the world is indeed a global village. The fact that almost every nation has developed an international radio service is a reflection of this and a gesture of conciliation toward world opinion (Hale 1975: xxii).

Soon after the war, the Soviet Union took the position that Western international broadcasting had begun to interfere with its internal affairs and that Soviet broadcasts were intended to counter hostile commentary. Following the communist takeover of Czechoslovakia, the possibility of a communist victory in the 1948 Italian elections and the Berlin Blockade, the United States responded with the creation of international radio services targeted to the Soviet Union and Eastern Europe. The services, which joined those of Great Britain and later would be joined by those of West Germany, purportedly were to bring reliable and credible programs from the West, eliminate distortion in the flow of information on world politics, and remove artificially created mistrust between East and West (Deutsche Welle 1982; Mickelson 1983).

Worldwide, over eighty countries now support radio broadcasting services addressed to listeners outside their national boundaries. Today, the stations of Russia (Radio Moscow), the United States (Voice of America, Radio Free Europe/Radio Liberty), and Great Britain (British Broadcasting Corporation) remain among the world's leading international broadcasting organizations (British Broadcasting Corporation 1990: 55). This book focuses on the so-called news presented by these and several other major broadcasters. It is this material that most IRB listeners tune in to hear (Abshire 1976: 80–81; Browne 1982: 332; Hachten 1987: 94–96). It is also the material to which international radio broadcasting organizations assign greatest importance (British Broadcasting Corporation 1990: 54–56; Browne 1983; United States Information Agency 1986: 12).

Throughout the world, all or almost all of what anyone knows about the political affairs in which he or she has any interest is not likely to be the result of direct personal experience. Rather, it is likely to come from direct or indirect contact with media of mass communications; it is the result of reading, hearing, seeing, discussing, or being told "the news." However, " 'news' is not what happens, but what someone [a source] says has happened or will happen" (Sigal 1973: 15). It is *language* about political actors, conditions, and events, and not actors, conditions, and events in any other sense, that people usually experience. Political language is political reality; there is no other so far as the meaning of political phenomena to spectators is concerned (Edelman 1988: 104–105). "Reality is created or constructed through communication, not expressed by it" (Nimmo and Combs 1983: 3). The symbolic constructions that are labeled news by international broadcasting organizations embody the appeals made to millions throughout the world through the use of Marconi's invention.

In cases where media audiences simply do not attend to the constructed nature of media accounts of politics, they are likely to label such accounts news. When they are more aware of their constructed nature, they are more likely to label such presentations editorials. When audiences understand media accounts of political phenomena as constructed explicitly to serve political goals, particularly goals that they do not share, they are more likely to label such presentations propaganda. However, whether people view themselves as confronting news, editorials, or propaganda, it is experiences with these symbolic materials that shape what they believe, question, or do not believe about political reality. Throughout most of the world today, hundreds of millions of people depend on IRB to provide such experiences.

In this book, and contrary to popular usage, to label messages propaganda is not to render a judgment about their truth or falsity, on whatever basis such an assessment might be made. Nor does the label suggest that the messages, if believed by their intended audiences, will benefit or disadvantage them in particular ways. IRB is not well understood as an effort to reduce misperceptions of one nation by another and thereby reduce the likelihood of international conflict. On the other hand, neither is it well understood as the transmission of intentionally deceitful statements by one nation to others on the assumption that deception is a useful and essential component of all international competition and conflict. Broadcasting propaganda can involve efforts at candor, deceit, or both. IRB is best understood as an effort to maintain or change perceptions through a variety of symbolic means and thereby produce some desired political effects.

Political behavior can be viewed as a response to political images that are shaped in a complex process of transmission and feedback involving various communication networks (Boulding 1961). IRB is an important component of worldwide communications networks. The images that are conveyed by IRB are constructed symbolic realities. They are accounts, in one form or another, of political actors, conditions, and events. The accounts can be understood as intended to serve political-economic and, occasionally, military interests.

The international media of countries with conflicting interest construct conflicting accounts of politically sensitive occurrences. This was vividly illustrated in September 1983 when a South Korean airliner was shot down by Soviet interceptor planes after intruding inside Soviet airspace. U.S. and Soviet reports of the event vastly differed (Herman and Chomsky 1988: 32–33; Edelman 1988: 70; Parenti 1986: 156–60). Similarly, during the Persian Gulf War, accounts by Radio Baghdad concerning the bombing of civilian targets directly contradicted accounts broadcast by the Voice of America (Freed 1991).

It is tempting to ask which, if either, nation told the truth about each of the occurrences. However, this question is quite misleading, for it rests on a number of problematic assumptions, which will be discussed in Chapter Three. Here, several related arguments, which are developed in that chapter and elaborated throughout the book, can be stated briefly. First, all broadcast accounts of politically relevant occurrences are symbolic constructions whose components derive their meaning from the political culture in which they are embedded. Language embodies cultural understanding, directing attention toward certain features of occurrences while obscuring others. Second, all broadcast accounts of politically relevant occurrences are socially negotiated and reflect political-economic interests and related institutional practices of information gathering and reporting. (Relevant interests range from those of the state, to dominant groups, including government, to the international broadcasting organizations and those who pursue their careers within them.)

Third, the formal, structural links of a nation's international broadcasting organization to its government influence the extent to which government interests are explicitly and deliberately considered in the construction of the organization's accounts of political affairs. However, no official international broadcast organization, whether it is located in a democratic or a nondemocratic state or in a state with a market or a nonmarket economy, is entirely free from the influences of government and/or of individuals holding positions of power and authority in the major institutions of its society. Fourth, the claim of commitment to broadcasting the truth, however sincerely that claim might be made and however it might be supported, nevertheless can be understood as a strategy for winning acceptance for constructions of political reality. It is a strategy employed more or less explicitly, more or less cynically, and more or less effectively by all international radio broadcasting organizations. Finally, all international broadcasting organizations claim, with varying degrees of explicitness, that constructions of political reality differing from those it offers are biased accounts of the political world.

This book explores the role that the use of Marconi's invention has come to play in the structure of world political, economic, and military competition. IRB has become an important means by which most of the nations of the world, and many opposition groups, attempt to define politically relevant actors, events, conditions, and structures, past and present, for foreign audiences that they consider politically, economically, and militarily important. Broadcasts are intended to influence target audience definitions of political situations and thereby have some influence on their future patterns of political behavior. Factual claims, official reports, political language, and national images all play important roles in this form of political communication: broadcasting propaganda.

Understanding the present structures, activities, and goals of the organizations that today carry on IRB is aided considerably by some familiarity with their social-political histories. Since the history of IRB is relatively obscure, the first two chapters of this book are devoted to describing the origins and development of the organizations that today are major participants in the international system of competition to win acceptance for their constructions of political reality via shortwave radio.

The third chapter examines the concept of propaganda. The term *propaganda* largely has fallen into disuse in social science literature, primarily as a result of the negative connotations it acquired long after its introduction in the seventeenth century. The term has been replaced by other less obviously pejorative terms such as *persuasive communication*. However, it will be argued that *propaganda* can be defined in a way that gives it considerable analytic utility. The chapter reviews two theoretical perspectives that together provide a basis for understanding propaganda as it is broadcast by international radio stations. The first, the social construction of reality perspective, is most commonly associated with the discipline of sociology. The approach speaks to two concerns essential to understanding propaganda: the relation between truth claims and the objects about which the claims are made, and the relation between truth claims and legitimation. The second, media system dependency theory, has developed primarily within the field of communication. The approach addresses questions concerning the role of the mass media in shaping both personal and socially shared beliefs about what is going on in the world. The chapter suggests that any distinction between news and propaganda is problematic, that the activity of telling the truth does not actually have some of the commonsense characteristics assigned to it, and that the claim of a media organization to be providing objective accounts of political affairs often is made in the service of legitimating its own, its government's, or its state's policies and actions.

Chapter Four presents a case study of broadcasting propaganda. The part played by IRB in the process by which political realities are constructed for developing nations by the international media of more economically developed states has received little attention. Radio serves a major source of understanding world politics for many people living in the developing areas (Hachten 1987: 10). The chapter empirically examines several systematic differences between the definitions of certain political realities that the Voice of America (VOA) and Radio Moscow transmitted to audiences in the Third World before the so-called Cold War ended.

Some portion of the international broadcasting of many governments consists of responses to criticisms directed at them by political adversaries. The regime of the Republic of South Africa long has been the object of verbal attack, particularly between 1948, when the National party came to power, extending and formally institutionalizing the policies of apartheid, and 1989, when a new government took office, subsequently lifted its ban on the African National Congress (or ANC, the primary black group fighting to end white minority rule), and initiated a sequence of events leading to some dismantling of the apartheid system. Criticisms have come from other African states and from nations throughout the world. South Africa has been condemned by international religious bodies, labor organizations, sporting groups, and human rights organizations (Tatum 1987).

Until 1990, when the South African Broadcasting Corporation (SABC) discontinued its IRB services except for those transmitting to Africa, Radio RSA, the Voice of South Africa, was a major instrument used by the South African government to respond to international criticism. The broadcasting organization stated as its goal the presentation of "balanced and objective information which enables [the] audience to make a more accurate assessment of South African affairs against a background of inaccurate and often one-sided coverage given events in South Africa by foreign media" (South African Broadcasting Corporation 1982: 96). South Africa's official construction of political reality, which it broadcast to international audiences in 1988, is analyzed in Chapter Five. This was a year marked by massive labor strikes and political action protesting the government's new labor laws and the banning of political activity by trade unions and antiapartheid groups. The chapter is an empirical case study of broadcasting counterpropaganda.

The final chapter proposes questions for further research on broadcasting propaganda. C. Wright Mills noted that between consciousness and existence stand communications that influence what consciousness people have of their existence (Mills 1951: 331). If the shaping of political consciousness is a subject matter for political scientists, political sociologists, and communication researchers, the study of broadcasting propaganda deserves consideration.

Since Marconi's time, the world's population has increased vastly, the supply of the earth's critical natural resources has been depleted significantly, competition among nations has become more intense, and the means of mass destruction have multiplied beyond measure. While some recent occurrences, such as the ending of the Cold War and the beginning of dismantling apartheid in South Africa serve as grounds for hope for the future, the need for mutual understanding among peoples of all nations has never been greater. Consequently, the need for a means of rapid, worldwide communication by which a nation might present its political perspectives for the consideration of the mass citizenry of other countries, particularly those living in antagonistic, formerly antagonistic, or highly competitive states has become essential. This book, which analyses the political uses to which Marconi's invention has been put, concludes with some speculation about the possibilities for realizing Marconi's dream suggesting that his device might be used to promote mutual understanding, trust, and peace among nations.

Broadcasting Propaganda

Chapter One

A Brief History of International Radio Broadcasting: 1915–1945

Historical accounts of the very beginning of organized international radio broadcasting (IRB) vary. Quite possibly, international broadcasting first was used systematically to advance political and military objectives in 1915 when Germany developed a regular radio news service that was employed by a number of neutral countries. Messages in code to German agents were incorporated into some of these transmissions. Since Germany's cable contacts had been cut, it had good reason to turn to radio (Whitton and Herz 1942: 8–9).

EARLY RADIO IN RUSSIA

Communication and its control have been fundamental concerns of the Soviet leadership from the beginning of the Soviet state. In an early work, Lenin had discussed its revolutionary value (Lenin 1902/1963). By 1910, his lieutenant in Baku, Joseph Stalin, was running a full-scale bureau of political information, financed by proceeds from bank raids. With the triumph of the October Revolution in 1917, the new government set up the Department of Agitation and Propaganda in Moscow, which took complete control of all information media (Rhodes 1983: 211–212).

The Russians were the first to establish a government-sponsored, continuous, and extensive system of radio broadcasting. The history of early broadcasting in Russia reveals that far-reaching systems of radio broadcasting were developed from the very start as a means of achieving significant political and economic goals.

The Russians attribute the development of radio not to Marconi, but to their countryman Alexander Popov (1859–1905) who, in February 1904, purportedly demonstrated the broadcasting of live human speech at a distance to the Third All-Russian Congress of Electrical Engineering (Paulu 1974: 29–31). In 1910, largely through Popov's efforts, a Russian national broadcasting company was created (Yaroshenko 1981: 52).

Russia had need of a centralized, far-reaching system of mass communication. It was a nation of enormous proportions, covering millions of square miles, comprising more than half Europe and nearly two-fifths of Asia. Its population, made up overwhelmingly of illiterate peasants, was ethnically fragmented and spread out unevenly over this vast area. Its agricultural economy was underdeveloped and industrialization was not advanced. Radio provided the Russian government with a potential means of communicating with its far-flung population. Radio solved the problem posed by illiteracy. It could make available throughout the land needed information about matters such as medical care, sanitation, and improved methods of agricultural production. It could also be used to advance the social and political integration of the nation and help overcome centuries of cultural isolation.

Vladimir Illich Lenin keenly appreciated the importance of radio for the new Soviet Republic he founded in 1917. He had always stressed the political significance of communication. In his central contribution to the Bolshevik theory of strategy and tactics, *What Is to be Done?*, Lenin (1902/1963) urged the establishment of an all-Russian newspaper for the purpose of advancing political, educational, and organizational objectives (Barghoorn 1964: 3–30). To Lenin, radio represented even more than a solution to some of the communications problems associated with the enormous domestic political and economic challenges his new regime confronted. He also saw that radio could serve as a way to spread the message of communism not only throughout Russia, but throughout the world. Communism always was conceived as an international movement aimed at ending the exploitation and alienation of workers worldwide.

In 1917 and following, Lenin and the Bolsheviks were hard-pressed to maintain themselves in power at the same time they were repelling foreign invaders. They needed to get their message to the population at home despite a breakdown in normal communications channels, and to reach foreign publics over the heads of their governments. Therefore, they enthusiastically seized upon radio as a medium to achieve these objectives. (Kaftanov 1961: 217)

On November 7, 1917, the first day of the Russian Revolution, the cruiser *Aurora*, in the harbor of St. Petersburg, broadcast messages to the "Citizens of Russia" containing decrees written by Lenin on "peace" and "the world." Five days later, another broadcast announced that the

Soviet government had been formed and that "decrees regarding land and peace had been adopted" (Paulu 1974: 33–34). The broadcasts were heard not only in Russia, but also in Germany, France, and Austria (Yaroshenko 1981: 53).

On February 4, 1918, Lenin addressed a radio report "to everyone" in which he debated claims made by foreign newspapers about conditions in the Soviet Union and about the decrees adopted by the Soviet government (Paulu 1974: 34). Later in that year, Russia periodically made political broadcasts detailing the Soviet view of the Treaty of Brest-Litovsk and the Bela Kun revolution in Hungary. In 1919, there were transmissions aimed explicitly at Great Britain, France, and Italy in which the Soviet Ministry of Foreign Affairs appealed to workers in these nations: "The workers and peasants of Russia, now freed from all oppressors and exploiters, first to have shed the capitalist yoke, ask you to be alert and not to slacken your pressure on your leaders who aspire to choke the people's revolution in Russia" (Paulu 1974: 200). A later broadcast called on workers of the Western nations to demonstrate against the "world reactionary forces" that were resisting the working people of Russia (Paulu 1974: 200).

To ensure wider distribution of his messages, Lenin supported experiments with radio. Soon after the revolution, a radio laboratory was established at Nizhni Novgorod (now Gorki). Lenin termed broadcasting "a thing of tremendous importance since it is a newspaper with no paper or wires, for by means of a transmitter and a receiver (adapted by B. Bruevitch, so that we will be able to get hundreds of them) all Russia will hear the paper read out in Moscow" (Yaroshenko 1981: 53).

In 1919, the radio laboratory started broadcasting experimental programs. By 1922, a central radiotelegraphy station was operating in Moscow whose transmissions of news bulletins could be received throughout Russia and much of Western Europe. In a letter to Stalin later that year, Lenin wrote about the great practical significance for propaganda, agitation, and education of the masses of being able to broadcast human speech over great distances by means of wireless radio. Lenin wrote a letter of support for the radio operation to members of the Politburo, who were asked to consider "the great service which it already performed as well as the considerable assistance which it may extend to us in the future both in a military sense and in the matter of propaganda" (Paulu 1974: 35).

Beginning in 1922, broadcasts from the Nizhni Novgorod station were transmitted on a more or less systematic, though not yet continuous, basis. On November 7 of that year, a special program was devoted to the fifth anniversary of the socialist revolution. The station's broadcasts now could be heard within a radius of 2,000 miles. Also in 1922, a 12-kilowatt transmitter, claimed to be the most powerful broadcasting station in the world, was installed in Moscow. By 1924, ten radio stations were functioning in Russia. A year later, central stations in Moscow and Leningrad were connected by line to a number of local theaters and concert halls, an arrangement that gradually evolved into a nationwide broadcasting network (Paulu 1974: 35). Subsequently, Russia developed the world's most extensive system of direct-to-home programming by wire.

In 1924, the Council of the Popular Commissars issued a freedom of broadcasting law which conceded to private organizations, as well as to individual collectivities, the right to establish and utilize radio stations. A joint stock company was formed to supervise broadcasting, and shares were issued in the names of trade unions and educational authorities. However, because such organizations were, in fact, arms of the government, in effect the government itself retained ownership of broadcasting facilities. By 1930 the fiction of independent ownership had disappeared and Soviet broadcasting had become a government operation in name as well as in fact (Head 1985: 58–59).

Early programming included education for would-be functionaries, who would receive work sheets from the government and then would return the exercises to appropriate agencies for correction; broadcasts encouraging friendly rivalry and cooperation between workers in various parts of the country; programs containing information on technological improvements in agriculture; transmissions for the Red Army; programs emphasizing Soviet ethics; and adult education programs on a wide variety of subjects (Grandin 1939/1971: 10–11).

Two major developments took place during the 1924–1929 period. First, Russian radio programming became more sophisticated and diversified. New principles of broadcast journalism were introduced along with presentations of music (particularly Russian folk music), drama, and features on daily life throughout the country. However, much of the content remained manifestly political, ranging from live reports on Party congresses and debates to programs serving as a means of early political socialization (Yaroshenko 1981: 56). Second, programs in regional languages were developed for the various national republics. These programs in particular were aimed at overcoming rural isolation, enhancing national political integration, and increasing worker productivity.

Domestic broadcast signals do not stop at national geographic borders. According to one Soviet historian, the political content of early Russian broadcasting was threatening enough to the governments of some Western nations as to prompt responses:

In capitalist countries around the Soviet Republic, where a very significant section of the population was familiar with the Russian language, it was prohibited to tune to such programs. In addition to that, the radio stations of many countries initiated what was called at that time "cat's concerts," that is, they aired artistic programs to jam Soviet broadcasting. (Yaroshenko 1981: 56)

Between 1927 and 1929, radio broadcasting specifically designed for foreign countries was initiated. Programs occurred at irregular intervals. In 1929, a department for broadcasting in foreign languages was created within the Soviet broadcasting system. In October of that year, Radio Moscow was formally inaugurated. One of its first programs, in French, celebrated the anniversary of the October Revolution. Later that year, German- and English-language programs were added. By 1930, Radio Moscow had regular daily programs in Russian, French, German, and English. Within three years, regular broadcasts in Czech, Hungarian, Italian, Spanish, and Swedish had been added, along with occasional programs in Turkish and Portuguese.

The early programming of Radio Moscow often was devoted to depicting the accomplishments of the revolution and the path of social development that Russia was following. In this regard, the international programming was little different from much of the domestic programming that was transmitted for the central station to the far reaches of the country.

Early international broadcasting contained few explicit attacks on opposing ideologies. However, occasional programs to Germany did contain ideological thrusts which would become a common feature of later Radio Moscow programs. "Programs frequently began with exhortations such as 'Police and soldiers of Germany, remember you are proletarians' and 'Remember in Germany, too, the October [Revolution] way is the right way.' Long live the German Soviet Republic" (Browne 1982: 242).

BROADCASTING TO THE COLONIES

Close to the time of the founding of Radio Moscow, other nations also began their international radio transmissions. Through their international broadcasts, the Soviets hoped to explain their revolution to both sympathizers and opponents in the West. The first Western nations to initiate international radio services, on the other hand, were colonial powers whose broadcasts helped maintain and strengthen their ties with overseas possessions.

The Netherlands began regular transmission in Dutch to the East Indies (now Indonesia) in 1927, France started French broadcasts to its colonies in 1931, the Belgians began broadcasting to the Congo that same year, and the British Broadcasting Corporation (BBC) initiated the Empire Service in English in 1932. Two of these colonial services, the Dutch and the British, ultimately developed into major contemporary international broadcast organizations. The early domestic radio broadcasting systems, from which international broadcasting organizations emerged, played a major role in shaping the relations of IRBs to their governments, the political role they were to play, and, consequently, the character of their programming. The vast majority of the early European national broadcasting systems had direct ties to governments. In 1938, for example, from among twenty-nine European systems, thirteen were state owned and operated, nine were government monopolies operated by autonomous public bodies or partially government controlled operations, four actually were operated by government, and only three were privately owned or run (Saerchinger 1938: 20).

Dutch Colonial Broadcasting

Domestic radio broadcasting in the Netherlands was initiated in 1919. Programming was produced by the Netherlands Radio Industry Company, a small, privately owned factory producing radio transmitting and receiving equipment. Regular broadcasts were made from the factory's transmitter from 1919 until the end of 1924.

In 1927, another private radio equipment company, the Netherlands Transmissions Apparatus Factory (NSF [Nederladdsche Seintoestellen Fabriek]) also began broadcasting. The company's comparatively great resources, (largely acquired from the foreign sale of naval radiotelegraphic equipment) made it possible to support both technical and program development. However, over time, the costs became prohibitive. In order to continue broadcasting, a separate organization was set up, the Hilversum Broadcasting Organization, which took over programming and its financing. Periodic appeals for contributions were made to listeners, whose donations entitled them to membership in the organization. Later renamed the General Radio Broadcasting Organization (AVRO [Algemeene Vereeniging Radio Omroep]), it became the first general broadcast organization in the Netherlands.

The construction of a second transmitter by the NSF in 1927 finally prompted the Dutch government to enact legislation regulating radio broadcasting. In that same year, the United States passed the Radio Act, designating broadcasting as a subject of federal control but leaving ownership and operation to private interests, and King George V signed a Royal Charter establishing a nonprofit, public organization to provide broadcasting throughout the United Kingdom as a public service, while insulating it from direct government intervention in daily operations. Like the United States and Great Britain, the Dutch confronted the twin questions of the ownership and content of radio broadcasting. As in the United States, early broadcasting in the Netherlands was developed by private companies. However, as in Great Britain, broadcasting was to be oriented toward public service rather than profit.

Nineteenth-century religious rivalries in the Netherlands had led major Dutch groups to reinforce their separate identities by developing separate, group-related institutions within the larger national framework. Each group set up its own schools, hospitals, trade unions, recreational clubs, and so on. This structure, known as *pillarization*, was imposed on Dutch broadcasting as well (Head: 1985: 109). By 1930, the Dutch government required, among other things, that the two stations devote equal time to programming for each of the four major Dutch political-religious associations: Protestant, Catholic, socialist, and one that was intended to be neither politically nor religiously committed. The broadcast activities of each of these associations were funded by voluntary contributions of its members. The government also established a special committee to ensure that programs did not contain anything that might, in its view, threaten national security or undermine public order. Furthermore, programming was to take into account what the committee saw as the social and cultural needs of the population that the broadcasting served.

The character of Dutch international broadcasting clearly reflected the history of that nation's experience with domestic radio. In 1925, the Phillips Company in Eindhoven began experimental radio broadcasts, including some using shortwave frequencies. By 1927, with most of the technical problems solved, regular shortwave radio programming was transmitted from the Netherlands to its colonies in the Dutch East Indies (now Indonesia). Phillips established a special broadcasting organization for this purpose, the Phillips Holland–East Indies Broadcasting Organization. In 1932, the NSF joined Phillips in broadcasting to the colonies.

Like domestic radio in the Netherlands, private enterprise was responsible for early Dutch international broadcasting. Again, programming was to reflect the diversity of Dutch society and to be a public service. In the context of international broadcasting, the question of what constituted public service was particularly complex. What public was to be served by the broadcasts: all those in the colonies who could understand Dutch, or, much more narrowly, Dutch settlers? What if any role was this remote audience to have in determining broadcast contents? What part was the state to play in the privately owned system of international broadcasting?

The answers to these questions initially appear to be somewhat surprising. Until the mid–1930s, Dutch programming was aimed exclusively at Dutch settlers living in the colonies. Virtually no consideration was given to the possibility that colonial people who had some understanding of the Dutch language also might listen to the broadcasts (Radio Nederland Wereldomroep 1982; Van Den Heuvel 1982: 298). Furthermore, although there might have been feedback from the audience for the international broadcasts (either the intended audience or the numerically much larger unrecognized audience of the Dutch speaking indigenous population), there is no evidence that any such feedback had an influence on programming. Failure of economically developed nations to attend seriously to the concerns of indigenous people in economically less developed regions to which they are transmitting is first seen in the broadcasts of the pioneer colonial services. Such neglect has been an enduring issue in IRB and is considered at length in Chapter Four.

While early Russian international broadcasting was government-controlled and explicitly aimed, at least in part, toward promoting an ideology worldwide, the Dutch government seemed content to leave international broadcasting in private hands and to remain largely unconcerned with program contents. The lack of direct government involvement in early colonial service broadcasting becomes particularly interesting when placed in historical perspective.

The Dutch had been reaping enormous profits from trade in the islands of the Malay Archipelago more or less continuously since the seventeenth century, when they replaced the Portuguese as the region's most important European power. By the early 1800s they were also benefiting from the production of export crops, and by the late 1800s, from investments in farmlands and privately owned plantations. While there was occasional resistance to Dutch rule, most of it had subsided by 1835. A modern nationalist movement, in which the East Indies sought greater power as a state, did not start until 1900. However, organized resistance to Dutch rule became serious in the late 1920s. A series of minor revolts occurred in 1926 and 1927. After 1926, numerous anti-Dutch parties developed, including the Indonesian Nationalist party, which was founded by Sukarno in 1927.

It was in the context of this serious challenge to Dutch authority that the colonial service was introduced. However, Dutch broadcasting to the East Indies was not initiated by the government as a communication medium aimed at reducing discontent in the indigenous population. Rather, it was a service, started by private enterprise, to provide a "home away from home" for Dutch citizens living in the colonies (Radio Nederland Wereldomroep 1982).

The absence of direct government ownership and control does not necessarily mean that an international radio service is not broadcasting messages serving government interests to an audience in a foreign land. Government and private enterprise have numerous common interests in nations with market economies. Such interests can override those based more narrowly on structures such as political-religious associations. Lack of direct government involvement in determining broadcast contents can be the reflection of the lack of any reason for the state to exercise direct control. Both the government of the Netherlands and Dutch business stood to benefit from the strengthening of ties with settlers in the colonies, particularly in a period of instability.

It seems reasonable to assume that providing a "home away from home" for Dutch settlers meant, among other things, constructing and broadcasting to them positive images of their native land, reminding them of their shared cultural heritage, presenting a particular view of the role of the Netherlands in the world political economy, and, most generally, offering a "Dutch perspective" on international affairs. The adoption of such orientations by Dutch settlers would encourage them to engage in patterns of political and economic behavior generally favorable to those "back home," in government and private enterprise alike.

British Colonial Broadcasting

In Britain, electronic telecommunication was regulated from its very inception, and market forces never were permitted to operate unrestrained. The 1869 Telegraph Act, drawing on earlier railway legislation, had conferred power on the postmaster general to control telegraphs, and the 1904 Wireless Telegraph Act, the first of its kind in the world, extended his power to control wireless transmissions as well (Briggs 1985: 10).

Initially, Parliament decided that the postmaster general should grant only one license for broadcasting at any one time. In 1923, the first license was awarded for two years exclusively to a limited company, the British Broadcasting Company, which had been founded by six wireless and electrical manufacturing firms. At first, the company derived its revenue partly from royalties charged on the sale of wireless receiving sets and partly from the sale of receiving licenses by the post office.

In 1925, the British government established a committee to make recommendations for the constitution of a national broadcasting service. Like the Dutch, the British also rejected both the idea of free and unregulated broadcasting by privately owned companies operating for profit and the idea of broadcasting being directly controlled and operated by the state. The committee proposed that broadcasting should be conducted by a public corporation acting as a trustee for the national interest and consisting of a board of governors which should be responsible for seeing that broadcasting was carried out as a public service.

With John Reith serving as director general, the British Broadcasting Corporation (BBC) was established by a Royal Charter in 1927, and the entire staff and all the equipment of the former company were taken over intact. Under the charter, the British government might have controlled fully the operation of the BBC. According to the provision of a license that accompanied the charter, the postmaster general retained authority to approve the location, wavelength, power, and broadcasting hours of radio stations and to take them over completely "in case of emergency." If government departments wished the BBC to make official announcements, it was compelled to do so. In addition, it was specified that the postmaster general might require the corporation to refrain from broadcasting specified subject matter (Briggs 1985: 93). Despite these restrictions, it became the policy of successive governments, and accepted by Parliament, to treat their powers as major reserve powers and to grant the corporation absolute independence in the day-to-day conduct of its business, vesting it with full responsibility over general administration and program content (Head 1985: 72–73).

The BBC began experimental international transmissions in late 1927. At Reith's personal initiative, its Empire Service was established in 1932. Selected programs, repeated from the domestic radio service, were broadcast to English-speaking listeners in Great Britain's many colonies, protectorates, and commonwealth partner nations throughout the world. Programming was designed to keep expatriates and loyal subjects of the king in constant touch with the mother country. News bulletins, planned in cooperation with Reuters News Agency and the Newspaper Proprietor's Association, were reported to be the most generally appreciated items in the daily programming (Briggs 1985: 138–140).

In the mid-1930s, fear began to spread that the unity of the empire was being threatened, not by movements toward self-government within some of the colonies, but by the rise of fascism in Europe. Germany had been engaging in international radio broadcasting since 1929, addressing Germans throughout the world and particularly in North America. After Adolf Hitler was named chancellor in 1933, Germany vastly expanded its radio operations, broadcasting to the Netherlands in Dutch and to Latin America in Spanish and Portuguese. Germany's broadcasts were interpreted as attempting, among other things, to weaken the British position in the Middle East and to extend German influence throughout Latin America (Radio Nederland Wereldomroep 1982).

In 1935, the year in which they invaded Ethiopia, the Italians built a powerful station in Bari, specifically for broadcasting in Arabic to the Arab world. (The Italians provided a vast number of cheap sets, tuned only to the frequency of the Bari station, to their intended audience.) Italian broadcasts contained virulent verbal assaults on the British, portraying them as the imperialistic oppressor and Italy as the protector of Islam (MacDonald 1977). They promoted Italian hegemony in the Mediterranean and constantly disparaged the Treaty of Versailles, the League of Nations, and, above all, communism (Grandin 1939/1971: 16). On May 9, 1936, after the Italian army's triumph in Ethiopia, Italian radio broadcast a speech of Benito Mussolini proclaiming: "The Italian people have created the empire with their own blood. They will nourish it with their own labor, and defend it against all comers with their own arms" (Rhodes 1983 Vol. 1: 81).

In an effort to counteract the influence of Radio Bari, the BBC initiated its Arabic service in January 1938. This was the first BBC service in a language other than English. The following month, the House of Commons belatedly passed a motion recognizing the need to counter both Italian and German broadcasts, "not by retaliation, but by the widespread dissemination of straightforward information and news" (Briggs 1985: 142). Many analysts had come to think of radio as a democratic weapon, providing the truth to present or potential victims of dictatorships (Qualter 1985: 220). Foreign radio was a principal medium that escaped a regime's monopoly on information transmission. Such a view was encouraged by the recognition that Radio Bari overtly promoted fascist ideology and reported events that had never occurred. The BBC presented itself in striking opposition to such policies when, in its first Arabic Service newscast, it reported an execution that morning of a Palestinian Arab, on orders of a British military court, for carrying a revolver (Briggs 1985: 143).

In their international broadcasts the British were trying to do more than contradict the claims of adversaries that they believed to be false. They were attempting to perpetuate the appearance of power in the eyes of foreign observers at a time when radio transmissions from hostile states were beginning to expose, by a variety of means, the harsh realities of British decline. Britain sought to create the image of power without investing in power's more costly substance (Shay 1977: 46). In March 1938, the BBC started Spanish- and Portuguese-language broadcasts. The transmissions were directed to Latin America, where Germany sent much of its anti-British radio programming (Soley 1989: 10). British radio broadcasting was used not only to provide reports about world conditions that were unavailable from other international sources, but also to construct a view of world politics that served its colonial interests.

With the establishment of foreign language services, (the BBC began broadcasting in Spanish, Portuguese, French, Italian, and German later in 1938), the Foreign Office assumed financial responsibility for the international operations of the BBC. Such control of finances, coupled with the right of Parliament (stipulated in the Royal Charter) to remove members of the BBC Board of Governors at will, created the potential for government control of BBC programming. However, while determining language services, there is no evidence that the government exercised its prerogative to influence the editorial policies or broadcast contents of BBC external services (Paulu 1981: 111–112; Radio Nederland Wereldomroep 1982).

The BBC's long and enduring history of independence from direct government control is, at once, both extraordinary and unexceptional. The relation of government control of international broadcasting organizations to broadcasting propaganda will be discussed in Chapter Three. However, because the BBC's independence was established with its very first domestic and international services, and because the BBC remains the model of politically independent international broadcasting committed to public service and to the presentation of putatively unbiased political information, some discussion of the relation of the BBC to the British government is appropriate here.

The BBC has engaged in a number of serious struggles against the efforts of Parliament to overtly control its operations and the contents of its broadcasts. These extend from opposition to Winston Churchill who, in 1926 as chancellor of the exchequer, was prepared to take over the BBC and mobilize broadcasting as a direct agent of the government to deal with a general strike (Briggs 1985: 97), to (and beyond) opposition to Prime Minister Margaret Thatcher who, in 1982, clashed with the BBC administration over coverage of the Falklands War (Holston 1987).

The outcomes of each of these struggles was politically important. BBC victories, though not entirely unambiguous in every instance, meant, in each particular case, that it would not serve passively as an agency transmitting accounts of certain political events that served immediate government interests. It seems reasonable to assume, for example, that accounts that the BBC presented of the general strike of 1926, various events in World War II, the 1956 Suez crisis, the 1967 military coup in Greece, aspects of the Vietnam War, continuing conflicts in Northern Ireland, and the Falklands War, would have been quite different had Parliament directly intervened in BBC operations. It is in this sense that the BBC enjoys an extraordinary history. Its historical experience stands in sharp contrast to that of most other international radio stations. It is largely this history that is responsible for the unequaled high level of credibility that the BBC long has been accorded (Browne 1982: 162; Hale 1975: 80; Head 1985: 75).

Not all students of BBC history have been impressed equally about the degree of independence of the organization from the British government. For example, reviewing the controversy surrounding BBC coverage of the 1926 general strike, English historian A.J.P. Taylor (1965: 246) commented that the vaunted independence of the BBC was secure as long as it was not exercised. Tom Burns (1977) has also raised a number of questions about the relationship. The point to be made here, however, does not so much concern the history of a particular broadcasting organization as it concerns the operation of all international broadcasting organizations, whatever the specific nature of their linkages to government.

Due to factors (identified and discussed in Chapter Three) that include the cultural frame of reference generally shared by members of the society of which an international broadcasting organization is a part and also to processes of information gathering and reporting that are institutionalized within an international broadcasting organization, the accounts of political affairs that such an organization transmits seldom are significantly at variance with the official views of its government. The Western conception of an adversary relationship between government and the mass media, with the media serving as a democratic check on government activities, ignores the high level of cooperation that exists between the two (Qualter 1985: 162). This is true of a nation's domestic and international media alike.

The original Dutch and British overseas services contributed to the integration of their respective colonial empires. They did so on their own, without significant direction from their governments. One explanation of their apparently extraordinary independence from government control (particularly that of the BBC) is simply that the governments had no reason to intervene in the colonial services. In this sense, independence was quite unexceptional. This interpretation is consistent with comments made by the first director general of BBC, John Reith. When asked what might happen if irreconcilable differences arose between the Foreign Office and the BBC, Reith responded that, while he would officially take the position that the BBC must have its way, personally he did not like to contemplate the BBC doing anything that the Foreign Office might oppose (Browne 1982: 179–180). Possibly the best strategy to employ in order to avoid conflict with government was to espouse a commitment to objectivity or impartiality. The new technology of radio broadcasting came to be housed in the institutions on which was imposed an ideology of a kind that would keep them out of trouble (Smith 1973: preface).

IRB IN WORLD WAR II

Much of the current character of international radio stems from what it became during World War II (Browne 1982: 62). In the 1930s, there were only three international radio stations in all Europe. By 1941, there were more than forty in full operation and many more under construction. Germany initiated most of the growth, aggressively using domestic radio broadcasts and transmissions to other countries from the time Hitler came to power.

World War I had made warfare no longer a question of relatively small professional military elites fighting against like armies on behalf of their governments. War had become a struggle involving entire populations pitted against entire populations, which now were required to supply the personnel and the materials and to endure the deprivations deriving from this total effort. At the beginning of World War II, for the first time radio was widely available as an instrument for mobilizing the domestic mass public and for waging verbal wars against mass adversaries of the state.

Radio had been used by Lenin and by the Germans in the 1914–1918 war. However, its impact had been limited because transmissions largely had been confined to Morse code. Nevertheless, even with this limitation, the potential of radio, particularly international radio broadcasting, had been sufficiently well appreciated that the representatives of the Allies at Versailles prohibited German broadcasting from Nauen, Hanover, and Berlin and the construction of any new station for a period of three months after the peace treaty had been signed.

By 1933, Germany had developed an elaborate system of domestic radio broadcasting. Most major cities had their own stations, each of which produced its own programming. Joseph Goebbels changed this decentralized pattern when he became Hitler's minister of popular enlightenment and propaganda that year. Goebbels himself wanted to call his office Ministry of Information, but was overruled by Hitler (Short 1983: 1). Goebbels concentrated the control of all German radio broadcasting, as well as publications, motion pictures, and the arts in Berlin, under his ministry. Control was so centralized and extensive that the ministry sometimes was referred to as the *Befehlszentrale*: the "center for issuing orders" (Rhodes 1983: 26). Goebbels never was able to establish his exclusive authority due to competition among members of his administrative staff and resistance from other ministries, most notably the German Foreign Ministry (Balfour 1979: 441). Nevertheless, the German broadcasting system embodied a model of direct government control exactly opposite that of the Dutch and the British, even going beyond the state-regulated system envisioned by Lenin. Goebbels expressed the view that the press was an exponent of the liberal spirit—the product and instrument of the French Revolution, whereas broadcasting was essentially authoritarian, and therefore a suitable spiritual weapon of the totalitarian state (Pohle 1955: 241).

The importance that the Nazi government attributed to radio can be seen in the fact that, like the Italians, the Nazis heavily subsidized the production of cheap wireless sets. Between 1933 and 1939 the number of privately owned radio sets in Germany quadrupled. In addition, speakers for communal listening were installed in factories, offices, and restaurants and at major street corners. By 1939, 70 percent of all German households owned a wireless set; this was the highest percentage in the world (Zeman 1964: 52). When a speech by a Nazi leader or an important government announcement was to be made, factories and offices were required to stop work so that all citizens could listen. In addition, party members designated as "radio wardens" attempted to ensure that all citizens seriously attended to the radio broadcasts. After the beginning of the war, such wardens also were given the responsibility of reporting those listening to foreign radio broadcasts (Rhodes 1983: 27).

Radio was Goebbels's instrument of choice for presenting National Socialist views both at home and to the world. He favored broadcasting for several reasons. Radio was easy to control centrally, it was not wasteful of manpower, it left no easily accessible record, it was immediate, and it penetrated. Broadcasts could not be controlled abroad by governments as easily as could other media (Zeman 1964: 104–117).

Domestic broadcasts included speeches by party and government officials, government proclamations, patriotic celebrations, lectures on military subjects, talks on history from the Nazi point of view, and racial doctrines (Graves 1941: 92; Kris and Speier 1944; Lazarsfeld and Stanton 1944/1979: 178–261; Pohle 1955).

The party paid attention not only to program content, but even to the very language that was used to convey its perspective. The National Socialists passed regulations that were intended to provide identical evaluation of events even as far as the use of language was concerned. New terms such as *Aufordung* (to enlarge the area of the Nordic race) and *Rassenschande* (marriage to or intimate relationship with a non-Aryan) were introduced, while the meanings or connotations of other terms were altered. For example, *fanatisch*, meaning fanatic, was an adjective having negative connotations during the Third Reich, while *Intellect*, which was defined as "creative capacity" during the Weimar Republic, was redefined to refer to "a critical, subversive and destructive quality" (Mueller 1973: 25–34).

Such manipulation of language, as well as general programming, can be understood better as being initiated to support primarily pragmatic rather than ideological objectives. Fascist movements, such as the one that developed in Germany, are characteristically hypernationalistic and define themselves by the things against which they stand. Hypernationalism was expressed, in the German case, in the form of hostility to philosophies, movements, groups, and organizations that possibly could be viewed as harmful to or diverting attention and energy from the ultimate goal of national social integration and greatness. It was expressed in its exaltation of the authority of the state and its supremacy over all other social groups. German fascists saw their cause as being above narrow class and party interests (Carsten 1969; Linz 1976). In German radio broadcasting, ideology was subordinate to the achievement of power (Speier and Otis 1944/1979: 240).

Germany's international broadcasts were similarly pragmatic. Goebbels lacked the ideological richness of the Soviet version of Marxism, which itself was a comprehensive worldview (Short 1983: 8). Early German radio transmissions were aimed at enhancing the legitimacy of the new regime abroad before it embarked on an ambitious foreign policy. At first, they were concentrated on the United States and the countries of Central America. The new regime needed markets for German goods as well as political credit. Broadcasts were used to instruct members of National Socialist organizations outside Germany to strengthen their faith and recruit new members (Zeman 1964: 104–117). The primary aim was to create a fifth column of believers in the Nazi cause and to use them as a lobby to back up the work of the German embassies (Hale 1975: 3).

During the first two or three years of the Third Reich, German radio to the West struck a peaceful note, avoiding, on the whole, the threatening language it employed later. Goebbels presented National Socialism as a respectable though revolutionary movement devoted to the preservation of peace. Emphasis was placed on the accomplishments of the regime in dealing with such serious domestic problems as rampant inflation, vast unemployment, and the lack of social and political integration. Broadcasts complained bitterly of the mistrust and misunderstanding of the new regime by the outside world and made much of the claim that the government had come to power by legal means. It was a complete misunderstanding of the principle of democracy, Goebbels suggested, to conclude from it that people wanted to rule themselves (Bramsted 1965: 144). Such a statement was consistent with fascist arguments that political systems in which the public participates only occasionally by voting and using the secret ballot permits a very low level of involvement in national decision making. In this view, national socialism offered a more genuine democracy by directly involving citizens through extensive personal participation in a political movement that represented the feelings and sentiments of the whole people.

German radio attempted to create close bonds between the broadcaster and the audience. The aim was to produce an atmosphere of friendship and confidence that was different in kind from the emotive relationship between a speaker and a mass audience (Zeman 1964: 114). Such a relationship could facilitate listeners' adoption of the view of the social and political world offered by the broadcaster.

Several campaigns were undertaken to convey an understanding of world politics that would serve regime interests. The first major effort was aimed at Austria after the Austrian National Socialist party was banned in summer 1933. From then until the forced annexation of Austria by Germany in 1938, the Austrians were told every evening by Berlin radio about the accomplishments of the Nationalist Socialists in Germany and what Hitler might do for Austria (Margolin 1946: 27).

After World War I, the Treaty of Versailles gave France control of the Saar in payment for French losses. A 1935 plebiscite was held to determine the region's political future. According to Zeman (1964: 108–117), while the National Socialists were unlikely to have lost the plebiscite over the return of the Saar to Germany, they were unlikely to have won by such an overwhelming majority without the effective radio programming. In the Saarland campaign, broadcasters successfully established the identification of National Socialism with German nationalism; the aims of the Germans in the Saar and those of Hitler's government were presented as being identical.

A third major broadcasting campaign was waged in connection with the 1936 Olympic Games held in Berlin. While the Saar campaign had been arranged for the purpose of national expansion, the Olympic Games were arranged to promote international recognition. By 1936, German international radio broadcasting was the most extensive in the world, overtaking the overseas services of the BBC. Germany continued to improve its position until the outbreak of World War II.

Germany's invasion of Poland in September 1939 and the immediate outbreak of war with Britain and France placed international radio broadcasting in the context of world war and changed the content of the messages of most stations. German radio efforts might have been more effective had the state not been using broadcasting for obvious political purposes in its Austrian, Saar, and Olympic campaigns for six years before World War II began. Germany's war effort was a continuation and intensification of its previous activities. Audiences outside Germany probably were more conscious of the political objectives of German broadcasts and more skeptical of program contents than they otherwise might have been (Bramsted 1965: 298).

The war involved incompatible interpretations of world politics. Through different accounts of political leaders, events, and conditions, each side sought to convince its own people, neutrals, and the enemy not only that it would win because it was stronger but also that its victory would be in the general interest because the principles by which it was motivated were more likely to bring peace and plenty. Each side set out to establish its own credibility and to destroy that of the enemy (Balfour 1979: 426).

A content analysis of German broadcasts to France from April to July 1940 (Speier and Otis 1944/1979: 214–215) found that German radio waged symbol warfare with several specific goals:

1. Undermining Allied confidence in victory by pointing out that Allied nations were weak or had failed while Germany's side was strong or had been suc-

cessful. For example, much was made of Dunkirk and considerable broad-casting time was devoted to Germany military achievements.

2. Convincing citizens of Allied nations, particularly the French, that they were divided socially from other Allied nations, such as Britain. Broadcasts contended that French national interests really were united with those of Germany.

3. Weakening Allied conviction of the right to victory by reporting Allied acts of brutality, while describing German military action in terms of attributes such as bravery.

4. Confusing Allied citizens' understanding of the complex world in which they lived by presenting certain Allied groups and leaders as internal enemies and exploiters. Efforts were made to present Germany as a real partner, friend, and protector who would treat the misled citizens of Allied nations with consideration.

5. Depoliticizing Allied audiences, not by confusing the roles of enemy and friend, but by emphasizing nonpolitical values and loyalties as more important than political ones. Discussions of the senselessness of war were presented; appeals were made to listeners' personal comfort and safety.

In its presentation of the war, German radio placed greater emphasis on adversary qualities than on the qualities of its own nation. More was said of British and French immorality than of German morality. However, more was said about German strength than about Allied weakness. The pattern of messages on German international radio was not, "We are strong and you are weak," but rather, "We are strong and you are immoral" (Speier and Otis 1944/1979: 223).

The BBC was in a difficult position to respond to German radio. In 1941, the British government established the Political Warfare Executive to deal with, among other things, communication to enemy countries. The department was responsible to the foreign secretary for policy, to the minister of information for administration, and to the minister of economic warfare for liaison with underground activities. While the agency issued regular directives to guide the BBC output to enemy and enemy-controlled countries, the BBC successfully waged a war with the agency and kept it from corrupting the presentation of its purportedly straight news. The BBC continued its policy of presenting so-called un-biased accounts as far as it could, while through other programming it encouraged resistance to Germany (Briggs 1985: 222–223).

The straight news that the BBC could send shortly after the outbreak of the war could not report dramatic British military victories. Early battles that were won by Britain, such as the Battle of Britain in the autumn of 1940 or the reverses of Field Marshal Erwin Rommel's troops in Libya in 1942, were largely defensive. The BBC could only emphasize the undaunted morale of the English people and express hope for future military success. Its main chance was to create belief in the accuracy and reliability of its news services in German and in other languages (Bramsted 1965: 290). In the time of war, the BBC followed the broadcasting policy it appeared to have established with its founding: a calculated strategy of admitting defeats in order to establish the confidence of its listeners in the integrity of its broadcasts (Crossman 1949: 333).

During the war, most international radio stations did not adopt the BBC strategy of assiduously avoiding deliberate deception in order to win acceptance for its claims about political and military affairs. Goebbels, for example, contended that in German broadcasts, anything was permissible that was successful. In his view, programming served the truth when it served German victory (Balfour 1979: 428).

Possibly even more deceptive than German radio were the so-called clandestine radio stations. Clandestine stations, which had been in operation ever since the 1930s, are operated by revolutionary or underground groups in a country or by adversary powers purporting to be indigenous opposition groups. The number of such stations increased dramatically with the outbreak of World War II (Browne 1982: 62–66). For their sponsors, clandestine stations often operate to harass a government, sometimes attempting to provoke it into repressive and self-defeating reactions. For guerrillas and active supporters of revolutionary or counterrevolutionary organizations, clandestine stations coordinate activities, reinforce beliefs, and provide information that is unavailable through aboveground channels. Clandestine stations also perform symbolic functions, enhancing the visibility and status of sponsoring organizations and serving as a means by which the politically powerless can release their frustration (Solely and Nichols 1987).

Two of the best-known clandestine stations operated by the Allies were Britain's Gustav Sigfried Eins and America's Radio 1212. Between May 1941 and October 1943, Gustav Sigfried Eins was Britain's major clandestine station, transmitting to Germany and its allies and directed at German officers. The station name was ambiguous so that listeners would provide their own interpretation. It purportedly broadcasted from German soil and was operated by a dissident noncommissioned German officer. The station offered interpretations of the Reich's problems, placing considerable emphasis on divisions between German military commanders and Nazi party leaders. Survey evidence suggests that the British station initially enjoyed a high level of credibility (Browne 1982: 63–64; Soley and Nichols 1987: 46).

Radio 1212 claimed to be a German-based station operated by loyal Rhinelanders. The station presented itself as promoting the German war effort while also providing news not available from official Reich stations. The station actually was operated by the Psychological Warfare Branch of the United States 12th Army group. Major news items in Radio 1212 broadcasts included reports of air raids on German cities, which the Nazi command had kept secret from frontline troops. The news generated distrust of the Nazi leadership among the troops and increased their reliance on accounts of the war emanating from Radio 1212 (Soley and Nichols 1987: 42–45).

Germany also had its clandestine stations, which were operated by a specialized department of the Reich, the Buro Concordia. Among other stations, the department operated Voix de la Paix, which broadcast defeatist messages to France before and during the German invasion. The station claimed to be operated by patriots who criticized the French defense industry as incompetent and claimed it would disintegrate in the event of an invasion (Soley and Nichols 1987: 34–35). In addition, Germany made considerable use of "personality" broadcasting to convey ideas and sentiments helpful to the Reich. The best known individual broadcasters included William Joyce ("Lord Haw-Haw") broadcasting to Britain, Mildred Gillars ("Axis Sally") broadcasting to U.S. military personnel in Europe, and Paul Ferdonnet transmitting to France (Browne 1982: 76–77).

During the war, German broadcasts increasingly were used to achieve specific goals, for example, to disintegrate the Czech will to resist from 1939 to 1943, to undermine French morale in 1939–1940, and to capitalize on historic French resentment of the British by claiming ceaselessly that Britain was using France to fight its war against Germany (Soley 1989: 84; Speier and Otis 1944/1979). Japan later joined Germany and Italy in waging such radio warfare, working primarily to divide America from its allies in Asia and the Pacific and to stimulate war-weariness, nostalgia, and a pessimistic view of the war among Allied troops. Undoubtedly, the best known broadcaster working to achieve this last objective was Ikuko Toguri ("Tokyo Rose"). The following suggests the general thrust of her program to U.S. military personnel in the Pacific:

How'd you like to go to the corner drug store tonight, and get an ice cream soda? I wonder who your wives and girl friends are out with tonight. Maybe with a 4F or a war plant worker making big money while you are out here fighting and knowing you can't succeed. Wouldn't you California boys like to be at the Coconut Grove tonight with your best girl? You have plenty of Coconut Groves, but no girls. (Tokyo Radio, sometime in 1943, quoted in Ryo 1983: 327)

In 1939, an American group called the Princeton Listening Center began the effort to understand the principles used by the Fascists to construct their programming (Graves 1941; Childs and Whitton 1942). The U.S. effort continued with the listening posts established in 1941 by the Federal Communications Commission and the Defense Communications Board (Kneitel 1982). Efforts to offset the effects of the broadcasts and wage a radio counterattack, initiated by the BBC in 1938, were later joined by the Free French and the Norwegians.

In 1940, the United States finally started to use IRB in support of the war effort. The State Department and the Federal Communications Commission secured the cooperation of the owners of the small number of shortwave stations to expand their overseas news programs. Two years later, under the Office of War Information, the Voice of America (VOA) went on the air. The United States was the last world power to initiate IRB. The reasons for the delayed development were largely political: The United States had lacked the motives that encouraged IRB by other countries. It was not politically isolated, as was Russia after World War I. It did not seek territorial expansion, as did Germany and Italy. It did not have a colonial empire to integrate, as did Great Britain and the Netherlands. In addition, largely as a result of World War I experiences, there was strong public opposition to anything that might be viewed as propaganda operations by the government. Finally, the U.S. commercial radio industry strongly opposed such broadcasts (Paulu 1974: 201).

By 1945, shortwave covered the globe, with broadcasts in forty languages transmitted from fifty-five countries (Abshire 1976: 21). Allied broadcasts in response to those of the Fascists involved attempts to discredit them as intentionally deceitful and malicious and to present Allied programming as depictions of the truth about the war (Abshire 1976: 201). Such presentations appear to have been sincere. For example, research on this period of BBC history brought to light no case in which the BBC put out statements believed by it to be false. Where it may be held to have engaged in deceit, such as the false reports it broadcast in 1940 and 1941 about successful British air attacks on Germany, the BBC was deceived itself by faulty intelligence reports (Balfour 1979: 428). While the VOA may not have been quite as fastidious as the BBC in its commitment to journalistic practices assumed to produce accurate accounting of the war, reports appear to have been generally reliable. When U.S. military strategy sometimes dictated that misleading information be broadcast, this was left to the Office of Strategic Services, lest VOA broadcasts lose credibility (Browne 1982: 95).

During wartime, the military context in which broadcasting occurs significantly influences its content. Whether a broadcasting nation is experiencing military victories or defeats influences the self-image it can construct. The contents of Radio Moscow broadcasts were qualitatively different in the winter of 1941 when the blitzkrieg almost reached the heart of the motherland, from 1944 when the massed Soviet armies were mauling the last vestiges of the Reich's defenses (Short 1983: 4). Similarly, after the battle of El Alamein in July 1942, the defeat of the German Sixth Army at Stalingrad in January 1943, as well as victories in Tunisia, Sicily, and Salerno, the Allies finally could define themselves as both united and powerful and could present a credible vision of Europe's future in which their political principles were likely to prevail. German radio, on the other hand, no longer could emphasize effectively the division of the British from their own leaders, divisions among Allied nations such as Poland, France, and the United States from the British, or divisions between the Western Allies and the Russians.

Allied victories also put them in a position to discredit official German statements about the course of the war. The credibility of German broadcasting was attacked successfully by contrasting earlier statements of Nazi leaders with the conditions of the present. Goebbels's biggest failure coincided with military failure: The BBC scored a notable victory by recording Hitler's pronouncements about the timing of the total collapse of the Soviet Union. When Moscow and Stalingrad survived and the tide of war subsequently turned, those recordings were played back (Hale 1975: 15). The BBC made additional use of Hitler's speeches. For example, on September 30, 1942, Hitler had termed the Allied Military Command "military idiots." A year later, a BBC broadcaster, reminding listeners of Hitler's derision, commented: "Military idiots. How does that sound today? It has different meaning from a year ago. Today, when Italy has collapsed, today, when British and American troops stand on the mainland of Fortress Europe" (BBC, September 30, 1943, quoted in Bramsted 1965: 297).

After Germany suffered a series of significant military defeats, its broadcasts turned to cultural attacks on the Allies, particularly the United States. Such attacks deplored America's failure to comprehend Western European political culture and the meaning of the National Socialist movement.

America, discovered by a European and spiritually nourished by European ideas, betrayed the mother continent by failing to understand the new spirit in Europe and allying herself instead with the capitalistic and plutocratic coalition. What do American skyscrapers know about the soil of Europe? American museums would be empty but for the treasure of European culture. The Metropolitan Opera had to close [it did not] as no more European works were available. Coca Cola and chewing gum will not replace European culture. That continent, once called a new world, is now an old world where reaction reigns. (Berlin Radio, October 1942, quoted in Ettinger 1943: 271)

Such broadcasting offered no vision to its worldwide audience of a new and better political order for the future. On the other hand, the Allies, particularly Britain, managed to convince the peoples of Western and Southern Europe that their victory, bringing with it the restoration to them of self-government, would be in the general interest (Balfour 1979: 439). Ultimately, German radio resorted to the cry for total war and apocalyptic hopes of "wonder weapons" to motivate Germany's supporters to fight on and defend the homeland from the invading Bolshevik barbarians (Short 1983: 5). After this point, German radio could no longer effectively serve the interests of the state as useful images could not be constructed from the rubble of the Third Reich.

It is instructive that, with the notable exceptions of Germany's Ministry of Popular Enlightenment and Propaganda and Italy's Ministry of Popular Culture, most of the agencies established by governments during World War II to oversee the domestic and international political communications of their countries had the word *information* in their titles: United States: Office of War Information; Great Britain: Ministry of Information; and France: General Commission of Information; and Japan: Central Information Bureau. Any distinction between *propaganda* and *information* was particularly difficult to make in the wartime context. The British definition of the purpose of their Ministry of Information as "propaganda with truth [facts]" reflects the realization of the near interchangeability and utilitarian nature of the words *propaganda* and *information* in time of total war (Short 1983: 1–2).

IRB AND THE ONSET OF THE COLD WAR

Immediately after World War II, shortwave broadcasting in the United States faltered. During the peak of its wartime operations, the VOA broadcast some 119 hours of programming daily, in fifty languages. However, in the last months of 1945, its personnel ranks were slashed by half and its programming reduced to less than 65 hours daily in twenty-four languages (Heil and Schiele 1986: 98–99). Some reduction was due to uncertainty about the role that IRB, which was sponsored by a democratic state, was to play during peacetime. However, the cutbacks were only temporary. After World War II the agencies of international political communication were being rearranged because their task had changed, but not because their task had been eliminated (Alexandre 1988: 9). When Nazi Germany collapsed and the former Allies of East and West stood facing each other across a divided Europe, their IRB was simply redirected (National Public Radio 1982).

World War II culminated in the emergence of the United States and the Soviet Union as the two most powerful nations in the world, with each nation working to consolidate a leadership role within its political-economic bailiwick. The United States perceived the entire "free world," with the limited exception of the area conceded to the Soviet Union at the Yalta Talks, as its legitimate sphere of influence. Even before World War II ended, Russia had taken over the Baltic states of Latvia, Estonia, and Lithuania, parts of Poland, Finland, and Romania, and eastern Czechoslovakia. Russian troops occupied a third of Germany and all of Bulgaria, Hungary, Poland, and Romania.

During 1945 and early 1946, Russia cut off most of the contacts between the West and the occupied territories of Eastern Europe. In March 1946, Winston Churchill, introducing a metaphor that was to be used countless times to legitimate Western IRB to Eastern Europe and the Soviet Union, warned that an "Iron Curtain" had descended across the continent of Europe. Behind this barrier, supposedly, Russia was steadily expanding its power. Indeed, in 1946, Russia organized Communist governments in Bulgaria and Romania, and in 1947, Communists took control of Hungary and Poland. Moreover, Communists seized full power in Czechoslovakia early in 1948.

In the fall of 1946, Greek communists revolted against their government. Great Britain, which had been giving military and economic aid to both Greece and Turkey, informed the United States that it could no longer provide enough resources to those nations to effectively help them resist communist subjugation. In March 1947, President Harry Truman declared that the United States would help any "free people to work out their own destinies in their own way" (Boorstein and Kelley 1986: 585). Congress granted his request for $400 million for aid to Greece and Turkey. The following year the United States initiated its European Recovery Program (the Marshall Plan). Over a three-year period the program sent about $13 billion in food, machinery, and other products to Europe in the belief that an economically strong and politically stable Europe would block the spread of communism.

By the late 1940s, the government of the United States defined itself as being in a state of war, short only of actual military exchanges, with the Soviet Union. The Soviet Union felt the same way about the United States (Council on Foreign Relations 1950, 1951, 1952; Fleming 1961; Horowitz 1965; LeFeber 1976). For example, United States under secretary of state Dean Acheson characterized Soviet foreign policy as "aggressive and expanding," while Soviet foreign minister V. M. Molotov claimed: "The Soviet Union is compelled to recon with the fact that the ruling circles of the U.S.A. and Great Britain have adopted an openly aggressive political course, the final aim of which is to establish by force Anglo-American domination over the world" (Barker 1972: 18–19).

The VOA inaugurated broadcasts in its Soviet Division in 1947. Programs were presented in Armenian, Azeri, Georgian, Russian, Ukranian, and Uzbek. Broadcasts in Estonian, Latvian, and Lithuanian were not part of the Soviet Division but were assigned to VOA's European Division because the United States did not recognize the incorporation of the three Baltic republics in the USSR (Alexeyeva 1986: 79).

Psychological warfare operations principally aimed at weakening Communist governments played an important part in the U.S. involvement in the so-called Cold War (Klapper and Lowenthal 1951–1952; Summers 1951). Immediately after World War II, the U.S. Congress had supported the view that privately owned media should be instruments of public information (Abshire 1976: 26). However, with the onset of the Cold War, Congress passed the 1948 Smith-Mundt Act, giving the VOA legislative sanction and funding it as a part of the U.S. State Department's program for international information and educational exchange.

In 1950, the VOA became part of President Truman's Campaign for Truth program, which was intended to serve as an integral part of the administration's "struggle against Communism" (Browne 1982: 101). According to Alexandre (1988: 10–11), the $121 million appropriation for the campaign in fiscal year (FY) 1950 added resources for an aggressive, anti-Communist course of action that included militarization of the economy, the expansion of covert Central Intelligence Agency (CIA) operations, development of a systematic effort to refute Soviet claims about the activities of the U.S. government and the intentions of its international policies, and attempts to hasten the demise of the Soviet Union. The clearly political role assigned to the VOA in the campaign was spelled out in a 1953 internal organizational document that stated:

[We] are not in business to amuse, entertain, or simply inform our listeners. Nor are we in business because news is an end in itself. The United States is in the midst of a serious struggle for the mind of mankind and the only purpose of the News Branch—as well as the entire Voice of America—is to contribute to winning the struggle. (quoted in Alexandre 1988: 12)

One of the most intensely contested battles of the Cold War was for the "middle ground" between East and West: first the war-devastated countries of Western Europe and then for what became known as the Nonaligned Third World. Having secured Western Europe through the Marshall Plan and selective military presence, as occurred in Greece, the United States was able to concentrate its efforts on the vast territory of Asia and Africa by the end of the 1940s. Latin America, which was shielded behind the Monroe Doctrine and associated economic relationships, was viewed separately from the countries of Africa and Asia.

The dissolution of the traditional colonial empires meant that the people and leaders of African and Asian states had the choice of continuing as members of the Western Bloc or exploring alternative political alignments and economic arrangements. In countries where forces arose in opposition to pro-U.S. governments, efforts were made in the United States to forestall their accession to power. Interest in neutralizing or ousting forces or values that were perceived to be inimical to the United States in the Nonaligned Third World prompted VOA sponsorship of research concerning the possible bearing of communication on political-economic changes (Gendzier 1978; Zartman 1976). According to Noam

Chomsky (1982), U.S. framing of international relations as a Cold War legitimated U.S. intervention to Third World nations and aggressive constraint strategies around the globe. Such actions enabled the construction of an international system suited to U.S. interests. The real issue, Chomsky argued, was not the "Soviet menace" but the danger of U.S. investments posed by the movements of political independence in the Third World.

The VOA was not the only U.S. international broadcasting organization that fully engaged early in the Cold War. Early in 1946, Radio in the American Sector of Berlin (RIAS) was created as a radio service for Germans living in that area. With the Berlin Blockade, in June 1948, the station began operating as an instrument of international political communication, carrying throughout Germany the message of Allied determination to resist the blockade. The station served as a prototype for two other U.S. stations that soon appeared (Browne 1982: 132–133). In 1948, in addition to the Berlin Blockade, a combination of political events, including the Communist takeover of Czechoslovakia, the threat of Communist victory in the Italian election, and a vast increase in the number of passionately anti-Communist Soviet exiles existing on a limited U.S. largesse in the U.S.-occupied zone in Germany, prompted the U.S. government to support additional broadcasting efforts (Mickelson 1983). The U.S. Department of State, Department of Defense, and National Security Council facilitated the development of Radio Free Europe (RFE) and subsequently Radio Liberation from Bolshevism (this was later shortened to Radio Liberation and finally to Radio Liberty or RL in 1953). (The stations were merged in 1976.) Both stations, with RL broadcasting to the Soviet Union and RFE to Eastern Europe, were to serve as outlets for exiles broadcasting back to their "captive homelands." They were to function independently of the U.S. government as "nonofficial instruments of American foreign policy" (Browne 1982: 135). During the Cold War, it was concluded that RFE and RL would have greater credibility if they appeared to be privately funded rather than supported by U.S. government funds (Abshire 1976: 32).

In an effort, supposedly, to support their independence, a massive advertising campaign, the "Crusade for Freedom," was launched. The U.S. public was asked to contribute "Truth Dollars" and school children were urged to contribute their pennies to "keep freedom alive in Europe" by "carrying the message of freedom beyond the Iron Curtain" (Mickelson 1983: 53). Remarkably, it was not until 1967 that the public finally learned, first from the oppositional periodical *Ramparts* and later from the *New York Times* and *Washington Post*, that the international broadcasting organizations were funded covertly by the CIA and that the funds raised by the public campaign contributed only a small fraction of their annual operating budget.

The carefully created illusion that the stations were free from formal government sponsorship diminished some of the public questioning that might have arisen concerning their strident tone. There may have been public support for the U.S. need to possess and use an aggressive weapon of political communication with which to engage the Soviet Union in a "war of words" as part of the Cold War. However, there was likely to be less public enthusiasm for an overt, government-sponsored propaganda effort.

In the Cold War, the mass public was told that the best official weapon of the U.S. government in the war of words was "the truth." The United States would tell the truth about world affairs, particularly to peoples lacking free access to information, through its VOA newscasts. The VOA would also present official U.S. government policy and accurately portray life in the United States for citizens of other lands through its feature programming. The very forceful expression of political arguments, opinions, and perspectives required other channels of international political communication.

A more emphatic voice than that of the VOA, it was argued, could undermine Soviet influence by exposing the more inhumane aspects of the system of rule practiced in the USSR and imposed on the Eastern European countries (Barker 1972: 19). Apparently, at least in the early days of the Cold War, news presented the truth, expressions of political opinion could and should be clearly differentiated from the presentation of news, and political propaganda differed from both in that it expressed political arguments in a particularly strident manner. Moreover, a democratic government was a truth teller and a dictatorship was a sinister manipulator of the public mind.

The tone of RFE/RL is illustrated in this broadcast from the early 1950s.

This is Radio Free Europe, the voice of freedom calling the captive countries behind the Iron Curtain—speaking to them in their own languages in more ways than the obvious. American propaganda of hope sizzling through the air with messages musical and spoken that the Communists don't want their slaves to hear—messages that should be a warning to the Reds that all their carefully canned dogma can't quite blot out the simple human urge to think and say what you please. (National Public Radio 1982)

This tendentious approach contrasted sharply with that established from its very beginning by the VOA. The dissimilarity, exemplified below, carefully embodies the distinction between news and propaganda that was widely accepted during this period: "Here in America we receive news from all over the world. The news may be favorable or unfavorable. Everyday we shall bring you this news—the Truth" (Voice of America, February 24, 1942, quoted in Heil and Schiele 1986: 98).

Radio Liberty, broadcasting to the Soviet Union, and Radio Free Europe, transmitting to Soviet-dominated Eastern Europe, were not conceived by their sponsors and administrators solely as instruments of symbolic warfare. Additionally, they were to provide their audiences with an alternative to media controlled by their government. They were to serve those living in Communist states as alternative sources of information, not only about world affairs but also about themselves. They were to be, in effect, the closest thing to a free press in the Communist world. The radios were to provide news as well as propaganda.

In broadcasting news to people lacking free access to information, RFE and RL proceeded from the assumption that informed societies can make more responsible judgments about their own and world affairs, while misinformed societies can more easily be manipulated in directions threatening peace. RFE and RL further assumed that the growth of an informed public opinion contributes to the moderation of repressive or adventurous policies (Alexeyeva 1986: 22). These assumptions echoed Marconi's ultimate hope for the utilization of his invention. RFE and RL also proceeded from the assumption that its propaganda could "confuse the enemy." Moreover, it would "embarrass its leadership and contribute to the roll-back of communist aggression in Eastern Europe." Their final goal was "liberation" (Mickelson 1983: 85). These assumptions echoed Marconi's initial and less idealistic reflection on the tactical uses of radio.

There are several ironies associated with the origin and operation of RFE and RL at the onset of the Cold War. First, public belief in the importance of media news operations functioning independent of government control, and in a sharp distinction between news and propaganda, were largely the result of an organized, nationwide effort covertly funded by a government agency. Second, as Jacques Ellul (1966) has pointed out, people who imagine they could not be victims of propaganda because they can distinguish truth from falsehood are actually extremely susceptible because when propaganda does "tell the truth," they are convinced it is no longer propaganda. Moreover, self-confidence makes people all the more vulnerable to attacks of which they are unaware.

Like the United States, Great Britain reduced its IRB at the end of World War II. By March 1945, total daily BBC broadcasting to Europe was decreased from fifty to forty-three hours, BBC staff was cut, and transmissions on a number of frequencies were eliminated. However, the BBC did initiate a Russian-language service to the Soviet Union in 1946.

Also like the United States, Great Britain significantly increased its broadcasting activity in 1948 in response to the events in Berlin and Czechoslovakia. During 1946 and 1947, BBC Russian-language broadcasts were very popular among many Soviet listeners. However, after 1948, goodwill deteriorated and, in 1950, a BBC-monitored talk on the Moscow Home Service described the leaders of the BBC, whom it identified by name, as "enemies of the cause of peace and democracy throughout the world" (Briggs 1985: 313). This certainly suggests that, at least in the view of Soviet authorities, during the Cold War, if not previously, the BBC was an instrument of Western propaganda.

From the very beginning, the organizational image maintained by the BBC was certainly not that of a political instrument. Its Royal Charter was intended to provide the organization with maximum insulation from government intrusion in its operations. Asa Briggs noted that this ideal was reaffirmed almost two decades later:

[The British government] categorically accepted the principle in its 1946 White Paper on Broadcasting (Cmd. 6852) that great care should be taken to insure the complete objectivity of the news bulletins which will form the kernel of all overseas broadcasting. "The Corporation's reputation for telling the truth," established in the darkest years of the war, it went on, "must be maintained and the treatment of any item in the overseas news bulletins must not differ in any material respect for its treatment in current news bulletins for domestic listeners." (Briggs 1985: 313)

The tone and content of broadcasts in the External Services of the BBC were less aggressive than that of the VOA, RFE, or RL. Despite the intent of the Royal Charter and despite the BBC's historical struggles to maintain its integrity, in the early days of the Cold War, the BBC's approach to news presentation prompted some in the British Foreign Service and Parliament to criticize the organization for not being "tough enough on Communism" (Browne 1982: 164).

After World War II, the Soviets did not reduce their IRB as did the Americans and the British. At the end of the war, the ruling bureaucracy exercised virtually total control of the flow of politically important information within the Soviet Union. The only significant gap in their ability to regulate communications were shortwave radio broadcasts from abroad (Lisann 1975: 2). The Soviets took the position that IRB from the West represented interference in the internal affairs of a sovereign state and that Radio Moscow broadcasts were intended to counter hostile propaganda (Hale 1975: 30). Specifically, the Soviets objected to Western IRB on grounds that it aroused dissatisfaction among various nationality groups; inculcated an apolitical attitude; dulled class consciousness; stirred up among Soviet youth feelings of admiration for the Western way of life, bourgeois values, and morality; spread imperialist ideology; and provoked dissatisfaction with Soviet reality (Paulu 1974: 214–15; Presidential Study Commission on International Broadcasting 1973: 17).

A study of Soviet objections to the Russian service of the VOA during the early period of the Cold War found approximately 1,000 references in the Soviet domestic media to VOA broadcasts between 1947 and 1951. Attacks tended to be more closely related to the state of the Cold War than to specific VOA programs. The research suggested that Soviet media tried to counteract the VOA by posing a negative counterimage of the United States rather than by seeking to refute the negative image of the Soviet system constructed and offered worldwide by the VOA (Inkeles 1953).

An additional Soviet response to Western IRB in the early Cold War period was *jamming*, transmitting a continuous noise on the same or an immediately adjacent frequency as an incoming radio signal in order to make the incoming program unintelligible. Soviet jamming of the VOA began in 1948, and during the next several years, other Eastern European countries followed their example. Soviet jamming of the BBC began several months after VOA jamming. The Soviet Union jammed RL from its very first day of broadcasting in 1953.

The Soviet policy of jamming has followed the ebb and flow of Cold War tension and crises (Browne 1982: 17; Short 1986: 6). For example, activity increased during the Hungarian and Suez crises in 1956, the 1967 Middle East War, and the 1968 invasion of Czechoslovakia. Jamming decreased during most of the period of nuclear test ban treaty negotiations from 1963 and 1968 and during the 1973 negotiations of the Conference on European Security and Cooperation at Geneva (Abshire 1976: 49).

In December 1950, the United Nations General Assembly adopted a resolution condemning jamming as a violation of the accepted principle of freedom of information and a denial of the right of all persons to be fully informed (Whitton and Larson 1964: 21). However, existing international law already had made illegal the transmission of any material that contained a threat to peace (Larson 1967: 4). The Soviets simply interpreted Western IRB as threatening material. "What Washington considers the simple truth [became] in the eye of Moscow harmful propaganda" (Whitton and Larson 1964: 219).

Jamming is poor strategy for responding to the IRB of a political adversary. First, it is relatively expensive. It has been estimated that the cost to the Soviets of jamming Western broadcasts was six times the cost of their own international broadcasts (Abshire 1976: 49) and twice as high as the funds appropriated by Western governments to produce and transmit them (Kirsch 1986: 162). In addition, jamming, like other forms of censorship, often calls attention to the existence of banned materials, making them more sought after. It also clarifies public perception of the extent to which the state controls the flow of political, economic, military, and other types of information. Finally, jamming suggests that the state cannot construct definitions and explanations of politically relevant conditions and events that are more compelling than those transmitted by its adversaries.

This chapter has suggested that, from its very beginning, IRB has been inseparably linked with world politics. Some of the political uses of IRB in World War I, the Russian Revolution, British and Dutch colonial administration, and World War II were described. The structure of world politics created immediately after World War II continued to shape IRB for more than forty years, and some of the important features of this history were foreshadowed by the events just discussed. Further details of IRB history from 1946 to 1989 are the subject matter of the following chapter.

Chapter Two

International Radio Broadcasting and International Conflicts: 1946–1989

The conceptualization of a Cold War existing between the Communist nations (led by the Soviet Union) and the Western capitalist countries (led by the United States) that was introduced at the end of World War II served as the dominant framework for understanding world events for more than four decades. Diplomats, journalists, novelists, filmmakers, broadcasters, and other shapers of public opinion worldwide, as well as social scientists, tended to assume the analytic division of the much of the world into Western and Soviet blocs. It is within the context of this framework that most of the history of IRB has unfolded.

IRB activity following World War II was a reflection of the history of overt Cold War conflicts that occurred between the time U.S. journalist Herbert Bayard Swope suggested the term in 1946 and the dramatic events in the communist world that began in 1989 with the Soviet withdrawal from Afghanistan and continue today. The Korean War, uprisings in Poland and Hungary, the Suez crisis, the Cuban missile crisis, the invasion of Czechoslovakia, and the Vietnam War each was associated with increased activity on the part of both Western and Soviet bloc international broadcasting organizations.

As will be shown in this chapter, a primary objective of such activity was to present, to selected audiences, particular understandings of the political, economic, and military actions of the international broadcasting organization's sponsoring state. Students of IRB have suggested that Soviet and Western broadcasts primarily are targeted to different audiences. While stations such as the BBC and the VOA generally seek varied publics worldwide, stations such as Radio Moscow tend to target those whose view of political reality already corresponds to that which they promote (Browne 1982: 235–236).

HISTORICAL CONFLICTS

The Korean War

The Korean War was the first direct military engagement of U.S. forces with those of Communist nations. It introduced limited warfare as a substitute for total (and possibly nuclear) war. Each side avoided attacking targets that could have led to the expansion of the war and limited the weapons it used as well as the territory in which it would fight. The war extracted enormous costs. For example, the South Korean and American troops suffered more than 580,000 casualties, the North Korean and Chinese troops suffered more than 1,590,000 casualties, and the United States spent about $67 billion on the war.

Remarkably, there appears to be little, if any, research on the role of IRB in the Korean War. That international radio was involved is suggested by the actions of the North Koreans, who initiated their international station, Radio Pyongyang, shortly before the war, adding English and Japanese services in 1950. It also suggested by the decision of the U.S. government to triple its funds for overseas communication during the war (Abshire 1976: 28). One detailed study of the VOA claimed that with the outbreak of the Korean War, "The VOA intensified its anti-Communist mission by broadcasting in Chinese designed to stir up discontent and disaffection in the Chinese homeland" (Alexandre 1988: 11).

Despite the absence of data, there seems little doubt that the international radio stations of the opposing nations invested the war with different meanings. The Communist nations claimed that capitalist countries had violated the Yalta and Potsdam agreements, which had been reached at the end of World War II, and that they sought to control world markets and sources of raw materials through limited wars (Grzybowski 1967). Western nations noted that they took military action only after North Korea invaded South Korea by crossing the thirty-eighth parallel and subsequently ignored a United Nations (UN) Security Council resolution demanding withdrawal of the troops. Each side charged the other with torture, starvation of prisoners, and other war crimes. The North Koreans and Chinese communists also were accused of "brainwashing" prisoners. After the 1953 truce, the West made much of the opposition of communist China and North Korea to UN insistence that prisoners of both sides be allowed to choose whether to return to their homeland. The refusal of approximately 14,000 Chinese and 8,000

North Korean prisoners to return home was presented by Western media as a dramatic repudiation of life in Communist societies.

The Uprising in Poland

In 1956, the call for "peaceful coexistence" and the campaign for "de-Stalinization" initiated by Nikita Khrushchev, then first secretary of the Communist party of the Soviet Union, encouraged many Eastern Europeans to expect greater freedom from Soviet Rule and an improved standard of living. In June, strikes and then riots broke out in Poznan, Poland. Workers in the ZISPO locomotive-building plant had been dissatisfied for several years about harsh working conditions, increasing work loads, and an increasing cost of living without improved wages. When they were informed that their work norms were to be increased yet again with no compensating increase in wages, they actively resisted.

Unrest soon spread to cities throughout Poland. Demands were made for the reinstatement to power of Wladyslav Gomulka, one of the early leaders of postwar Poland. Tension heightened and the distinct threat of a Soviet military invasion was present. The Polish Service of RFE encouraged citizens to be firm in their demands for political liberalization and the removal of some of the government's more repressive measures. However, RFE also cautioned the Poles to be realistic enough to recognize the ability of the Soviets to intervene (Browne 1982: 138). RFE's Polish Service reported the Polish uprising from the very first hours of the strikes in Poznan. Apparently, events were described in a careful and dispassionate manner and in a way that "counselled against hasty or dangerous action that could damage the cause but encourage keeping the spirit of freedom alive" (Mickelson 1983: 95). Such an approach involved broadcasting a view of the political situation in which, in the foreseeable future, it was not only just but also possible for citizens to overthrow their Communist regime. In the case of the 1956 RFE Polish transmissions, there may have been little, if any, distinction, between broadcasting news and broadcasting practical suggestions for political strategy.

The Poles were successful in avoiding direct military conflict with the Soviet Union and in returning Gomulka to his post as the head of Poland's Communist party. The reforms that followed included improving working conditions, abolishing forced collectivization of farmland, and ending the government's campaign against religion. These changes were widely reported by RFE in its many Eastern European language services and may have had a stimulating effect on Hungary, where fighting erupted days later in the streets of Budapest (Browne 1982: 138).

The Hungarian Uprising

Open revolution against Communist rule in Hungary spread rapidly. A new government was quickly established and declared Hungary to be a neutral nation like its neighbor Austria. However, the new government lasted only a few days. Over 200,000 Soviet troops and 2,500 tanks and armored cars poured into the country and suppressed the uprising. Countless Hungarians were killed or imprisoned, and approximately 200,000 fled their homeland.

RFE, whose Hungarian Service identified itself as "the voice of Free Hungary," was accused of discouraging a peaceful settlement of the conflict and demanding that all Communists resign from government. International radio stations of the Soviet Union, Czechoslovakia, and East Germany further contended that the rebels were "counterrevolutionaries and fascists" (Soley and Nichols 1987: 64–65). Many, in the West as well as in Soviet Bloc nations, also claimed that RFE had encouraged the rebels, whom it termed "freedom fighters," to endanger their lives by suggesting that they fight on, as Western military help would soon arrive (Heil and Schiele 1986: 101; Mickelson 1983: 96–103).

The extent to which RFE "fomented, organized and directed the revolution," as Soviet media charged, remains unclear. The perception of RFE as a "Cold Warrior" and a "propagandistic troublemaker" persists to this day (Mickelson 1983: 100–101). There are two ways in which RFE did become directly involved in the 1956 Hungarian uprising. First, it broadcast the list of the rebels' formal demands for sweeping reforms and reported their victories. Second, RFE helped unite the resistance movement by providing it with a central channel of communication. Rebels had taken over a number of local radio stations. However, their signals were too weak to be heard outside their local areas. The stations were monitored by RFE in Munich and their messages were broadcast back into Hungary (Browne 1982: 138–139; Mickelson 1983: 96; Soley and Nichols 1987: 64–67). RFE's activity, therefore, involved more than broadcasting news. It also involved the use of IRB as a tactical instrument.

Crisis in Suez

At the time of the Hungarian uprising, the Soviet Union was attempting to expand its influence in the Middle East. Both the Soviet Union and several Western nations courted Egypt's allegiance by offering economic aid for its development plans, which included construction of the Aswan High Dam. However, after Egypt actively sought Soviet aid for the dam and also purchased Soviet arms, the United States and Great Britain withdrew their offers of assistance. In retaliation, Egyptian president Gamal Abdel Nasser seized the Suez Canal from international control and accepted Soviet aid for the Aswan project.

In October 1956, when the Soviets were militarily involved in Hungary, Israel invaded Egypt. Great Britain and France immediately joined the attack, seeking to return the Suez Canal to international control. While both the United States and the Soviet Union supported a United Nations resolution calling for an immediate truce, the Soviets threatened to send troops to help Egypt. The United Nations did arrange a truce after several days of fighting, but, by backing Egypt against Israel, the Soviets had effectively portrayed themselves as supporters of the Arab nations in the affairs of the Middle East.

The Soviets were fortunate in having the Suez situation to deflect, at least partially, world attention from their invasion of Hungary. IRB from Soviet Bloc states claimed that Suez was a flagrant example of interference in the affairs of a sovereign state. When a BBC commentator unfavorably compared the Hungarian "intervention" to the Suez "campaign," Radio Prague responded:

Can he claim that the Israeli, British and French troops were invited into Egypt by the government of that country, as was the case in Hungary? Can he maintain that the Soviet troops entered Hungary to capture a Suez Canal for a bunch of shareholders, as was the case in Egypt? And, lastly, is it not clear that the Soviet troops are in Hungary to put an end to murder and terror, whereas the Western forces entered Egypt to start a war and to establish a reign of terror? (Radio Prague, November 11, 1956, quoted in Hale 1975: 24)

The situation in Suez presented the greatest difficulties for the External Services of the BBC. Problems stemmed from the deep divisions in British public opinion over the conflict. "As [Sir Kenneth] Clark succinctly put it, 'at no time since broadcasting began had there been such a lack of agreement in Parliament and in the country on a major matter of foreign policy' " (Briggs 1985: 317).

Prime Minister Anthony Eden expected the BBC to rally a nation at war, and not to report (and thereby possibly widen) the internal political differences. Nevertheless, the BBC broadcast a variety of views on the conflict, including some that were directly opposed to official government policy. For a time, the whole position of the BBC as an institution seemed to be in jeopardy. However, the Suez operations were so brief that it is impossible to tell whether, had they been prolonged, the cabinet would have used the provision of the license that accompanied the BBC's charter to exercise direct control over the organization (Briggs 1985: 317).

The BBC's refusal to engage in deliberate deception by creating and broadcasting a view of Britain as politically united on the Suez issue was not without political consequences. As Donald Browne noted:

The next few years saw considerable questioning of the External Services by parliament in the course of appropriations hearings, and the Services did not fare well in terms of budget increases during this period. Also, the Foreign Office, which served (and which continues to serve) as the main channel through which the External Services requested and received their budget, appointed an "observer" to assist in coordinating activities between itself and the External Services. (Browne 1982: 165)

Cuba and the Bay of Pigs

The United States and its international broadcasting organizations faced their own crisis five years after Suez. When John Kennedy became president in 1961, Cold War tensions were high. A new challenge had been presented to the United States in 1960 when Cuban leader Fidel Castro declared his government Communist, seized millions of dollars worth of U.S. property in Cuba, and began to receive military aid from the Soviet Union and other communist states. The United States ended diplomatic relations with Cuba in January 1961.

Prior to Castro's rise to power, the VOA had devoted less than 1 percent of its broadcast schedule to Latin American programming. However, following the Cuban Revolution, Congress authorized and provided funds to the United States Information Agency, the VOA's parent organization, to increase its Spanish-language broadcasts in order "to cultivate friendship with the people of Cuba and to offset anti-American broadcasts in that country" (Frederick 1986: 16).

In addition, the CIA financed a clandestine station, Radio Swan, which was named for its location on Swan Island, a barren piece of land off the coast of Honduras. The island long had served as a relay base for United Fruit Company's radio system. The station's purpose was to discredit the Castro government and to help prepare the way for the "liberation" of Cuba by Cuban exile forces (Browne 1982: 149). The station featured many well-known Cuban journalists, radio announcers, and opposition leaders who were living in exile in the United States (Soley and Nichols 1987: 178).

In April 1961, the CIA sponsored an invasion of Cuba by anti-Castro Cubans at the Bay of Pigs. A few hours after the insurgents landed on the beaches of Cuba, the VOA increased its Spanish-language, Latin American Service from two hours to nineteen hours daily. News and commentary stressed official pronouncements. Speculation regarding the role of the CIA in the invasion was scrupulously avoided (Frederick 1986: 17). Radio Swan became strategically involved in the military action. As the invasion force landed, it reported: "The invaders are steadily advancing on every front. Throughout all Cuba, people are joining forces with the underground rebels fighting Fidel Castro. Castro's forces are surrendering in droves" (Radio Swan, April 17, 1961, quoted in Soley and Nichols 1987: 181).

The Bay of Pigs operation was poorly planned and failed badly. Within three days, the Cuban militia had killed or captured most of the invaders. The unsuccessful military effort strengthened Castro's control of Cuba and delivered the United States an embarrassing foreign policy defeat. The failure of the invasion and revelations of The CIA's role in the affair forced the VOA to retract much of what it had claimed about the event and destroyed whatever credibility Radio Swan might have enjoyed. In response to the radio campaigns that had been waged against it, the Cuban government established its own international broadcasting organization following the Bay of Pigs invasion. By the 1980s, Radio Havana Cuba was broadcasting in eight languages for a total exceeding 400 hours a week, more than any other government station in the Americas.

The Cuban Missile Crisis

In October 1962, the United States determined that the Soviet Union secretly had installed missile bases in Cuba and was in the process of shipping missiles to them. President Kennedy demanded that the Soviet Union remove the missiles and set up a naval quarantine of Cuba. The Soviet Union tried to bargain, offering to remove the bases if the United States would dismantle its missile bases in Turkey. The United States refused, and the world waited for a possible nuclear confrontation.

In order to make the position of the U.S. government on the presence of missiles in Cuba clearly known throughout the world, the VOA patched together a network of commercial AM stations that flooded the Cuban AM dial. In Europe, the VOA, together with RFE, used fifty-two transmitters on eighty different frequencies to broadcast information about the U.S. position and related actions (Abshire 1976: 83).

One of the most interesting aspects of the VOA's involvement in the Cuban Missile crisis concerns the United States government's use of a network of privately owned commercial radio stations to saturate Cuba. The VOA is forbidden by its charter from broadcasting its programs within the United States. This provision is intended to prevent the government from "propagandizing" within the country. Critics of the Kennedy administration claimed that the VOA acted illegally in using domestic AM stations for its broadcasts to Cuba. The administration responded that the action did not violate the provision of the charter because the privately owned stations had volunteered their services (Frederick 1986: 19).

Whatever the merits of this argument, it does pose an important question: How would the commercial stations' presentation of the events comprising the Cuban Missile crisis have differed had they not been serving as part of the ad hoc VOA radio network? In the United States, or, more generally, in the context of a capitalist political economy, are the contents of reports that are prepared and delivered by privately owned media likely to differ in any important ways from the contents of reports prepared and delivered by government supported agencies? Is news that is constructed and broadcast by an agency of a capitalist state likely to differ from news constructed and broadcast by the privately owned media within that state? These questions will be explored in the following chapter.

After the Cuban Missile crisis, Cold War tensions eased somewhat. In 1963, the United States, the Soviet Union, and the United Kingdom signed a treaty limiting the testing of nuclear weapons; the United States and the Soviet Union also established a direct communication link between the White House and the Kremlin to reduce the risk of accidental nuclear war. In 1964, the United States and the Soviet Union signed their first bilateral treaty creating consular relations, and in 1966, direct air service was established between New York and Moscow. The following year, the two nations extended an agreement for educational, scientific, and cultural exchanges.

The Invasion of Czechoslovakia

Hopes for easing Cold War tensions in Europe were jolted on August 20, 1968, when Soviet, Bulgarian, East German, Hungarian, and Polish troops invaded Czechoslovakia. As with the Hungarian situation, the invasion was preceded by a period of liberalization. In January 1968, Antonin Novotny, long the Stalinist ruler of Czechoslovakia, was deposed as party leader and succeeded by Alexander Dubcek, a Slovak, who declared his intention to democratize the system of Communist rule. During the first eight months of 1968, a period often referred to as the "Prague Spring," Dubcek did transform Czechoslovakia into the most liberal of the Communist Bloc countries. Among other changes, Czech mass media were given considerable freedom from direct government control.

The invasion of Czechoslovakia was justified by Moscow as regional self-defense against foreign-influenced incursion, a right and duty established by the Warsaw Pact. The Soviets claimed they had entered Czech territory at the request of the Czech government, which had appealed for military aid in view of threats to the sovereignty of the state and its socialist system that were posed by domestic and foreign forces.

It was the contention of the Soviet Union that: "Czechoslovak reactionary leaders were being 'influenced' by 'American press, television and radio—these mass media [were using] the whole arsenal of misinformation, slander, [and] calumny in interpreting the events in Czech-oslovakia in a determined direction, incitement to further [undermine] the socialist order in Czechoslovakia' " (Franck and Weisband 1972: 105). As Radio Moscow put it:

Recently Czechoslovakia has been the subject of special attention from bourgeois propaganda. Press, radio and television pursue a clear course: first, to encourage those forces in Czechoslovakia who are following their own aims alien to the people; and, second, to undermine the friendship and fruitful cooperation be-tween the countries of the socialist community, and to sow distrust in the relation between fraternal peoples. (Radio Moscow Foreign Service to Czechoslovakia, May 16, 1968, quoted in Paulu 1974: 321)

At first glance, the explanation offered by the Soviets for their invasion of Czechoslovakia seems quite curious. No claims were made that West-ern troops were massed on the Czech border, that leaders or members of a Western-sponsored internal counterrevolutionary movement had been identified, or that a major cache of arms or vast sums of money available for the possible use of insurgent forces has been uncovered. Rather, the Soviet Union claimed that its military had been called into Czechoslovakia because of increasing Western influence in the nation. Franck and Weisband (1972) have referred to such a justification for armed intervention as "vicarious aggression," which is not aggression in an objective sense but rather exists in the subjectivity of the beholder. It all depends on how sensitive, how vulnerable, how paranoid the leadership of a superpower is; what on one occasion may be shrugged off as nuisance propaganda can on another be termed vicarious aggres-sion. There can be no objective standards for defining so subjective a circumstance (Franck and Weisband 1972: 106).

The United States and the Soviet Union have both asserted the principle that they may each decide at their own discretion to use force in a neighboring state when forces within that nation, "inspired" by an "alien" power or philosophy, appear to be taking control, even though the only external element is ideas, ideology, propaganda and perhaps moral or even financial support. (Franck and Weisband 1972: 108)

The authors contend that the United States employed such a justification for its military actions toward Guatemala in 1954, Cuba in 1962, and the Dominican Republic in 1965.

The Soviets defined the reform movement in Czechoslovakia as serv-ing the imperial intentions of the United States and West Germany. Czech reformers were depicted as agents of Western states seeking to expand their sphere of military-economic hegemony to the common danger of the socialist commonwealth.

It cannot, of course, be known whether those were the real reasons for the Soviet invasion, or whether this was really how the Kremlin perceived the Prague Spring and the intentions of the West. But they were the reasons advanced by Soviet apologists, and they were apparently accepted by all but a tiny radical minority of the Soviet population. (Franck and Weisband 1972: 164)

Another imponderable is the extent to which the Soviets constructed their view of the political situation in Czechoslovakia from materials presented by Western international media. To the extent that they did, Western news may have had unintended and undesired political consequences from the perspective of the West. Perhaps, a recognition of this possibility was responsible for the "cautious restraint" demonstrated by RFE's Czechoslovak desk during the Prague Spring and the subsequent Soviet invasion. RFE appears to have altered its approach to political turmoil in communist states as a result of its 1956 experiences in Hungary. Direct involvement in the uprising was left to clandestine stations. For example, numerous Russian-language clandestine broadcasts were designed to demoralize the invading troops (Soley and Nichols 1987: 12).

The Vietnam War

The Vietnam War threatened to turn the Cold War into a full-fledged conflict. France sought to reestablish its colonial control of Vietnam after the defeat of Japan in World War II. In 1950, as France began to suffer military reverses at the hands of communist and nationalist troops, the U.S. government started authorizing appropriations in support of anticommunist forces in Vietnam. Beginning with these early appropriations, "[The] VOA had its concomitant ideological role. Within a few months after Congress approved $75 million in March 1950 to contain Asian communism, the VOA added, not coincidentally, Vietnamese language programs to its broadcasts" (Alexandre 1988: 62).

The United States began sending military advisors to South Vietnam in the 1950s. During the early 1960s, the United States stepped up its support of South Vietnam, finally sending combat troops in 1965. Also in 1965, the United States began large-scale bombing of North Vietnam. By 1968, over 500,000 U.S. troops were in Vietnam.

The U.S. government explained its military involvement as an effort to stop the advance of communism in Asia and to defend democracy against aggression. "[American domestic] media coverage and interpretation of the war took for granted that the United States intervened in the service of generous ideals, with the goal of defending South Vietnam from aggression and terrorism and in the interest of democracy and self-determination" (Herman and Chomsky 1988: 169).

Throughout the Vietnam War, the insurgent forces were described as the "enemy," although it was never explained why they deserved to be so considered; it being assumed that the "Communist" label was sufficient explanation. Reporters who prided themselves on their objectivity saw cities "fall" to the "enemy" when they could have as easily viewed them as "liberated" or merely changing political hands. (Parenti 1986: 175)

Through 1967, the U.S. domestic media presentation of the Vietnam conflict reflected the official version expressed by the U.S. government. It appeared to be the view of members of the administration that the role of commercial media news in reporting the Vietnam situation was to support government activities. For example, Dean Rusk, then secretary of state, in response to a question that he considered unhelpful from ABC's diplomatic correspondent, John Scali, answered "Whose side are you on?" Thus, the very loyalty of a reporter who asked a critical question was challenged (Greenfield 1990: 76). Data indicate that commercial media coverage did encourage a decisive majority of readers, viewers, and listeners to support the war (Epstein 1975). Many had questioned U.S. involvement in Vietnam from its very beginning. When early dissent found public expression in the form of the organized protest of student, church, union, and peace groups, it was occasionally treated with some sympathy and insight. However, the cumulative impact of media coverage was to discredit protest (Gitlin 1980; Hallin 1986a).

The rightness of the war as a response to aggression and the nobility of intent to defend democracy were rarely subject to question. Any discussion of opposition tended to focus not on the legitimacy of the war but rather on the possibility of military success. A 1968 survey by the *Boston Globe* of thirty-nine leading American newspapers with a total circulation of 22 million showed that not one advocated withdrawal from Vietnam (Aronson 1973). This certainty contributed to the fact that, during the height of the Vietnam War, there were nearly 1,000 "underground" newspapers and 400 counterculture radio stations in the U.S. (Graber 1984: 347). Obviously, many Americans felt that commercial media did not reflect the full spectrum of opinion on the war.

If, at least through 1977, U.S. commercial media, independent of government sponsorship and protected by the First Amendment of the U.S. Constitution, accepted and disseminated the government view of the U.S. role in Vietnam, it is extremely unlikely that the VOA, the official international voice of the U.S. government, would do otherwise. Like domestic media, the VOA broadcast the statements and described the activities of government officials. It also presented official reports on the course of the war originating from the State Department, the Pentagon, the CIA, and the White House. Private and government-sponsored media alike constructed a political reality in which the United States had selflessly intervened to stop communist aggression and support political democracy. "Left out of this view was any thought that the United States had waged a horrific war in support of a dictatorship and against a largely civilian population to prevent a popularly supported non-capitalist alternative social order from gaining power" (Parenti 1986: 176).

In the United States, commercial media coverage of Vietnam began to change with the 1968 Tet offensive. U.S. military defeats made it increasingly difficult to continue disseminating optimistic reports about the course of the war and the "light at the end of the tunnel" that supposedly was seen by the administration. It also became increasingly difficult for the media to largely ignore domestic expressions of dissent and the dramatic growth of the antiwar movement.

The media emphasized the government's position until respected sources widely voiced their dissent. At that point the media continued to give the largest amount of coverage to the administration's views. But they coupled it with coverage of the story of growing dissent in America about the merits of Vietnam policies, including ample attention to anti-administration voices and to anti-war demonstrations. (Graber 1984: 327)

As America's commercial media unavoidably increased their coverage of U.S. military reverses in Vietnam and domestic opposition to the war (including the dissent of an increasing number of political elites), politically conservative critics of the media began to charge that such coverage was undermining public support for the war, encouraging a speedup of troop withdrawals, and subverting President Lyndon Johnson's program of "Vietnamization"—destroying indigenous assistance and its civilian base and expanding the war in Laos and Cambodia (Braestrup 1978).

There was no condemnation of the media for uncritical acceptance of the doctrine of U.S. benevolence and for adherence to the official line on all central issues, or even awareness of these characteristics in media performance. Rather, given that the U.S. government did not attain all of its objectives in Indochina, the issue was whether the media were to be faulted for undermining the noble cause for adopting too "adversarial" a stance and departing thereby from fairness and objectivity. (Herman and Chomsky 1988: 169–70)

Given the existence of such conservative criticism of commercial media coverage of Vietnam and its widespread acceptance by the U.S. public, it is hardly surprising that even more forceful attacks would be waged against the VOA. In 1967, John Daly, who had just taken over as director of the VOA, expressed his intention to have the VOA report "fully and fairly" the division in the country over Vietnam. A member of Congress, Charles Joelson (D-NJ), voicing the opinion of many government officials, responded by saying: "The Voice of America is to promulgate our government policy. If that policy is wrong, we ought to change it here, not broadcast statements opposing that policy." Another Congressman, John Rooney (D-NY), added that Daly "should realize that his job is to promote our way of thinking" (Browne 1982: 105).

As domestic debate on the war became more widespread and acrimonious, government pressure on VOA news to present a view of the Vietnam situation supportive of, or at least consistent with, administration objectives probably intensified. As the war was coming to a conclusion in 1975, VOA's coverage of congressional debate and conditions in Vietnam was subjected to censorship. Laurien Alexandre provided this example of censorship of Vietnam coverage:

On April 14, 1975, an internal VOA newsroom directive officially prohibited the use of any stories that spoke of, or were reflective of, a U.S. withdrawal from Saigon. Only administration sources were to be quoted on the evacuation. The comments of congressional leaders—statements which other international news agencies broadcast—were left unreported. . . . While the possibility of saving lives certainly played into the decision affecting VOA's coverage, the restraints must be viewed as compliance with diplomatic requests which attempted to disinform the Vietnamese about the American government's plans in order to save face as long as possible. (Alexandre 1988: 71–72)

Political considerations clearly played a major role in VOA's Vietnam coverage. Politicians and diplomats tried, and sometimes succeeded, in manipulating news gathering and in managing news dissemination to bolster the foreign policy objectives of the U.S. government. VOA news broadcasts, then, presented constructions of political reality that served government interests. VOA news personnel themselves may have opposed such a consequence.

It wasn't that VOA news staff were intentionally sabotaging American policy objectives nor that they necessarily even opposed U.S. actions in Vietnam. Simply, VOA news personnel did not want to be told what to do, or how to do it, by Uptown officials or State Department bureaucrats whom they felt were insensitive to the ethics of a professional news outlet. . . . It was over this Vietnam coverage that the tension between diplomacy and journalism became most pronounced by mid-decade. (Alexandre 1988: 64)

IMPLICATIONS OF SUEZ AND VIETNAM COVERAGE

The fundamental problem confronting the VOA in reporting political dissensus in the United States over the Vietnam War was similar to that facing the BBC in reporting political dissensus in Great Britain over the Suez conflict. Both organizations faced the threat of losing organizational integrity. Due to provisions of its Royal Charter and to the brevity of the Suez episode, the threat to the BBC was less than that challenging the VOA. However, it does seem reasonably clear that had the Suez crisis continued, the British government would have intervened in the framing of Suez coverage in the same way as the U.S. government intervened in the VOA newsroom during the later months of U.S. involvement in Vietnam.

The Suez and Vietnam cases suggest two generalizations about the operation of Western media, whether domestic or international, and state-sponsored or privately owned, during periods of extensive domestic political protest. First, when political dissent is reported, accounts will focus on dissent within the national elite. Attention will be paid to the expression of opposing views of members of Parliament, senators or members of Congress, or those representing dominant economic interests. Only rarely will the views of those associated with challenge groups receive comparable attention. For example:

When President Richard Nixon justified America's invasion into Cambodia during the Vietnam War, three groups immediately demanded time to broadcast counterarguments. One was a group of Democratic senators; another was the Democratic National Committee. The third was a group of business executives organized to oppose the war. The three groups differed in their assessment of the errors committed by the president, and none was willing to yield to any of the others. . . . The courts settled the problem of choosing among opponents by ruling that no group has the right to expound its particular brand of opposition. Rather, it is up to the media to decide which opposition group will be heard. (Graber 1984: 107–108)

It is extremely unlikely that only the three groups mentioned by Graber sought media access to respond to President Nixon's statements. However, it appears that they were the only groups considered to have a legitimate claim to media access. The media limited its own choice from among the severely limited set of opposing viewpoints that it had created. Such limitation was a form of self-censorship.

A second generalization about the performance of Western media proffered by the Suez and Vietnam situations concerns the response of the media to their perception of a threat of direct government involvement in determining the content of their news broadcasts. Journalists at the BBC and the VOA strenuously objected to any suggestion of government activity that could be interpreted as censorship. However, the objections seemed to be based more on a concern for some loss of apparent autonomy than for the substantive contents of the accounts that their governments would have them broadcast. This suggests that maintaining organizational and professional autonomy are the primary values of these Western media. Reliance on government sources for information, focusing almost exclusively on elite opinion, and broadcasting materials that support state interests and legitimize state action apparently are not interpreted by news professionals as inconsistent with their belief in their autonomy and the integrity of the organizations for which they work. It is primarily when a government explicitly threatens some form of direct censorship that the tension between the roles of the news organization as an information outlet and as a policy advocate is felt and elicits some response.

BROADCASTING THE TRUTH

To claim that those working in Western media organizations generally, or in Western international broadcasting organizations in particular, are concerned primarily with maintaining organizational and professional autonomy is not to assert that they are not committed to disseminating the truth. Accurate and objective reporting long has been accepted as the prime responsibility of news work and has been incorporated into the ideology of the profession. Certainly, most of those working in Western international broadcasting organizations would object to the argument (elaborated throughout this book) that they are engaged, in some phase or other, in the process of broadcasting propaganda.

It would be an oversimplification to suggest that the selection of issues to cover and the choice of sources to present to the public in news stories is politically motivated. While it is true that news legitimizes and supports the existing politico-economic system, it is not true that journalists' selection of news stories reflects a conscious desire on their part to report the news in such a way that the status quo is maintained. (Soloski 1989: 214)

Nevertheless, as Anthony Smith noted, everywhere in the world today:

news reporters are concerned with the collection of "facts," the selection and pre-digestion of information, the writing of descriptions of events. The problem lies in that "facts" do not exist in isolation from other facts or from wide-ranging sets of assumptions. The "facts" of news come to us embedded inside perspective from which their selection proceeds. (Smith 1973: 97)

The implication of this from the perspective of broadcasting news as broadcasting propaganda is this:

Insofar as we rely on news in forming our mental pictures of what is going on in the world, what we are seeing is not a neutral body of information, but rather information gathered and presented to illustrate certain ways of seeing the world based on certain values and favorable to certain courses of action. (Smith 1973: 100–101)

The professional ideology espousing commitment to the truth serves several related functions for news organizations and their employees. First, at least in the West, publicly proclaimed support of this value makes it difficult for government or private media owners or sponsors to intervene directly in the news-making process; an acknowledged commitment to telling the truth facilitates professional and organizational autonomy. Intervention would violate an important cultural value.

Second, constant emphasis on disseminating the truth can impede recognition of the point made by A. Smith (1973) and others (Edelman 1988; Gans 1979; Herman and Chomsky 1988; Manoff and Schudson 1986; Parenti 1986; Tuchman 1978) that all news reflects a social perspective and serves identifiable interests. Effectively denying or obscuring the point not only can improve organizational and professional self-image, it can enhance the credibility of the organization's constructions of political reality. This is particularly important in the highly competitive context within which international broadcast organizations operate, in which worldwide audiences commonly are exposed to conflicting historical, social, political, and economic perspectives associated with the conflicting political agendas of competing states.

Third, by obscuring recognition that news accounts inherently embody some perspective that supports political interests, the professional ideology of Western media organizations denies that they in fact have an identifiable perspective. Hence, it denies the very possibility of congruence between the perspectives of the news organization and government. However, it is precisely this congruence that accounts for the historical infrequency of direct interventions of Western governments into the news-making activities of their international broadcasting organizations. That is, Western governments tend not to censor, not because they are inhibited by cultural norms or by the legal provisions of charters from interfering in the affairs of organizations that broadcast "the truth" to the world, but because they seldom have any real need to do so. The history of IRB (traced in this chapter as well as in Chapter One) supports such a contention.

BROADCASTING TO THE THIRD WORLD

As noted earlier, transmissions by colonial powers to their territories were among the first international radio broadcasts. Such broadcasting was to provide a "home away from home" for colonial administrators and expatriates and to contribute to the political integration of colonial empires. Later, indigenous peoples in colonial and other dependent and economically underdeveloped regions became target audiences for economically and politically dominant states seeking to spread their social, political, and economic perspectives worldwide.

While IRB served for decades as a major source of information for many of the nations of Asia, Africa, and Latin America, it was only after the decolonization that followed World War II that the penetration of Western news and mass culture into the regions came to be perceived by some regional leaders as problematic (Hachten 1987: xvi).

The first formal declaration expressing concern about the structure and content of international communication was adopted at the Fourth Summit Conference of the Non-Aligned Movement held in Algiers in 1973. The agenda of the conference suggested the need of nonaligned nations to reorganize their colonially inherited communication channels which, it contended, hampered information exchanges among them. It also called on the nations to counteract what it claimed as the often tendentious, incorrect, nonobjective, and inadequate coverage given Third World nations in the international media. These media are controlled by agencies of developed countries and effectively monopolize the dissemination of world information and news (Samarajiwa 1974).

Since the original 1973 declaration, numerous academic studies have explored its basic thesis (United Nations Educational, Scientific, and Cultural Organization 1979; Lee 1980; McPhail 1981; Nordenstreng and Schiller 1979; Rosenblum 1979; Schiller 1976; Smith 1980; Tunstall 1977). Researchers have investigated the consequences of Third World reliance on Western news agencies, films, books, magazines, television programs, broadcasting norms, communication hardware, engineers, and technicians, and also on Western trained journalists. Reports have detailed the specific ways in which the phenomenon that was coming to be known as media imperialism, cultural domination or electronic colonialism appears to operate.

International radio broadcasting organizations, such as the BBC and the VOA, long have had audiences numbering in the millions throughout Asia, Africa, and Latin America. Nevertheless, little empirical research has systematically investigated the possible impact of IRB in the Third World. If the programming of an international broadcasting organization tends to promote the political and material interests of its nation and protect its value orientations and cultural assumptions without serious regard for the potentially damaging effects of such programming on the receiving culture, then its transmissions to other nations reasonably might be viewed as part of a process of media imperialism. Certainly it might be viewed as such if the transmitting nation were in the industrialized West and the target nation or area were part of the Third World.

The extent to which the programming of any given international broadcasting organization promotes its national political, material, and cultural interests can be treated, at least in part, as an empirical question. So too can the question of the amount and character of what it says about Third World nations. International broadcast organizations may differ in these regards, and the nature and extent of these differences among international broadcasting organizations can also be treated as questions for empirical research. These and related topics will be discussed in some detail in Chapter Four. Using original data, the chapter presents the first attempt to understand empirically the impact of IRB on the Third World through the use of comparative content analysis.

IRB IN A RADICALLY CHANGING WORLD

Political, military, and economic conditions clearly have determined the history of IRB. As we have seen, in World War I, Germany used it to carry military messages. Later, shortwave broadcasting was employed by the Russians to declare to the world the accomplishments of their revolution and help with their task of national economic development and political integration. In the following decade, colonial powers, such as the Dutch and the British, initiated international radio services to strengthen profitable ties with their colonies. The broadcasting organizations' historical experiences had long-lasting effects on the language services they developed and maintained and on their relations to their sponsoring states.

World War II prompted a vast expansion of IRB. In that historical context, its service as an instrument for political mobilization and for symbolically attacking state adversaries was firmly established. Techniques for writing messages for international audiences that served state interests were developed and refined.

While throughout the war, some international broadcast organizations continued to practice deliberate deception in their presentation of news, experiences in World War II made it clear to many broadcasters that the long-run consequences of this strategy tended to be counterproductive from the perspective of the interests of their nations. During World War II, national self-images broadcast by the international radio organizations of the Allies, as well as the images of the Axis nations they transmitted, for the most part probably represented neither organization-initiated attempts at deception nor the results of direct government intervention. Rather, it seems more likely that the program contents reflected newsmakers' adoption of their own nation's dominant political culture.

Newsmakers, as well as the political elites of their countries, generally see the political world in the same general terms. Nevertheless, journalists do not tend to understand or to represent their accounts as bearing the imprint of a political culture, but see them rather as fundamentally undistorted reflections of political reality. Historically, journalists often have worked deliberately to provide people living under oppressive systems of rule with the only view of political situations they might have as an alternative to the official view of their state. It is difficult to exaggerate the importance of making available such an alternative. Remarkably courageous men and women have willingly accepted great personal risks and hardships so that they might "tell the truth as they see it." However, even in these cases, the problematic nature of the last four words, "as they see it," often has not always been fully appreciated.

After World War II, there was near universal acceptance of the idea that the United States and the Soviet Union were engaged in a Cold War. Worldwide adoption of this notion provided the interpretative framework within which most accounts of major international events were presented by the world's international broadcasting organizations for more than forty years—most of the history of IRB itself. Chapter Four presents an original study that illustrates, details, and explains some of the impact of the Cold War on the contents of Voice of America and Radio Moscow newscasts.

In 1989, a series of extraordinary events initiated changes in the structure of the world political order that eventually prompted political elites and news organizations throughout the world to proclaim that the Cold War had ended. The Soviet Union withdrew its troops from Afghanistan, the Solidarity Movement acceded to power in Poland, and mass protests demanding fundamental political, economic, and human rights were staged in the heart of Beijing, followed by similar action in East Germany, Czechoslovakia, Bulgaria, Rumania, and, finally, the Soviet Union itself. Whether or not the Cold War had ended (whatever that might mean), it became clear that the framework within which the condition and the events of the world political economy had been interpreted for more than forty years was no longer serviceable.

One event that was widely interpreted as signaling the emergence of a new international order and the demise of the Cold War as a viable framework for understanding world politics was the joint reaction of the United States and the Soviet Union to Iraq's annexation of Kuwait in the late summer of 1990. The implication of both nations' condemnation of Iraq's military action and their agreement to cooperate in halting further Iraqi expansion was interpreted in unambiguous terms by the VOA:

Since the fall last year of the Berlin Wall, and the dramatic easing of East-West tensions that followed, there has been much talk about establishing a new world order for a post–Cold War era. For the Bush administration, the crisis prompted by Iraq's invasion of Kuwait represents a test of how the post–Cold War world will work. (Voice of America, English Service to the Americas, September 7, 1990)

At least two major international broadcasting organizations have already started to claim a role for themselves in the "post–Cold War era" and to request resources for the performance of that role. VOA director Richard Carlson made the appeal for his organization this way:

This is a time of matchless opportunity. The VOA staff of the 1940s was eager for the day when they would have victories to report—the victory of western armies over the Axis powers that held much of the world enslaved. This generation of VOA broadcasters is eager to report on the world's most recent victory, the victory of freedom. Millions in China, Poland, Hungary, Czechoslovakia, Burma, Romania and Bulgaria—as well as sub-Sahara Africa—will tell you how VOA has inspired them in the past year and for many years before that. Their quest for freedom continues and so does the VOA's indispensable mission as an intellectual greengrocer to the world, providing food for the sustenance of common ideals. Given the resources, we welcome the opportunity. (Voice of America 1990: 1)

The BBC made a similar case:

The opening up of previously closed societies did not lessen the hunger for BBC broadcasts. In Eastern Europe generally the demand for reliable objective information is, if anything, greater than during the past 40 years. "The Spectator" wrote: "There is a huge need for popular re-education here, much greater than that which faced the Allies in Germany after the war. Far from being wound down, the external services of the BBC and their sister services (Radio Free Europe, Deutsche Welle, etc.) should be extended and funded more generously than ever before." (British Broadcasting Corporation 1990: 56)

As new international conflicts arise and as others are resolved, and as new political-economic alliances are formed and as others are terminated, international broadcasting organizations will introduce new reifying terms and phrases to refer to the changed conditions. New typifications and new frameworks for understanding and responding to political actors and events will appear in their newscasts. New political realities will be created for IRB audiences and, if sustained by state resources, international radio stations will go forward with their business: broadcasting propaganda.

Chapter Three

News, Propaganda, and International Radio Broadcasting

Erving Goffman began his major essay on the basic frameworks available in our society for making sense out of events in the following manner:

There is a venerable tradition in philosophy that argues that what the reader assumes to be real is but a shadow, and that by attending to what the writer says about perception, thought, the brain, language, culture, a new methodology, or novel social forces, the veil can be lifted. That sort of line, of course, gives as much a role to the writer and his writing as is possible to imagine and for that reason is pathetic. (What can better push a book than the claim that it will change what the reader thinks is going on?) (Goffman 1974: 1)

Clearly intending to avoid this tradition, but nevertheless working to develop another analysis of social reality, Goffman asserted that he would try

to follow a trend established by William James. . . . Instead of asking what reality is, he gave matters a subversive phenomenological twist, italicizing the following question: *Under what circumstances do we think things are real?* The important thing about reality, he implied, is our sense of its realness in contrast to our feeling that some things lack this quality. One can then ask under what conditions such a feeling is generated, and this question speaks to a small, manageable problem having to do with the camera and not what it is the camera takes pictures of. (Goffman 1974: 2)

The analysis of broadcasting propaganda developed in this book has to do with the accounts of politically relevant phenomena that are carried on IRB. The study focuses on the political realities created by international broadcasting organizations and not on the political realities created by the actions of governments and states. At times, the study does deal with the relation between IRB accounts and the political actors, events, and conditions of which they tell. On these occasions, concern is not with the truth or falsity of the accounts, however that might be assessed, but with the circumstances under which, and the methods by which, certain political actions, conditions, and events are presented as realities by various international broadcasting organizations.

This study does not argue that what people assume to be real about the political world as a result of listening to IRB is but a shadow and that, by attending to its arguments, readers will be in a position to assess what is or was really going on. However, the study does argue that any distinction between news and propaganda is problematic, that the activity of telling the truth does not have some of the commonsense characteristics often assigned to it, and that the claim that one is telling the truth historically has been made in the service of organizational, governmental, and state interests.

Reporting the history of IRB in Chapter One and Two required the use of analytically difficult terms such as news and propaganda and extensive questioning of many phrases such as *Cold War* and *political crisis* to indicate the need to explore tacit assumptions about their referents.

This chapter examines these and several related concepts. It begins with a description of a theoretical perspective on the relation between truth claims and the objects about which these claims are made. The perspective also concerns the relation between truth claims and legitimation. Next, a recent theoretical approach to the role of the mass media in shaping both personal and socially shared beliefs about what is going on in the world is described. The chapter then moves to an analysis of news and propaganda. Discussions focus on the application of those concepts to the contents of IRB. To paraphrase Goffman, the chapter speaks to a reasonably manageable problem having to do with IRB and not directly with what it is that the broadcasts are talking about.

THE SOCIAL CONSTRUCTION OF
REALITY PERSPECTIVE

Those with philosophical interests in epistemology, ontology, and language have explored questions about the nature of truth for centuries. Those with anthropological interests in the interplay of language, thought, and culture also have created a venerable intellectual history in confronting the topic. The concern here is considerably more modest.

Discussion will proceed on the basis of a comparatively recent theoretical perspective that finds its immediate source in the sociology of knowledge and its application in the academic fields of sociology, communication, and political science. The general theoretical orientation is often referred to as the *social construction of reality*. As a theoretical orientation within sociology, it is common associated with the writings of Alfred Schutz (1932/1967; 1962), Peter Berger and Thomas Luckmann (1966), and Erving Goffman (1974).

Alfred Schutz's inquiries focused on the way in which people create the world of everyday life. In exploring this topic, Schutz raised William James's questions about what people accept as reality. All human beings, he asserted, carry in their minds a "stock knowledge of physical things and fellow creates, of social collections and artifacts, including cultural objects" (Schutz, 1932/1967: 81). This stock of knowledge, which they have acquired through the process of socialization, provides a frame of reference or orientation with which they can interpret objects and events as they conduct their everyday lives. Moreover, the objects and events of the world have no inherent or universal meaning apart from this imposed framework.

For Schutz, people's stock of knowledge *is* their reality. It is experienced as the objective world existing "out there," independent of their will and confronting them as fact. The stock of knowledge has a taken-for-granted character and is seldom the object of conscious reflection. It is understood by people in a commonsense fashion as reality itself. Although people can doubt this reality, they very seldom do so—and they cannot do so when they are engaged in their routine activities.

People assume that other members of their society generally share their stock of knowledge and will experience the world in the same way they do. They assume that others will see the world as being made up of the same types of objects and events, that these objects and events will have the same meaning for them, and that they will respond to them in the ways they themselves have learned are appropriate.

For Schutz, objects and events have no inherent, universal meanings apart from the meanings that actors impose on them. People rely on *typifications* or "recipes" for action that exist in their culture. These typifications which are part of their stock of knowledge, provide them with ready-made courses of action, solutions to problems, and interpretations of the social world. While the typifications constitute a cultural framework that is experienced as requiring no further analysis, problematic situations can arise that call the typifications into question.

Some inferences about social discourse can be drawn from Schutz's perspective. The approach suggests that in everyday conversation, people use typifications about objects and events. Their statements are meaningful to others who have learned the same stock of knowledge of which the typifications are a part. To the extent that listeners share the speaker's interpretation of the world and the speaker avoids using typifications in idiosyncratic or unconventional ways, listeners will assume that the speaker is telling the truth. This is the routinely unquestioned assumption that speakers themselves also make about their own statements. The assumption of truth is likely to be made by an audience except in those unusual contexts in which there are some independent grounds for doubting the veracity of the speaker.

Some discourse between a speaker and an audience whose members are not participants in a common culture with the speaker can have a very different character. If the audience has not learned the stock of knowledge of which the speaker's typifications are a part, the assumption that it will accept, in an unquestioned manner, the speaker's interpretation of the world is not warranted. The reality of the speaker and the reality of audience members are less likely to fully coincide. While there may be no doubt in the mind of the speaker that he or she is telling the truth, members of a foreign (culturally different) audience, in particular, are not likely to be so certain. If, in addition, audience members have some reason to suspect that the speaker has an interest in manipulating them, then, no matter how truthful the speaker sees him- or herself as being, he or she will not be entirely credible. The important point, however, is that differences in the constructed realities of the speaker and a foreign audience may lead the audience to view the speaker's assertions as lacking meaning or credibility. He or she will not be routinely accepted as an agent who tells the truth.

Recognition of the observable differences between societies, in terms of what is taken for granted as knowledge in them, is the point of departure for Peter Berger and Thomas Luckmann's analysis of

the process by which any body of "knowledge" comes to be socially established as "reality." Sociological interest in questions of "reality" and "knowledge" is initially justified by the fact of their social relativity. What is "real" to the Tibetan Monk may not be "real" to an American businessman. . . . It follows that specific agglomerations of "reality" and "knowledge" pertain to specific social contexts. (Berger and Luckmann 1966: 3)

In addition to discussing, in a manner similar to that of Schutz, processes by which people create the realities of their everyday lives, Berger and Luckmann considered the construction of symbolic realities. While language, with its typifications, has its primary reference to objects and events that individuals routinely experience and share with others in a taken-for-granted manner, it can be used to transcend the here and now. Language can bring to life not only objects and events that are physically absent at the moment but also objects and events in the remembered or reconstructed past as well as objects and events that are projected as imaginary figures or occurrences in the future. Language also is capable of constructing symbols that are highly abstracted from everyday experience. It can create symbol systems (such as religion, philosophy, ideology, and science) that become essential constituents of everyday life and the conscious experience of this reality (Berger and Luckmann 1966: 38–42).

Berger and Luckmann observed that social institutions appear to have an objective reality of their own as given, self-evident aspects of the world. The social world, which is a human product, confronts its producer as an external reality—as something other than a human product. New generations learn about this reality through the process of socialization, just as they learn about the other things that make up the world they encounter daily.

New generations also learn a meaning of the social order, which bestows on it not only cognitive validity but normative legitimacy as well. Socialization involves the simultaneous transmission of knowledge and values. All understandings of the social world carry with them evaluations. Berger and Luckmann's position thus eschews the traditional distinction between the explanation and the evaluation of the social world. This position is developed in their discussion of "levels of legitimation" (1966: 94–104).

Incipient legitimation involves assigning labels to objects of experience. As an example, Berger and Luckmann noted that the transmission of a kinship vocabulary pro facto legitimates the kinship structure. The second level of legitimation contains practical explanatory schemes such as proverbs, adages, moral maxims, legends, folk tales, and so on. The third level of legitimation contains explicit and relatively complex theories that explain the structure and operation of the given social order. The theories provide a frame of reference for understanding institutionalized patterns of conduct. Because of their complexity, they often are transmitted by specialized personnel in formal socialization contexts.

Symbolic universes constitute Berger and Luckmann's fourth and most comprehensive level of legitimation. These abstract symbol systems are social products whose history must be understood in order to have a full grasp of their meaning. A symbolic universe provides meaning for realities other than those of everyday experience and "puts everything in its right place." Since that "right place" is the reality of everyday life, and since the social order is a part of it, "the symbolic universe provides the ultimate legitimation of the institutional order by bestowing upon it the primacy in the hierarchy of human experience" (Berger and Luckmann 1966: 98).

Features of VOA coverage of international events between 1946 and 1989 serve to illustrate the involvement of IRB in the social construction and legitimation processes identified by Berger and Luckmann. Again it must be emphasized that discussion concerns accounts of the actions of governments, armies, civilian populations, and so on, and not the actors and actions themselves.

As Laurien Alexandre (1988: 8–13) pointed out, the VOA originated as part of the Truman administrations effort to "sell the 'Cold War.' " The very use of the term *Cold War*, in VOA newscasts, bestowed both cognitive validity on an interpretation of exciting relations between the United States and the Soviet Union and normative validity on the policies and actions of the United States as depicted within the interpretation (incipient legitimation). Presentations of the Korean War, uprisings in Poland and Hungary, and the invasion of Czechoslovakia included the use of maxims asserting that the international role of the United States was to help any "free" nation resist "communist aggression" (second level of legitimation). Countless discussions of U.S. foreign policy by government officials, academics, foundation representatives, authors, and so on, as presented in the context of programming represented as in-depth analyses of the Vietnam War, offered third-level legitimations.

According to Robert Bellah (1975), Americans share a "civil religion." This is a national religious self-understanding that is expressed in a set of beliefs (Americans as the chosen people), symbols (the Statue of Liberty) and solemn rituals (a presidential inauguration) and also has its own prophets (George Washington and Thomas Jefferson), martyrs (Abraham Lincoln and John Kennedy), sacred events (Memorial Day), sacred places (Arlington National Cemetery), and sacred scriptures (the Declaration of Independence and the Constitution). The civil religion has served to reaffirm the religious legitimacy of the highest political authority, to provide symbols of national solidarity, and to mobilize deep levels of personal motivation for the attainment of national goals. In Berger and Luckmann's terms, such a civil religion constitutes a symbolic universe.

Under Ronald Reagan's administration, a considerable segment of VOA's broadcasting to Western Europe was aimed at undermining support for oppressed people in parts of the Third World that had developed as a consequence of the Vietnam War, and at restoring the image of American benevolence that had been shaped by CARE (Cooperative for American Relief to Everywhere) packages, the Marshall Plan, and the Berlin airlift experiences of an earlier generation (Alexandre 1988: 102–104). Programming presenting U.S. policy toward certain "Third World" nations (e.g., Nicaragua) as the policy of a nation depicted in terms of this symbolic universe involved efforts at establishing Berger and Luckmann's fourth level of legitimation.

Legitimation processes explain the social world by ascribing validity to socially created meanings (Berger and Luckmann 1966: 93). This proposition suggests that an audience will tend to view a source of communication as telling the truth when its claims appear to audience members to be consistent with the set of socially constructed meanings they share. The perception of such consistency subsequently will promote audience acceptance of the normative components embodied in the claims as well. The perception of inconsistency will lead an audience to reject the credibility of the source of communication. The rejection of a message from this source will not be experienced as a choice of one social construction of reality and a rejection of an alternative, but rather as acceptance of the truth and the rejection of a lie or half-truth or (under conditions specified later in this chapter) an acceptance of the truth and a rejection of propaganda.

From the perspective of the source of the communication, unless it deliberately was attempting deceit, rejection of its message is likely to be explained in terms of its audience being "out of touch with reality" and being unable to recognize the truth. The audience may be seen as the victim of lies, half-truths, brainwashing, indoctrination, and propaganda. Neither communicator nor foreign audience is likely to give any serious consideration to Berger and Luckmann's fundamental point that what is real to the Tibetan monk may not be real to the American businessman.

Much of the work of Erving Goffman shares with that of Schutz and Berger and Luckmann the premise that the social world is fundamentally ambiguous: Objects, actors, conditions and events have no inherent meaning. Rather, meaning is imposed through human action that organizes, characterizes, and identifies experiences in terms of shared definitions. The meaning that is imposed is limited by, and relative to, the social context in which it is created. Once meanings are learned through the socialization process, people tend to act on them without continual reassessment and without awareness of the social forces that created them. In Goffman's terms, we use these institutionalized meanings to "frame" or interpret our everyday experience (Goffman 1974).

A *frame* is a scheme of interpretation in which features of the world to which we attend are organized and made intelligible. A frame provides an answer to the question, "What is going on?" Any event can be described in terms of a focus that is wide or narrow and close or distant. Furthermore, in most situations, many different things are simultaneously occurring—things that are likely to have begun at different moments and that may terminate dissynchronously. Hence, to ask the question, "What is *it* that is going on?" biases the answer in the direction of unitary exposition and simplicity. Finally, characteristics of any event may differ widely because an individual or organization's role in an undertaking can provide a distinctive evaluative assessment of what sort of an instance of the type the particular undertaking was (Goffman 1974: 8–10).

Lang and Lang (1983) provided an important example of applying the concept of framing to the analysis of media construction of news and the political implications of the construction process. Their research, which concerns U.S. media coverage of the Watergate burglary, found that, while there was extensive discussion of the topic in the press, almost all of it presented Watergate as a partisan issue of the sort that commonly arises during heated political campaigns. When democratic candidate George McGovern's comments about Watergate were presented, they were "balanced" by the presentation of White House denials of McGovern's claims and interpretations. Possibly as a consequence of such a presentation (framing), public opinion polls showed that Watergate failed to become an issue in the 1972 presidential campaign. It was not until late in 1973 when Watergate case Judge John Sirica was presented by the media as a credible, unbiased spokesman for a cover-up scenario that the press abandoned its practice of "balancing" Watergate reports and instead presented information that more or less exclusively supported the cover-up narrative. Watergate, once understood as a caper, finally came to be perceived by the public as an important and politically relevant problem.

In most communication situations, a source offers an audience a frame that the source itself has adopted. The communication is intended to lead all participants to have the same view of something that is going on. Obviously, however, there are occasions when one or more individuals intentionally make an effort to manage activity so that others will have a false belief (i.e., one employing a frame different from that adopted by the communicators themselves) about what is happening. Goffman (1974: ch. 4) noted that when two or more individuals cooperate in presenting a deception, covert communication among them is likely to be required and, even when it is not required, the grounds for it are present. This he termed *collusive communication;* those in on the deception are a *collusive net* and those against whom the net operates are the *excolluded*.

Goffman identified several varieties of deceptions. First, there are those that are benign; these are not injurious to fundamental rights. Here, not only is the structure of framed activity in question, so too is the moral attitude of the community to such activities. A second class of fabrications consists of those that are exploitive: One party constrains others in a construction that is clearly inimical to its interests. In addition to such direct fabrications involving two essential parties—a fabricator who does the manipulation and a dupe whose world is fabricated and who is molded as a consequence, Goffman identified a class of indirect constructions involving three parties. A fabricator can construct a definition of a second party in order to be in a position to dupe a third party into certain false beliefs concerning the second. The second party—the victim—need not be taken in, and is unlikely to be. What is required is that the party that had been misrepresented be unable for some reason to convince the third party of the facts.

Situations such as these introduce the notion of frame conflict. As an example, Goffman cited a well-known study indicating that what is considered horseplay for inner-city adolescents is often seen as vandalism and thievery by officials and victims. In this case, and in countless others, Goffman noted, there is no way in theory to bring everyone into the same frame (Goffman 1976: ch. 9). The power position of the contending parties then becomes relevant. The more powerful party may be able to dominate coercive forces sufficiently to induce a show of respect from the other party. To this it can be added that the more powerful of two parties in a frame dispute involving public issues is more likely to have access to the means of mass communication through which public framing of the issue can be influenced.

In sum, the social construction of reality perspective, as presented in the works of Schutz, Berger and Luckmann, and Goffman, views purposeful human activity as taking place within structures of meaning. The objects and events of the everyday world have no meaning that is inherent and universal, but only what is socially created and socially imposed. Those imposed meanings, these theorists assert, reflect the structure of the social-historical contexts in which they were created. However, people routinely experience the world in a "taken-for-granted way"; meaning appears to be both inherent and universal. People generally conduct their everyday lives under the unreflective assumption that everyone's experience of the world is fundamentally the same. This assumption is misleading for two related reasons. First, it obscures the extent to which the objects of experience are social creations and not "givens" with the same ontological and epistemological status as the objects they symbolically designate through the use of words such as *tree* and *rock*. Second, the assumption leads to an identification of truth with a particular, learned set of socially shared meanings. The implications of this approach and its associated concepts such as *typification, reification, legitimation, frames,* and *collusive nets* to the analysis of IRB will be identified on the following pages.

MEDIA SYSTEM DEPENDENCY THEORY

Media system dependency theory provides the conceptual link between the social construction of reality perspective and empirical research on the role that mass media play in shaping both personal and socially shared beliefs about social objects, particularly those social objects that are remote from people's everyday lives (Adoni and Mane 1984: 327). In developing this position, Hanna Adoni and Sherrill Mane noted that the media of mass communication are referred to only in a tangential way by Schutz and Berger and Luckmann. (They did not mention Goffman.) However, it is clear that, to a considerable extent, what people in modern societies believe about what is going on in the world is influenced by their exposure to mass media.

With respect to specifically political beliefs, Dan Nimmo and James Combs contended that: "few people learn about politics through direct experience; for most persons political realities are mediated through mass and group communication, a process resulting as much in the creation, transmission and adoption of political fantasies as in realistic views of what takes place" (1983: xv). This argument expresses the basic premise that Nimmo and Combs share with the social construction of reality theorists: "Reality is created or constructed through communication, not expressed by it" (Nimmo and Combs 1983: 3).

An example of this process is provided by a cross-national study conducted in the United States, United Kingdom, Germany, Israel, and South Africa (Cohen, Adoni, and Bantz 1990). Researchers found that respondents' perception of a foreign conflict's complexity (number of issues, number of participants, duration of history, and magnitude of possible consequences), intensity (physical aggression, verbal aggression, and expression of feelings or emotions exposed by participants in a conflict), and solvability (nature of the issues, desire of involved parties to solve the conflict, willingness of involved parties to compromise, and the presence of parties actually engaged in solution-oriented activity) was related to the presentation of social conflict in general on television news to which they were exposed.

Analysis of the U.S. public's perceptions of its political leaders provides a further illustration of the creation of political reality for audiences by the mass media. Edelman (1988: 104–105) pointed out that it is language about political actors and events, not the actors or events in any other sense, that people experience. Political language is political reality; there is no other so far as the meaning of events to actors and spectators is concerned. Media offer accounts of political leaders to the mass public, which accepts or rejects these constructions in accord with their perception of their own material and ideal interests. For example, in some media accounts, Ronald Reagan was presented as a well-meaning and effective leader who represented the common people's aspirations against elitist liberals and intellectuals, while in other accounts he was characterized as a front for mean-spirited corporate executives and a menace to the poor. There was no way to establish the validity of either of these positions to the satisfaction of those who had a material or ideological reason to hold a different view.

The difference between the two examples of media construction of political reality is subtle. Audiences probably were aware that there were alternative accounts of the Reagan presidency and that they had a choice in determining for themselves which among them represented the truth. Audiences probably are less likely to be aware that their understanding of the complexity, intensity and solvability of some given international conflict is one of a number of alternatives perspectives on what is really going on. However, in both cases, audiences are presented with socially constructed realities, whether they are recognized as such or not.

In cases where individuals simply do not attend to the constructed nature of accounts of political actors, events, or conditions, they are likely to label such presentations news; where they are more aware of their constructed nature, they are more likely to label such presentations editorial; and where they view presentations as accounts intentionally constructed to serve political goals, they are more likely to label such presentations propaganda. However, whether people view themselves as confronting news, editorials, or propaganda, experiences with these symbolic materials shape what they believe, question, or do not believe about political reality. In modern societies people depend on the mass media to provide such experiences.

Melvin DeFleur and Sandra Ball-Rokeach (1989: 302–327) identified three "dependency–engendering" information resources, controlled by the media, to which individual groups, organizations, and institutions require access in order to attain many of their goals. First, media have the capacity to gather or create information. Second, media can transform the raw information they gathered or created into forms useful to other social actors. Third, media have the capacity to deliver information to mass audiences. This information is used by actors to understand themselves, the world of their everyday experiences, and the world beyond their direct experience, and to orient their actions and interactions with others.

Social understanding dependencies develop when actors use media information resources to comprehend and interpret people, culture, and events of the past, present, and future. *Action orientation dependencies* appear when actors use media information resources as guides for their own behavior, such as voting. *Interaction orientation dependencies* are established when actors rely on information from media about behaviors that are appropriate or effective in dealing with others, such as members of groups with whom they have had little experience or contact. In any society the broader the range of goals that require access to media information resources, the greater will be the power of that society's media.

An example of the application of media system dependency theory is provided by a study of the response of the directly affected population to the eruption of Mount St. Helens in May 1980 (Hirschburg, Dillman, and Ball-Rokeach 1986). Researchers found that average citizens and official agencies lacked a frame of reference to interpret the event. Neither the public nor their officials knew what to expect or what action to take. (People did not know that the cloudy ash from the eruption would deposit up to several inches of ash in areas hundreds of miles from the volcano site. Once the ash fell, no one knew what impact it might have. Was it harmful to breathe? Would it damage property? How did you get rid of it?) The eruption provided an ambiguous situation—one in which there is insufficient information to create a definition or to select one definition over others. Attaining individual and collective safety and security goals was dependent on the resources of the media system. Leaders and average citizens knew the media system was in a far better structural position eventually to obtain, process and disseminate ambiguity-resolving information than were their interpersonal communication networks. The researchers concluded that in any situation in which ambiguity is experienced and interpersonal communication networks lack the information or expertise needed to resolve the ambiguity, the media system becomes the major alternative information source. They also suggested that, in the same way, rapid social change catches people without an established reality to use in defining and interpreting events going on around them. In the case of rapid social change, we should also expect to find the media system dominant in people's search for information to make the world interpretable and, therefore, less threatening.

Media system dependency theory also specifies that the media have their own set of dependencies. In particular, they depend on the political system for the resources necessary for the attainment of important goals, including their stability and economic welfare (DeFleur and Ball-Rokeach 1989: 304–305). The polity includes regulatory agencies controlling, among other things, frequency and transmission power (in the case of electronic media), patterns of ownership, and tariff and trade policies. At least in the West, the polity also legitimizes the media by granting it constitutional and other legal rights as an information system. It does this on the ground that the media are essential to democracy because they stimulate citizens' political interest and provide the specific information they need to hold government ultimately accountable to the governed. In apparent support of this goal, some political systems, such as those of Norway and Sweden, go so far as to subsidize the newspapers of various parties in an effort to make available to the public a diversity of political views (Hachten 1987: 22).

DeFleur and Ball-Rokeach (1989: 309) pointed out that individuals construct their own media systems. That is, people put together particular combinations of the media that are available to them: newspapers, magazines, radio, television, and so on. The researchers noted that these components, and the relative importance people assign to them, change with individuals' changing social circumstances. For example, during a crisis, people construct out of available components the kind of media system that appears to them to have the greatest potential for realizing their goals under the altered circumstances. Once the crisis is over, however, they may return to everyday media systems that are germane to the attainment of their everyday goals.

In the United States, very few individuals include IRB as a part of their media system. However, throughout the rest of the world, levels of regular listenership (once a week or more) are significantly higher. For example, in Central and Eastern Europe and the former Soviet Union, regular listenership ranges from 25 to 50 percent (Browne 1982: 330), while the proportion may be still higher in Third World countries where rural populations rely heavily on radio. Audience research conducted by the BBC in April 1990 indicated that the BBC World Service had approximately 120 million regular adult listeners, including 2 million in Latin America, 20 million in Africa, 10 million in the Arab world, 31 million in Europe, and 53 million in South Asia (British Broadcasting Corporation 1990: 54). Equally large audiences have also been found for VOA broadcasts. The United States Information Agency's Office for Research estimated that as of December 1989, the VOA had 127 million regular adult listeners, including 6.2 million in the American Republics, 15.6 million in Sub-Saharan Africa, 6.3 million in Northeast and North Africa, 27.7 million in Europe, 19.0 million in South Asia, 32.0 million in East Asia and the Pacific, 17.0 million in China, and 32.1 million in the Soviet Union (Voice of America 1990: 4). Such figures suggest that throughout the world, IRB is a component of a very substantial number of people's media systems.

Consistent with media system dependency theory, evidence indicates that listening to IRB vastly increases during major world crises, often doubling the usual audience figures (Browne 1982: 330). As noted in Chapter one, Allied governments recognized, much to their dismay, that some of their citizens had relied to some extent on German IRB for their understanding of World War I. During World War II, many in Western nations tuned to the BBC for war news because of their confidence in the integrity of its broadcasts. In 1946, audiences throughout Europe listened to RIAS for information about the Berline Blockcade. RFE played a highly active and controversial role in the 1956 uprising in Poland. Throughout the world, listeners tuned to special networks patched together by the VOA to get the latest information on the 1962 Cuban missile crisis. Czech reliance on Western IRB was cited as a provocation by the Soviets for the Prague Spring of 1968. The South Vietnamese relied heavily on VOA reports on the fall and evacuation of Saigon in April 1975. Similarly, it seems likely that, surrounded by the collapse of the old order in Eastern Europe in 1989, tens of millions of Czeches, Bulgarians, Romanians, Latvians, Lithuanians, Estonians, and others turned to Western IRB to provide a framework for understanding what was going on and ways to respond to the revolutionary transformations of the political-economic systems under which they were living.

In all the cases mentioned above— the eruption of Mount St. Helens, the two world wars, the Berlin Blockade, and the uprising in Poland— people confronted ambiguous situations; they lacked information sufficient to interpret the events and guide their responses. That is, on the basis of their own information resources, they could not determine adequately what was going on or what they should do about it in order to attain their relevant goals. Such goals might range from simply locating events within their established cognitive framework, to achieving values such as personal freedom and living under a system of democratic rule, to the basic goal of survival.

The notion of ambiguity is central to both social construction of reality theory and media system dependency theory. The first perspective argues that the objects and events of the world have no inherent meaning; their only meaning has been socially imposed. Further, they contend that imposed meanings reflect the specific social contexts in which they are created. As we have just seen, the second perspective asserts that, in modern societies, people routinely turn to the media to provide meaning for objects and events in the world when they lack the resources to do so themselves.

A limitation of social construction of reality theory was its lack of adequate attention to the contribution of media to individuals' perceptions of social reality (Meyrowitz 1985). Media system dependency theory can be used in empirical research, in conjunction with this perspective, to remedy the neglect. A limitation of media system dependency theory was its lack of adequate attention to the question of what constitutes information. It does not explore an important variant of Goffman's question ("Under what circumstances do we think things are real?"), namely, "Under what circumstances do we believe what we are told by the media?"

NEWS

In the Mount St. Helens study (Hirschburg, Dillman and Ball-Rokeach 1986), the nature of information received from the media appeared to be entirely nonproblematic. Readers, listeners, and viewers depended on the media to understand what was happening and to learn how they might respond. In a nonreflective, commonsense way, media were providing facts: People were being told the truth about what was going on rather than being provided with mere rumors. They sought news rather than opinions. From the social construction of reality perspective, the situation is not quite so commonsensical. Media provided typifications (constructed accounts or interpretations of events), along with a course of action. Audiences encountered language about a volcanic eruption that they accepted in accord with their interests, such as safety and security. What media present to their audience "is not a mirror image of truth, but a coherent narrative of the world that serves particular purposes" (Romano 1986: 42).

In modern societies people routinely turn to the media for information about wars, uprisings, impending military and political conflicts, and institutionalized political events such as elections. Here, too, they seek news rather than opinions, although, in addition, some may want to learn about the personal views of elites such as public officials, religious leaders, journalists, political commentators, and so-called experts. In the Mount St. Helens example, it seems unlikely that anyone (with the possible exception of highly anxious individuals) tended to question the facticity of the reports they received. If they did, they probably believed that the reports did present the best information available at the time. In the examples of accounts of political conflicts, however, the situation may be somewhat different. Individuals may be more likely to raise some questions about the accuracy of the accounts or about the meaning attributed to reported events. Media accounts of clouds of volcanic ash, ash deposits, and health risks associated with the presence of volcanic ash in the atmosphere probably were understood by audiences as involving straightforward statements of facts. Such accounts reported news. Reports of the complexity, intensity, and solvability of a war or some revolutionary action are somewhat more problematic, however. While such reports may be labeled news, in Western nations it is not uncommon to encounter criticisms of the bias of certain media accounts. Such criticisms are most likely to find public expression in times of political controversy such as during elections (Adams 1983; Arterton 1984; Joslyn 1984; Linski 1983; Robinson and Sheehan 1983), domestic labor disputes (Glasgow University Media Group 1976, 1980) or unpopular wars (Glasgow University Media Group 1985; Gitlin 1980; Herman and Chomsky 1988).

Despite periodic concern about media bias in Western nations, Western mass publics tend to accept most media accounts as undistorted symbolic representations of the world of experience. Those who produce and communicate the accounts to the public seem to share this view. With respect to U.S. journalists in particular, Carlin Romano commented:

Ever since Kant argued in the *Critique of Pure Reason* that the nature of human thought makes it impossible to perceive things in themselves without shaping by the mind's categories, the idea that language or thought can precisely mirror the world has been skeptically received. In the twentieth century, the doubt about "naive realism" seems to have gained the upper hand in every field except American journalism. Therefore the American journalists' belief in the possibility of objectively representing reality seems as naive as thinking the whole world operates in English. (1986: 76)

Throughout the world, it is generally those whose political orientation differs significantly from that of their government who are most likely to regard their society's media as unreliable sources of information (Denver and Bochel 1973). Political outsiders such as members of racial, ethnic, and religious minorities; supporters of minority political parties; members of the working class; and members of organizations related to social movements are among those most likely to view what is conventionally labeled as news in their society as symbolic constructions serving specifiable interests. It is they who are most likely to reject a sharp distinction between the news they encounter daily and propaganda.

Naive realism and widespread trust in media contents persists throughout much of the West, despite a vast theoretical and empirically grounded literature specifying and documenting bases for rejecting the assumption of a generally nonproblematic correspondence between objects and events in the world (particularly political objects and events) and their symbolic representations constructed by the mass media and transmitted by them as news. As Smith observes: "Credibility in the mind of the audience is the *sine qua non* of news. All else is either propaganda or entertainment" (1973: 109).

A number of analysts of the mass media, including Bennett (1983), Edelman (1988), Entman (1989), Epstein (1973), Fishman (1980), Gans (1979), Gitlin (1980), Graber (1984), Herman and Chomsky (1988), Lee and Solomon (1991), Parenti (1986), Qualter (1985), Real (1989), Schudson (1978, 1983), Sigal (1973), Smith (1973), and Tuchman (1978) have identified a primary reason to question the meaning of the objectivity of news and therefore to question the plausibility of any simple equation of *reporting the news* with *telling the truth* and to sharply differentiate news from propaganda. That reason, in Sigal's words, is that " 'news' is not what happens but what someone (a source) says has happened or will happen" (1973: 15).

The sources of much of the material that is reported as news are officials representing government, military, and corporate bureaucracies. Today, news gathering is largely a matter of the representatives of one bureaucracy (the news organization) picking up prefabricated items from representatives of another bureaucracy (Schudson 1986: 81). Reliance on such sources of information as a basis for the news has at least three major consequences. First, under certain conditions, views of officials come to define social reality; objective news comes to be identified with reports originating from official sources. Second, news tends to be framed in such a way that it serves to legitimate the social order dominated by the existing government, military, and corporate bureaucracies. Third, despite appearances to the contrary, the vast number of newspapers, radio and television stations, and news magazines present in most Western nations do not offer citizens a genuine diversity of political content and perspectives.

Tuchman noted: "News is located, gathered and disseminated by professionals working in organizations. This is inevitably a product of news workers drawing upon institutional processes and conforming to institutional practices. These practices necessarily include association with institutions whose news is routinely reported" (1978: 4–5). News organizations, Tuchman remarked, place reporters at legitimated institutions where occurrences supposedly of interest to contemporary news consumers may be found easily and routinely. Occurrences are more likely to be defined as news when reporters witness them or can learn about them with little effort. "Newsworthiness is a negotiated phenomenon rather than the application of independently derived objective criteria to news events" (Tuchman 1978: 46). To a considerable extent, this accounts for the finding that, during the Cold War, the press in the United States tended to reflect official interpretations and foreign policy positions of its government (Herman and Chomsky 1988).

There is, as Tuchman put it, a "mutual embeddedness of fact and source" (1978: 90). W. Lance Bennett (1983) has described the dynamics by which official versions of reality become dominant news content, and the news, in turn, comes to seem objective. He observed that, at least in the United States, mass media news is remarkably uniform, despite the enormous variety and number of its carriers in the form of newspapers, magazines, television and radio stations, and so on. Four characteristics tend to prevail. First, news is *personalized*; political events are presented as reports about individual actors such as government, military, and corporate officials. Political processes, power relations, and economic forces underlying events tend to be ignored. Second, news is *dramatized*. Political events are symbolically represented as stories constructed so as to present problems and solutions with rising and falling action. Abstract and technical aspects of events are seldom discussed. Typically, events are trivialized and separated from their political context. Third, news is *fragmented*. Bits of information are presented with few coherent connections. Trends and historical patterns are seldom made part of the news. Western journalism's prohibition against commentary and interpretation results in face-value reporting of separate events, no matter how interrelated they may be. The news presents events rather than issues. Fourth, news is *normalized*. Official sources often get the last word in a news story, providing comforting images of authority and security. The range of acceptable or even thinkable modes for political action is narrowed. Alternatives to the political-economic status quo are seldom, if ever, considered. According to Bennett, official perspectives are legitimate because they dominate news content, and the news, in turn, seems objective because official versions of events fall into familiar, standardized patterns with normal themes.

Using Schutz's terminology (introduced earlier in this chapter) Bennett's analysis concludes that mass media offer their audiences typifications that provide ready-made courses of action, solutions to problems, and interpretations of the social world. Audiences will tend to think of news as a fundamentally undistorted reflection of political reality. In publishing or broadcasting the news, western domestic mass media will be understood as telling audiences what they understand as the truth.

Using Berger and Luckman's terminology, Bennett's analysis indicates that media impose meaning on events and, in so doing, engage in the processes of reification and legitimation. For example, from 1946 through 1989, Western media referred to the Cold War as if it were essentially a fact of nature rather than a convenient, simplifying label for a highly complex set of international relations primarily involving the United States and the Soviet Union. The abstraction ipso facto legitimated much of U.S. political, economic, and military strategy during the period. Bennett recognized the serious implications of these processes:

Even though the news may be illusory, the world it helps legitimate is not. War is an ever-present possibility. Oppression is a fact of political life. Capricious economic cycles dictate the quality of existence. Many people accept those aspects of reality as inescapable tragedies of the human condition. A review of the effects of mass media news suggests that the "inevitability" of our existence is more a product of how that existence is communicated to us than it is the result of tragic human nature. The newsworld simply does not contain a vision of human alternatives; it presents, instead, a picture of an inescapable status quo. (1985: 27)

Media organizations, including international broadcasting organizations, do not present themselves, in any terms, as engaging in definition, reification, or legitimation processes. With a possible and important exception discussed later in this chapter, those who work within media organizations generally do not view themselves as constructing social and political reality. Rather, they view their work as gathering, organizing and disseminating objective information. The products of their work are understood as veridical representations of social and political reality, the existence of which is apprehended in a commonsense way. There are related historical, organizational, and psychological factors that account for the general acceptance of this view of news and its production. The perspective is generally shared throughout Western nations with capitalist economies.

In the United States, general support for the principle that media of communication should present objective accounts of the social and the political world can be traced to the publication of the *New York Sun* in 1883, the start of the era of the "penny press" (DeFleur and Ball-Rokeach 1989: 46–61; Jowett and O'Donnell 1986: 65–72; Schudson 1978: 12–60). Prior to that time, the so-called colonial press produced and distributed small papers and pamphlets to educated elites. These publications, all with limited circulation, commonly were sponsored by political organizations and explicitly gave voice to a particular group's interest and perspectives. However, technical advances in printing and paper making soon made possible the relatively quick and inexpensive production of vast numbers of newspapers. Increasing urbanization, along with the growth of commerce and a marketplace ideology, provided opportunity and incentive to develop newspapers as commodities for sale on a mass market.

The penny press was written to have broad appeal. This involved the publication of information and the adoption of a perspective that could not be readily identified as partisan or biased. The material needed to be consistent with widely shared assumptions about the order and operation of the social world of people's everyday experience. The penny press required sponsorship, for it lacked the support of partisan organizations, and the penny charged for a paper (hence its name), even with a large circulation, failed to cover even the cost of production. Commercial advertising came to fill the need.

The colonial press had provided politically relevant information and a readily identifiable perspective to a supportive audience under the sponsorship of political organizations and parties. The goal of its publication was the cultivation of an informed, partisan elite. The penny press presented news to a mass public under the sponsorship of commercial enterprise. Its goal was to provide business advertisers with large audiences of potential consumers, and its objective was profit for its sponsors and itself. This profit orientation remains predominant among privately owned mass media. Observing this point, Terence Qualter commented:

The media are far from being the sinister manipulator of the popular mind suggested by some conspiracy theorists. Their major functions seem to be to support the system, to uphold conformity, to provide reassurance, and to protect the members of society from excessively disturbing, distracting or dysfunctional information. The mass media are almost entirely commercial, profit-making institutions. Their *raison d'être* is the promotion of consumerism, and the development of secure, confident, materialistic society in which consumerism flourishes. (1985: x-xi)

In the mid-1880s, six New York newspapers formed the first wire service as a cooperative association to share the cost of collecting foreign news. The service also came to subscribe to the idea of proclaiming objective reports.

The wire services conjured into being a race of neutral journalists in order that news could be added to papers of differing political persuasions. As industrialization grew, as newspapers involved an ever-larger investment of capital to bring them into existence, the press gained a greater and greater sense of itself as a kind of natural resource; its ideology of truthfulness increased accordingly. (Smith 1973: 39)

Finally, as advertising started to become a dependable source of revenue for radio broadcasts around 1922, "the same socioeconomic forces that led newspapers to turn to selling space to advertisers so they could sell their products to a mass audience were to result in a parallel pattern for radio" (DeFleur and Ball-Rokeach 1989: 106). Radio, too, carried so-called objective news, much of it from wire service sources.

However Western newspapers, wire services, or radio broadcasting organizations characterized their accounts of the political and social world, those accounts were social constructions that tended to be personalized, dramatized, and fragmented stories. Above all, the media depended on official sources for the information contained in such news stories. Nevertheless, recognition of such dependence did not convince most journalists that their accounts were other than truthful representations of social and political affairs. Two factors account for the persistence of this view.

First, newsmakers follow guidelines designed to enhance their objectivity (one of which is dependence on purportedly reliable and authoritative sources). They do not feel that they operate as conduits for elite perspectives because their own views and those of the elite generally tend to correspond. They are not presenting views at variance with their own. Rather, they are telling the truth as they see it.

Reporters tend over time to adapt the outlook of the news sources with whom they are associated; they ask questions appropriate to their sources' world. Inasmuch as questions contain their own answers, guiding where one may look for an answer and thus what one may find, the questions may be said to reconstitute not only a topic but a world. (Tuchman 1978: 152)

Second, operating in the context of capitalist nations with competitive party systems, the Western media developed an ideology according to which it performed two essential functions. It created a "marketplace of ideas" from which the public chose what it wished to read, listen to, and believe. It served as a watchdog for the public, holding government accountable for its policies and actions.

Operating as a gadfly would seem to be inconsistent with media dependence on elites for information or journalists' personal adoption of elite perspectives. The problem is partially overcome by the occasional opportunities for the media to report on political "crises"—political situations in which elite concensus either fails to form or breaks down, or in which there is widespread and deeply felt sentiment on the part of the mass public that a political actor, action, or policy significantly violates a cultural value or values. In the United States, the Vietnam War can serve as an example of the first situation and the Watergate events can illustrate the second. In both these political occurrences, the American media appeared, at some point, to take an adversarial stance toward government in their coverage. It is crises such as these (similarly, the British media have had the Suez crisis and several major labor disputes) that provide opportunities for media to demonstrate an independence from elites.

Two aspects of such apparent demonstrations of autonomy are noteworthy. First, in general it is only during such crises that claims to autonomy can find more than incidental, anecdotal support. On such occasions, the media make much of this adversarial stance, while elites conspicuously protest the bias of the media. Elites may go so far as to blame the media for the crisis. In the example cited, some U.S. government officials, in fact, claimed that the American media had "lost" the war in Vietnam (Hallin 1986). Others asserted that it was the American media that were responsible for the downfall of Richard Nixon (Molotch, Protess, and Gordon 1983).

Not only is the ability to illustrate media independence generally limited to such situations, but, on closer inspection, even in these situations the media actually continue to play a role in support of the political-economic status quo. For example, studies of media coverage of the Vietnam War concluded that the media tended to support the war effort, imposing a frame according to which the United States had selflessly intervened to try to install a Western-style democracy in one nation and to halt the spread of communist tyranny throughout Southeast Asia (Herman and Chomsky 1988: 169–252). "Left out of this view [presented by the American media] was any thought that the United States had waged a horrific war in support of a dictatorship and against a largely civilian population to prevent a popularly supported but noncapitalist alternative social order from gaining power" (Parenti 1986: 176). In the case of Watergate, Bennett (1983) pointed out that the meaning of the events conveyed to the American public by the mass media was that "the system worked." That is, the media constructed a political world in which the constitutional order and political processes of the United States keeps democratically elected officials from betraying public trust. "It is ironic that such conclusions often accompany revelations of political deception. In the case of Watergate, the 'system' pardoned the worst

offender, gave light sentences to most of the others and made archvil-
lians into media celebrities and millionaires in the process" (Bennett
1983: 33). In general, "misconduct and poor policies are treated as de-
viations from the norms prescribed by the American political system"
(Graber 1984a: 94). Such treatment certainly cannot be characterized as
an adversarial stance.

There is one additional condition under which Western audiences, or
at least American audiences, are likely to question media accounts. This
is during time of war. Most citizens in the West seem to be sensitive to
the point of Winston Churchill's remark that: "In wartime, truth is so
precious that she should always be attended by a bodyguard of lies."
There seems to be general agreement among government, the military,
journalists, and the public that some wartime restrictions on the dissemination of certain information, such as troop movements and targets,
occasionally are appropriate. Beyond this, however, there often is widespread skepticism toward media reports of a war. Such doubt stems
from a recognition of the media's dependence on the military for war
information and on the realization that it is not always in the interest
of the military to tell the public everything it knows.

The American media themselves complained about this almost total
dependency on the Pentagon during wartime. For example, during the
1991 Persian Gulf War, *Newsweek* commented on Pentagon rules re-
stricting press coverage: "The problem is that the Pentagon's policy is
not only about military security. It's also about protecting the military's
image. The result is that the press won't be able to accurately report the
conduct of the war" (January 14, 1991: 19).

Similarly, a Gannet News Service report noted that journalists covering the Gulf War were: "distrustful of Pentagon assessments—particularly in view of deception during the Vietnam War, the Watergate
scandal and the more recent Iran-Contra affair" (February 3, 1991).

During wartime, publics recognize that they are spectators of a war
of words between military adversaries. Doubtless, it was not surprising
for the American public to find that, during the Gulf War, American
media carried reports that U.S. commanders boasted of precision bombing and devastating victories over Iraqi forces, while Radio Baghdad
carried the speeches of Saddam Hussein, offering a vastly different reality in which Iraqi tanks surged into Saudi Arabia to inflict heavy casualties on coalition troops.

There are several factors that possibly account for lower public confidence in reports on military affairs based on material supplied by official
military sources than in other accounts. The military would seem to have
a clearer interest in and ability to control the flow of information than
other elites. Also, while political and business elites might sometimes

be expected to reveal some variety of perspectives within their ranks that becomes public knowledge, the tighter organization of the military makes similar revelations less likely. Speaking with one voice may lead some to wonder if information and viable, alternative views are being suppressed. Finally, military affairs often involve enormous resources in terms of dollars and sometimes in terms of human lives. Hence, there is likely to be public anxiety about the accuracy of their coverage. Such anxiety may generate some distrust.

However, what is grasped by Western audiences in times of war seems to be forgotten at almost all other times. Media dependence on the military for information during wartime is only one aspect of their general dependence on official sources of information at all times. Approximately 70 to 90 percent of news stories are drawn from situations over which the news makers have either complete or substantial control (Sigal 1973: 124). Dependence on the military briefing officer is not unlike dependence on the corporate spokesperson or the elected public official. Like the effective briefing officer, "the effective public official does not attempt to educate or convey 'objective' images; the official's goal is to represent issues and events in ways that gain support, shape action and influence outcomes" (Bennett 1983: 34).

In the West, clear realization by the public of the interdependence of business, the military, government, and the media is hampered not only by commonsense ideas about the nature of objectivity and the failure to understand the constructed nature of the reality presented as news but also by the professional ideology of the media serving as the Fourth Estate—the guardian of the public against government wrongdoing.

To maintain the image of a Fourth Estate without undermining its relations with government, on which it depends for information and legitimacy, the media take what Bennett (1983: 82) termed a "ritualistic posture of antagonism" rather than a genuinely adversarial stance. The position both mystifies and legitimizes the reporting of a narrow range of political messages from a narrow range of sources. The ritualistic nature of the oppositional stance, Bennett noted, is suggested by several empirically documented conditions: incidents of media criticism occur on a highly regular basis, the media favor interelite confrontation, and criticisms of officials will be restricted to them personally and will not be directed at their office or at the institution that they represent (Bennett 1983: 82). The posture of antagonism is maintained even under conditions such as existed in the United States during the Reagan administration, when considerable pressure exerted by the government was largely effective in creating a compliant media system (Hertsgaard 1989). Government sources and journalists so commonly interact intimately that any notion of genuinely "free" press is rendered inaccurate (Entman

1989: 29). This is not to say that there are no significant differences between the media systems of nations with democratic and nondemocratic politics. As Herman and Chomsky observed:

The U.S. media do not function in the manner of the propaganda system of a totalitarian state. Rather, they permit—indeed encourage—spirited debate, criticism and dissent, as long as these remain faithfully within the system of presupposition and principles that constitute an elite consensus, a system so powerful as to be internalized largely without awareness. (1988: 302)

While all media systems tend to support the institutional order of which they are a part, it is possible, if extremely rare, for even a state-controlled media system to respond to the expressed demand of a mass public and genuinely take on the role of government adversary. For example, in 1984, Brazilian television, although highly dependent on Brazil's military regime, telecast enormous antiregime demonstrations in Rio de Janeiro and Sao Paulo, thereby helping to support a popular campaign for direct presidential elections. Brazilian television subsequently expressed explicit support for the regime's opposition, the coalition movement of the Democratic Alliance (Guimaraes and Amoral 1988).

Worldwide audiences of IRB are likely to be aware of the direct links that exist between the intentional broadcasting organizations to which they listen and the governments sponsoring the broadcasts. Even though some international stations, such as the BBC and the VOA, have a degree of formal autonomy from their national government, the international media do not maintain any equivalent of a posture of antagonism toward their governments. To do so would be contrary to the widely understood raison d'être of such organizations. The clear presence of a government-media linkage and the absence of ritualistic antagonism between media and government puts audiences of IRB newscasts in a better position than Western audiences of their own domestic commercial media to have some insight into the constructed nature of political realities being presented as news by the media to which they are attending.

It appears that, universally (with the possible exception of the United Kingdom and democracies such as Norway and Sweden, in which government provides subsidies to the newspapers of the various political parties), the perception of government-media linkages generates far greater distrust of media contents than the perception of business-media linkages. This occurs despite the general coincidence of the interests of business and government in private-enterprise, market-oriented economies (see Lindbolm 1977).

Trusting their own society's enormous media system to provide comprehensive and objective information about the political world, Americans do not tend to depend on any foreign information sources. The media systems that individual Americans construct for themselves do not usually contain IRB. However it is *only* in the United States and the Anglo-Saxon West that IRB receives little attention.

Throughout the world, lack of confidence in their domestic media to provide what is perceived to be reasonably accurate, reliable, and comprehensive political information is a major reason why people turn to IRB (Abshire 1976: 80–81; Hachten 1987: 94–96). Distrust of domestic media is particularly widespread in nations whose governments directly control or frequently intervene and censor the media, deprive opposition groups of access to media, and attempt to manage the flow of information back and forth across its borders. For example, historically, audiences for Western IRB in the former Soviet Union and Eastern Europe have been large. In 1982, a year when the West took a particularly critical stance toward the Soviet Union as a response to Soviet military involvement in Afghanistan, the Soviet role in Poland's imposition of martial law in December 1981, and East-West disagreement over nuclear disarmament, data indicate that the cumulative weekly estimate of listeners to the VOA in the Soviet Union was almost 30 million, while 15 million tuned in Radio Liberty and another 15 million listened to the BBC. Corresponding figures for Poland were approximately 13 million for the VOA, 18 million for Radio Free Europe, and 6 million for the BBC (Board for International Broadcasting 1985: 17).

Research based on random sample surveys, analyses of listener mail, listener panels, and a variety of anecdotal material indicate that news is the clear programming preference of IRB listeners, while political commentary and analyses finish at or near the bottom of programming interest lists (Browne 1982: 332). The sharp distinction between news and political commentary that is apparently made by IRB audiences parallels the distinction made by U.S. and other Western audiences with respect to the political content of their domestic media.

The suggestion that IRB audiences make such a sharp distinction is surprising given that: (1) Worldwide, many people depend on IRB for political information because they distrust their own domestic media system, and (2) IRB audiences are aware that international broadcasting organizations are the official voices of their nations. Why should those who distrust their own country's media system, particularly because of its government ownership and dependency, place greater trust in the government-sponsored medium of another country? Put in more colloquial terms; why should citizens in nations with government-controlled media systems (approximately half the world's broadcasting systems are state owned; Head 1985: 603) tend to view their own domestic media as publishing and broadcasting propaganda and turn to IRB for news? On the other hand why should citizens in nations with predominantly commercial, public corporation, or mixed media systems rather than with government-controlled media systems tend to view their domestic media as producing news and generally ignore IRB, possibly because IRB is thought to present little more than propaganda?

The second of these two questions was considered previously. North American audiences, and possibly audiences elsewhere (such as Australia, Western Europe, Scandinavia, and Japan), generally view their media systems as making claims that are consistent with the set of socially constructed meanings that they share. They tend to understand media constructions from the perspective of naive realism. Such constructions generally are not seen as legitimations; those who produce and transmit them usually are not seen as part of a collusive net. On the occasion when political events seem so ambiguous to the mass public that they are widely understood as susceptible to alternative framing, during periods of such as war, economic instability, or elite dissensus, audiences in nations with media systems that are not monopolized by their government tend to act as though their media offered reasonably comprehensive information and a real diversity of content and perspectivies—a veritable "marketplace of ideas." From these they are free to make their own selections and subsequently construct their own understanding of political reality. Under the conditions of apparently considerable choice and self-directed reality construction, the political images that emerge are taken as real. On the other hand, political claims from foreign sources, such as IRB, are likely to be seen as involving efforts at legitimation and as the products of collusive communication. Historical experiences with the broadcasting operations of various communist and fascist regimes, with clandestine stations, and with American efforts (particularly during the early days of the Cold War, the uprisings in Poland and Hungary, the invasion of Czechoslovakia, and the Vietnam era) are likely sources of this orientation.

Quite the opposite is found in states with government-dominated media systems. In such states, there tends to be widespread cynicism with respect to media content; news reported by the domestic media is not always taken seriously. For example, according to Smith (1976: 365), some Soviet intellectuals made a point of boasting that they never read the Soviet press. Soviet data quoted by Lisann (1975: 144) indicate that the main reason why many Soviets listened to or watched their domestic broadcasts about international affairs was to compare the Soviet reports with those of foreign radio. The least interest was in Soviet analysis and commentary. The acquisition of facts fell in between. Reports carried on Soviet radio and television were not routinely accepted as veridical accounts of political reality largely because of their obviously tendentious mode of presentation (Paulu 1974: 210). Soviet citizens who turned to Western radio tended to do so because of its apparent comprehensive coverage and its speed. Occupation, education, and social class were more powerful predictors of such media experience in the Soviet Union than anti-Soviet sentiment (Lisann 1975: 114–124).

IRB makes its possible for citizens of nations with government-dominated media to construct their own media systems to provide content independent of the control of their state. From materials presented by such a diversified system, they are free to make their own selection and subsequently construct their own images of political reality. Under the condition of the apparently considerable choice provided by IRB, rather than the limitation of domestic sources, self-directed reality construction will produce political images that are taken as real.

Various international audiences may not depend on IRB to learn the truth from a particular selected source. Rather, they may be seeking what they understand as several alternative constructions of political reality, each of which serves the political, economic, and ideological interests of its source. From these, they can select materials that together make the political world intelligible for them. Such intelligibility involves constructing a political reality consistent with the social, economic, and political relationships they experience daily and with the socially shared stock of knowledge they routinely use to interpret objects and event as they conduct their everyday lives.

From the perspective of the individual consumer, news can be understood as media material that he or she selects to make sense of the political world. The more or less integrated set of beliefs that together constituent the individual's understanding of political affairs is itself a construction of symbolic constructions. However, personal constructions (what Adoni and Mane, 1984, termed *subjective realities*) tend to be experienced in an unreflective way as knowledge of an objective political world.

From the perspective of its organizational source, news can be understood as politically relevant media material that is presented to mass audiences without regard to its political implications, that is, without conscious consideration of the individuals, groups, movements, organizations, institutions, or governments that its dissemination might possibly benefit or damage. The ability to present news entails the freedom to disregard implications of communicating politically relevant materials to mass audiences (Gans 1979: 182–213). The manifest function of broadcasting news is to inform a mass audience.

PROPAGANDA

News for one person may be propaganda for another. From the perspective of the individual consumer, propaganda can be understood as politically relevant media material that he or she refuses to incorporate into the more or less integrated set of beliefs that together constitute his or her understanding of political affairs. Media material is particularly likely to be labeled propaganda by audiences when it is widely believed that the primary intent of its organizational source is to manipulate the political orientations of the audience rather than to inform.

From the perspective of its organizational source, propaganda can be understood as politically relevant material that it presents to mass audiences with the primary intent of influencing political orientations. Organizational criteria (which are sometimes explicit and sometimes implicit) for the selection and framing of material to be published or broadcast includes some conscious consideration of the individuals, groups, movements, organizations (including itself), institutions, or governments that its dissemination might possibly benefit or harm.

From the perspective of the individual working for a media organization that has the achievement of some political impact as a primary goal, the media materials that he or she creates are not necessarily seen as propaganda. News writers and reporters routinely may select topics and frame them on the basis of manifestly journalistic rather than clearly political criteria. Within the organization, they may seldom experience any pressure to do otherwise.

In his study of the international newsrooms of the West's three largest international radio stations, the Voice of America, the BBC, and Deutsche Welle, Browne claimed that:

There was nothing in the newsroom practices I saw to indicate that stories were organized in a manner to conform to ideological considerations whereby, for example, newscasts might be expected to always lead with a story illustrating one's own strengths or one's enemy's weakness. Selection of specific items for inclusion seems not to conform to any easily identifiable patterns. Few items from anything other than what most central newsroom editors regard as traditional sources—wire services and one's own correspondents and/or correspondents from one's own domestic media—seem to be used by the newsrooms. (1983: 219)

Absence of conscious political interest on the part of those directly involved in producing and disseminating politically relevant media material, however, does not mean that the material they produce and communicate cannot be used to serve the political goals of the organization for which they work. Their ideas of objectivity, the typifications on which they rely, and the frames they employ in a non-self-conscious manner lead newsmakers to an understanding of the political world that often embodies legitimations of their own political-economic order. The news that they produce is the propaganda that their media organizations broadcast.

As noted in Chapters One and Two, all major international radio organizations broadcast in a wide variety of languages. For example, during the 1980s, the Soviet Union, the United States, the People's Republic of China, West Germany, and the United Kingdom each broadcast regularly in more than thirty-five languages. Many language services are semiautonomous. In the case of the VOA:

Some observers have described the Voice of America as being 42 individual radio stations. To an extent this is true. For while all VOA language services broadcast centrally prepared news and editorials, service chiefs exercise considerable autonomy and independent judgment as they select, commission, or create other broadcast ingredients to satisfy the informational appetites of their respective audiences. (United States Information Agency 1986: 23)

What is true of news production processes in the international newsrooms of international broadcasting organizations is also true of news production processes in their language services. News makers tend to understand and report political ideas in terms that serve the goals of the international broadcasting organization. Historically, there have been occasions when language services have pursued political interests so vigorously that they have undermined the credibility of the products of the central newsroom. For example, as seen in Chapter Two, the strident tone of RFE/RL language services, which are often staffed by émigrés from the countries to which broadcasts were directed, seriously compromised the U.S. government's efforts to maintain a sharp distinction between news and propaganda in the minds of Eastern European and Soviet audiences.

The preceding discussion suggests that much of the news broadcast on international radio is constructed by those intending to inform audiences by following the rules of objective journalism. However, the news makers inadvertently provide media products that further the interests of the state in whose service the international broadcasting organization is operated. Much of what is constructed as news is broadcast as propaganda.

While this characterization is intended to apply to much of the news that is broadcast by international radio organizations today, particularly by the international organizations of Western democratic nations with market economies, it certainly is not intended to be a characterization of the news-making and reporting processes that constitute most of the history of IRB. That history (reviewed in Chapters One and Two), contained numerous accounts of stations intentionally engaging in deceit to achieve political objectives. The 1935 broadcasts of Italy's Radio Bari, fascist Germany's international broadcasts under the direction of Joseph Goebbels, the operations of World War II clandestine stations such as Britain's Gustav Sigfried Eins and America's Radio 1212, and the 1961 broadcasts of Radio Swan, sponsored by the U.S. government in support of the Bay of Pigs mission, serve as ready examples of the continuous and systematic use of deliberate deception in IRB to achieve political ends. More recently, the domestic and international media of both the former Soviet Union and the United States were accused of engaging in disinformation campaigns with respect to their reporting on topics as diverse as the 1979 Soviet invasion of Afghanistan; a 1981 plot to kill the Pope; the destruction of a Korean airliner by a Soviet fighter plane in 1983; the U.S. invasion of Grenada in 1983; elections in Nicaragua, El Salvador, and Guatemala throughout the 1980s; and U.S. air attacks against purportedly terrorist-related targets in Libya in 1986 (Alexandre 1988: 113–122; Herman and Chomsky 1988: 87–296; Parenti 1986: 148–185).

While maintaining any precise distinction between news and propaganda is untenable, nevertheless, it is useful to have some working definitions to facilitate further discussion of IRB. In the pages that follow, *propaganda* will be understood as sets of messages that are deliberately intended by their sender (the party that has the ultimate authority to establish and to supervise the realization of the goals of an international broadcasting organization) to have some politically relevant effect or effects on a defined audience or audiences.

This definition says nothing about the truth of falsity of the broadcast messages. Nor does it specify that the messages, if believed by their intended audiences, will benefit or disadvantage them in particular ways. The definition is consistent with conceptualizations of *political propaganda* that appear widely in the literature (Davison 1965: 47; Ellul 1966: 62; George 1959: 4; Jowett and O'Donnell 1986: 16; Martin 1958: 10–20; McQuail 1969: 12; Mitchell 1970: 4; Murty 1968: 34; Qualter 1985: 121–124; Whitaker 1962: 5). It is the presence or absence of political intent on the part of a communicator that determines whether the resultant message is propaganda or news. A total absence of political intent appears to be rare in the case of IRB. The IRB history reported in Chapters One and Two can be viewed as support for this claim. The presence of political intent makes intelligible the fact that almost all governments invest considerable resources not only in IRB, but also in other varieties of international communication such as publishing and distributing various films, magazines, and newspapers worldwide; maintaining libraries throughout the world; and sponsoring cultural exchange programs.

The working definition of propaganda that focuses on sender intent does not disregard discussions of news and propaganda occurring earlier in this chapter. Whatever the political intent of those who exercise authority within an international broadcasting organization, those who work for the organization may continue to understand their products as news. Whatever the political intent of those who exercise authority within an international broadcasting organization, audiences throughout the world may continue to depend on the organization to bring them the news. This approach encourages further research into the problem of identifying the social and psychological conditions under which people think the media materials they either produce or consume represent the truth. These points can be developed further through a discussion of the varieties of propaganda broadcast by international radio stations.

BROADCASTING VARIETIES OF PROPAGANDA

Factual propaganda involves the presentation of truth claims in order to: (1) establish or reinforce support of a particular political actor, action, policy, or institutional structure; (2) change audience orientations toward such a political object or event; (3) contradict truth claims made by political opponents; and (4) accuse political opponents of unpopular political, military, or economic acts or polices. Each of these objectives can be illustrated by references to IRB history.

Cases of presenting *supporting truth claims* are seen in the early programming of Radio Moscow which depicted the accomplishments of the Russian Revolution, in 1940 German broadcasts that made much of Nazi military successes (such as that at Dunkirk), and 1947 programs of the VOA that presented details of the Marshall Plan. Instances of *reorienting assertions* include Nazi Germany's broadcasts to France in which French national interests were depicted as united with those of Germany and opposed to those of Britain. Radio Moscow presented reorienting assertions in 1968 when it claimed that Russian troops had entered Czech territory at the request of the Czech government which had appealed for military aid in views of threats to the sovereignty of the state and its socialist system being posed by domestic and foreign sources. Throughout the Vietnam War, the VOA sought to reorient much of world opinion by maintaining that the United States had militarily intervened to defend South Vietnam from aggression and terrorism and was acting in the interests of democracy. Presentation of *contradicting assertions* was a major strategy of the British and the French during World War II. As the Nazis began to suffer military reverses, British and French programs pointed out inconsistencies in claims broadcast on German international radio. During the Persian Gulf War, Radio Baghdad contradicted VOA accounts of Allied bombing which had stated that, as a matter of policy, civilian neighborhoods in Baghdad had been avoided (Henderson 1991). (Contradicting assertions are more accurately understood as a form of counterpropaganda, as will be explained in Chapter Five.) Examples of *accusing assertions* include VOA reports of Chinese soldiers "brainwashing" prisoners during the Korean War, Radio Moscow claims that Great Britain's involvement in the Suez Crisis constituted flagrant interference in the affairs of a sovereign state, and the VOA's account of a 1983 incident in which a Soviet plane shot down a South Korean civilian airliner.

There are two defining characteristics of *factual propaganda*. First, the claims are intended by the communicating agent (such as an international broadcasting organization) to be understood by an audience as verifiable or falsifiable by whatever method or methods are routinely used by that audience (such as the canons of scientific inquiry) for making such an assertion; the assertions are presented as demonstrably true. Second, the claims are intended to achieve one or more of the goals specified above. Whether the claims are "really" true or false, whether the direct producers of the messages believe them or not, and whether the direct producers of the messages intend simply to inform or to achieve some other or additional objectives are all questions irrelevant to the classification.

Bureaucratic propaganda, a second major category, was identified by Altheide and Johnson (1980). In their analysis, bureaucratic propaganda consists of seemingly factual reports, produced by an organization, such as a government, to maintain its legitimacy and the legitimacy of its policies and actions. Such official reports do not present lies, but rather, information without context. That is, the reports contain few, if any, cues concerning the research methods and editing processes that shaped them. According to Altheide and Johnson, official reports also divert attention from the primary reason for which they were prepared: organizational self-justification and promotion. Their self-serving character is masked by their apparent conformity to norms of objectivity.

Bureaucratic propaganda becomes possible when access to direct sources of experience or alternative sources of information is not available. Diverse examples of official reports, or bureaucratic propaganda, cited by Altheide and Johnson include: reports on the effectiveness of welfare programs issued by welfare agencies and by the federal government, reports on religious conversions prepared by evangelical crusades, reports on television ratings presented by commercial networks, and reports on military preparedness presented by the United States Pentagon.

Altheide and Johnson pointed out that it is the political context of competition that makes the presentation of official reports a self-serving activity. Reports are performances for an audience, and they are rhetorical rather than scientific. They present the organization, movement, or government to spectators. For example, the various U.S. Bureau of Labor Statistics indices of economic trends are not just matter-of-fact reports on the state of the economy. Rather, they reflect the success or failure of an administration. They set off waves of response in business, financial, and political circles. How they are constructed is not without considerable consequences.

Presentation or reference to official reports comprises a substantial part of the fare of IRB. Inclusion of such material is necessitated, indirectly, by the constitutions of some international broadcasting organizations. For example, Clause 13 (2) of the BBC's constitution obliges daily reporting of the proceedings of both houses of Parliament. Such proceedings routinely include the discussion of official reports. Similarly, the third provision of the VOA charter (Public Law 94–350) requires the VOA to present and discuss the policies of the United States. Such discussion regularly makes use of official reports.

The distinction between factual propaganda and bureaucratic propaganda is not always clear. Generally, bureaucratic propaganda reflects a more organized and deliberate effort to construct a set of truth claims for legitimizing purposes. (In Berger and Luckmann's terms bureaucratic propaganda offers "third level legitimations".) The grounds for collusive communication are more likely to be present in the process of constructing bureaucratic propaganda. Moreover, when an audience confronts bureaucratic propaganda, it is in a somewhat different position than when it confronts factual propaganda. Lacking details of research methods and editing process, there is little the audiences can do in terms of critical evaluation. However, the more sophistication among the audience might understand the nature of bureaucratic propaganda and hence be highly skeptical of its message.

Taken together, factual propaganda and bureaucratic propaganda make up much of what IRB audiences understand as news. It is when audiences believe that there is political intent underlying the transmission of factual propaganda or bureaucratic propaganda, or when the claims appear to be inconsistent with their stock of knowledge, that they are most likely to understand the material as propaganda and reject its messages. Under these conditions, people will not think the things they hear on the newscasts of an international broadcasting station are real.

Linguistic propaganda constitutes a third major category. Symbols undergird authority by legitimating the distribution of power (Elder and Cobb 1983: 18). Since this is so, all organizations have an interest in appropriating legitimating symbols. Examples of the use of such symbols can be found in domestic U.S. newscasts.

References in the news to the corporate sector of the economy as "big business," rather than "corporate capitalism" or "monopoly capitalism," reinforces corporate power. As metaphor, "big business" invokes images of the corporate marketplace of an earlier era, not the contemporary economic situation. Linguistic practices such as these hamper an analytic understanding of social issues.

... Such practices unintentionally create and control controversy by limiting analyses of the interrelationship between and among phenomena. (Tuchman 1978: 164)

There are at least three different forms of linguistic propaganda. Each is an instance of what Mueller (1973: 24–42) termed "directed communication": the overt, organized effort to manipulate language to meet political needs and goals.

One type of linguistic propaganda, *rationalizing terms*, consists in categorizing a political relationship that has been characterized as unjust in such a way as to rationalize perpetuating the relationship. Categorization, perception, and politics go hand in hand. Verbal constructions contribute to the long-term maintenance of exploitive relationships between social groups or nations that blatantly violate the moral codes to which their adherents subscribe. For example:

Whites define their personal posture toward blacks as a caring one or as offering blacks the conditions in which they feel comfortable, even if the blacks are slaves, living in impoverished ghettos, or able to find alienating work or no work at all.

Indeed, a moralistic discourse typically is central to the transaction between enemies; reaction formation complements rationalization. In consequence, unequal relationships become stabilized, each group learning its expected form of action and each episode in the sequence of hostilities rationalizing later ones and long-standing differences in material resources and privilege. (Edelman 1988: 83)

The use of rationalizing terms is illustrated in the contents of newscasts by Radio RSA, the Voice of South Africa. Sometime in the mid–1980s, the phrase "democratic development" was introduced to refer to the South African government's economic and political polices toward its various racial groups living under apartheid. (This example will be discussed at greater length in Chapter Five).

Redefining terms is another form of linguistic propaganda. It consists in denying a critic exclusive use of a political symbol by redefining the symbol in such a way that the critic cannot lay claim to its use in the redefined sense. An example of this variety of linguistic propaganda is provided by Frederick in his study of Cuban-American "radio wars" (1986: 166–69). On the VOA, the word *democracy* consistently was defined in terms of the presence of free elections. This is an understanding of the concept that is common in the United States where voting is viewed as the key mechanism of consensus (Lipset 1981: 12). In the United States, elections draw attention to common social ties and to the importance and apparent reasonableness of accepting public policies that are adopted (Edelman 1964: 3). On Radio Havana Cuba (RHC), on the other hand, the word *democracy* consistently was used in a broader context to include opposition to imperialism and support for revolution. Similarly, "freedom" on the VOA generally referred to personal liberties such as freedom of expression, assembly, and religion, while on RHC, "freedom" generally referred to collective rights such as freedom from poverty and hunger and access to guaranteed housing, health care, and education. These examples illustrate this form of linguistic propaganda, which involves the introduction of what C. L. Stevenson termed "persuasive definitions" (1958: 279). A persuasive definition of a term changes its descriptive meaning without substantially changing its emotive meaning—the emotion that the term expresses.

Conceptual justification, a third form of linguistic propaganda, involves the use of a political adversary's verbal strategy to justify one's own political policies and actions. During the Cold War, this approach was used on several occasions by the Soviet Union in response to news presented in the American mass media and on the VOA. For example, the conceptual justification offered by the U.S. government for its interventions in Guatemala in 1954, Cuba in 1962, and the Dominican Republic in 1965 was precisely the justification presented by the Soviet Union for its 1956 intervention in Hungary and its suppression of the Dubcek regime in Czechoslovakia in 1968 (Franck and Weisband 1972). (Borrowing conceptual justifications can also be employed as a strategy of counterpropaganda, as noted in Chapter Five.)

Sociological propaganda comprises the fourth major category. Every society is integrated, to some extent, by the commitment of its members to a common set of values, beliefs, and attitudes. In modern societies, these shared orientations are transmitted, learned, and internalized through gradual and continuous socialization processes carried out in the context of family, church, and school and reinforced in the workplace and by the mass media. The shared orientations define a collective self-image for members of the society. They also provide an image of the society for foreign populations. Ellul (1966) used the phrase "sociological propaganda" to refer to the set of orientations by which any society seeks to integrate maximum numbers of individuals into itself, unify members' behavior according to a pattern, and spread its style of life abroad, imposing itself on other groups. In the terms of Berger and Luckmann (1966), sociological propaganda presents a "symbolic universe" providing ultimate legitimation of the institutional order and explanation of the world that universalizes a particular social perspective.

Herbert Gans's study of the "CBS Evening News," "NBC Nightly News," *Newsweek*, and *Time* demonstrated the presence of sociological propaganda in U.S. commercial media material. In general, he found that American media promote the view of the United States as the good society. The nation's political system generally is presented as an altruistic democracy that follows a course based on public interest and public service, ensuring individual freedom and liberty as well as political and legal equality. Its economic system generally is characterized as responsible capitalism in which there is little gross exploitation or unreasonable profit and in which competition creates the possibility of increased prosperity for all (Gans 1979: 42–69).

Sociological propaganda appeared with greater than usual frequency on the VOA during the years of the Reagan administration. At that time, United States Information Agency (USIA), the parent organization of the VOA, emphasized the importance of disseminating worldwide a view in which "the United States is presented as dedicated to the goals of world peace, abiding by the edicts of world order, and morally, ethically and politically dedicated to the betterment of human kind" (Alexandre 1988: 121–122).

Discussion thus far had focused on news programming.

The broadcasting of news is the core of virtually every international radio station. Survey after survey and poll after poll, whether by BBC, VOA, Deutsche Welle or any other international broadcaster, reveals the news is the major reason offered by the vast majority of listeners for why they tune to that particular station. (Browne 1983: 205)

Nevertheless, the presentation of news constitutes only a fraction of the material regularly broadcast by any international station. More hours are spent on the presentation of cultural features, policy discussions, plays, music, language lessons, verbal travelogues, shortwave hobbyist programs, and other features than on news per se. Propaganda, particularly sociological propaganda, is embodied in this manifestly nonpolitical programming as well as in the news.

The diverse programming of international broadcasting organizations can be understood as having as its goal the development of a reservoir of positive affect toward the broadcasting nation. Several examples of such efforts are presented in the following chapters. Considerable research is needed to specify the ways in which positive affect toward a foreign nation, based on exposure to manifestly non-political materials such as the nation's music, literature, and art, might influence the political orientations of audiences toward that country.

The first section of this book has provided some historical and theoretical context for understanding IRB. The following section draws on these materials to empirically examine, among other things, news broadcasts in the World Services of the VOA and Radio Moscow, the newscasts sent to the Third World by the regional services of these stations compared to those broadcast in the World Service newscasts of the BBC, Radio Beijing, and Swiss Radio International, and some diverse materials broadcast by Radio RSA, the Voice of South Africa. The studies are intended to demonstrate the analytic value of understanding the enterprise of IRB as that of broadcasting propaganda.

Chapter Four

A Case Study of Broadcasting Propaganda: International Radio Broadcasting toward the End of the Cold War

This chapter discusses U.S. and Soviet IRB to the Third World in 1986, about three years before monumental changes in World Politics led to almost universal adoption of the statement: "The Cold War has ended." Analysis of original data derived from VOA and Radio Moscow newscasts is presented to indicate how the international broadcasting organizations defined the social and political world for listeners in the developing areas at a time when the United States and the former Soviet Union still clearly defined each other as political adversaries. At issue is the extent to which the VOA and Radio Moscow newscasts were structured in such a way that they appear to have served the competing political and economic objectives of the United States and the Soviet Union rather than the information needs of their target audiences in the developing nations.

IRB, THE COLD WAR, AND MEDIA IMPERIALISM

There is a considerable body of literature on communications to the developing nations. Many of these studies have examined the influence of Western news agencies such as the Associated Press, United Press International, Reuters, and Agence France Presse (Tunstall 1977; Rosenblum 1978; Nordenstreng and Schiller 1979); films (Guback 1969); television (Lee 1980; Varis 1984; Hallin 1986b); and communications technology, including direct broadcast satellites (Smith 1980; McPhail 1981). However, little attention has been given to Western IRB directed to and about Third World countries themselves. Even less consideration has been given to the former Soviet Union's communications to the Third World—through any channel.

Although economic measures of domination such as control of capital, markets, and the infrastructure of international finance are reasonably well documented, the sources of power for cultural communications are just beginning to be understood. Each of the studies cited above proceeded from the realization that the forces that define social reality are important determinants of a society's outlook and the nature of its goals. This principle is fundamental to both the social construction of reality perspective and media system dependency theory. It is for this reason that communication and the flow of messages between and among nations—especially between developing and dominant states—assume a special significance.

Much of the research on communications between the West and Third World nations is highly critical. The studies labeled the operation of the structure of international communications variously as *media imperialism* (Tunstall 1977; Lee 1980), *cultural domination* (Schiller 1976; Smith 1980), and *electronic colonialism* (McPhail 1981). Some called for a new world information order (United Nations Educational, Scientific, and Cultural Organization 1979). Critical works suggested that the image of the world that Western media presented was extraordinarily biased. Although Western media vigorously espoused commitment to doctrines of impartiality, accuracy, and objectivity, critics contended that the Western media worked to promote self-serving values and forms of world domination and control.

Such critical analysis is consistent with the perspective on media (developed in preceding chapters) as active creators of symbolic realities that serve identifiable political-economic interests. However, the critical analysis is at variance with the position taken here to the extent that it maintains that accounts of the social world *can* be constructed to be entirely independent of the social context in which they are created. This study takes as its point of departure the theoretical assumption that all media accounts bear traces of the circumstances in which they originate.

In addition, critical analysis is inconsistent with the perspective developed throughout this book to the extent that it assumed that the bias it identified was fundamentally the result of conscious and deliberate efforts on the part of Western media to construct a particular, self-serving image of the Third World. The unreflective use of typifications plays an important role as well. In the case of IRB, there may have been little, if any, collusive communication among those within a Western IRB who were responsible for the contents of its newscasts to the Third World.

Analysts who were critical of the world information order said little about IRB. They also failed to consider the contents and objectives of

Soviet communications to the Third World. In addition, there was a tendency to engage in polemics rather than systematically investigate empirical hypotheses. For example, Schiller (1976), Smith (1980), and McPhail (1981) all devoted considerable attention to the presentation of anecdotal evidence in support of the normative conclusion that Western media have disregarded their responsibilities of reporting fairly and accurately, particularly with regard to respecting the values and viewpoints of their audience in the developing areas.

COMMUNICATION AND DEVELOPMENT THEORY

In 1952, Leo Lowenthal announced the birth of a new "discipline of international communication research" in a special issue of the *Public Opinion Quarterly*. Lowenthal himself noted that the field was born of practical expediency, citing two trends that fostered it: the spreading of technological means of communication into the nonindustrialized areas of the earth and the expanding activities of governments in spreading their information and ideology throughout the world.

Also in the early 1950s, interest in neutralizing or ousting forces or values perceived to be inimical to the United States in the nonaligned world prompted VOA sponsorship of research concerning the possible bearing of communication on political economic change (Zartman 1976; Gendzier 1978) and for more effective means of conducting psychological warfare against Soviet Bloc and pro-communist Third World countries (Samarajiwa 1984). The countries included in the study—Turkey, Lebanon, Egypt, Syria, Jordan, and Iran—were all of great political significance at the time.

The research turned out to be unusually important, for the data, which were gathered originally for audience research, served as the basis for Daniel Lerner's *The Passing of Traditional Society* (1958). Lerner's book long served as a paradigm for studies of the role of communication in development, clearly influencing subsequent work such as David McClelland's *The Achieving Society* (1961), Lucien Pye's *Communication and Political Development* (1963), and Wilbur Schramm's *Mass Media and National Development* (1964). These studies suggested that Western communication to the Third World encouraged economic development and, subsequently, political democracy in these regions. Economic development was sought through providing political and economic information that is essential to informed decision making, promoting "modern attitudes" (particularly the value of economic achievement in the context of free-market economies), encouraging increased trade with the industrialized West, and importing Western technology to modernize economies. Information and ideals were targeted at Third World elites who were found to be moving away from traditional values, heavy consumers of foreign communications, and critical of their local media, particularly radio. Western communications were seen as advancing the social and economic integration of the region and its growth in the image of the United States and its Western democratic partners. These outcomes, and the processes that lead to them, were presumed to be obviously desirable to all parties concerned.

NEW WORLD INFORMATION ORDER THEORY

By the early 1970s, Third World leaders had begun to question the actual impact of international communication on the course of development. In 1973, a formal declaration was adopted by the Fourth Summit Conference of the Non-Aligned Movement that was highly critical of Western international media. The declaration claimed that Western reports of Third World affairs tended to be not only inadequate but also tendentious, incorrect, and "non-objective" (Samarajiwa 1984).

In 1977, the United Nations Educational, Scientific, and Cultural Organization (UNESCO) established the International Commission for the Study of Communication Problems (the MacBride Commission). Its report, issued two years later, concluded that Western attitudes toward economic development actually impeded the understanding of Third World nations and their problems, not only in the West but also among people in Third World countries themselves. Third World leaders perceived that what was being communicated about developing countries worldwide were their negative aspects, such as poverty and political instability. Little coverage was being given to long-term gains in educational, social, or humanitarian features of Third World development, and complex problems were being ignored. The report concluded that a new form of neocolonialism was being perpetuated by Third World nations when they imported foreign news (UNESCO 1979). Soviet writers supported the commission's findings (Zassoursky and Losev 1984).

Independent scholarly interest in the problems identified by Third World leaders appeared in the late 1970s and early 1980s (Schiller 1976; Tunstall 1977; Cherry 1978; Nordenstreng and Schiller 1979; Rosenblum 1979; Smith 1980; McPhail 1981; Hedeboro 1982). What does it matter, some scholars asked, if a national movement has struggled for years to achieve liberation if that goal, once achieved, is undercut by definitions of social and political realities derived from its former oppressor? According to this point of view, the messages of Western international media served the commercial and political interest of Western-controlled multinational corporations that dominate the world economy (Varis 1975; Mattelart 1979). In the view of many critics, this "media imperialism" of the twentieth century was to be just as dreaded as the mercantile colonialism of the eighteenth and nineteenth centuries.

Most of those critical of the world information order focused exclusively on the influence of Western media in the Third World. However, the Soviet Union, as well as the West, had long established elaborate patterns of communication and information dissemination to the developing areas (Kecskemeti 1956; Fisher and Merill 1976; Gerbner and Siefert 1984). There was no compelling reason to assume that Soviet media, unlike their Western counterparts, did not seek to promote their own political and economic objectives through broadcasting particular symbolic constructions of the political world. The history of IRB (presented in Chapters One and Two) suggests that they did. Nor is there good reason to assume that the Soviet media seriously attended to the potentially negative effects of their messages on the receiving cultures.

MEDIA IMPERIALISM, THE VOA, AND RADIO MOSCOW

In order to determine the extent to which some of the criticisms of international media such as news agencies, newspapers, films, and television applied to U.S. and Soviet IRB to the Third World while the Cold War was still being waged, it was necessary to identify verifiable claims about international media specified in the literature. Six of these claims are discussed below. This particular set is not intended to be exhaustive; however, each of the six claims is commonly encountered in literature that is critical of the international media. Following the discussion of each claim, criteria used for testing the claim in this chapter will be specified.

Criticisms of the International Media

1. *International media do not define the conditions and events occurring in Third World countries as being as important as the conditions and events occurring in more economically developed nations.* One contention, frequently found in critical studies of the international media, concerned the amount of coverage given the Third World. As an example of geographic bias in news coverage, Adams (1986) reported that Western coverage of natural disasters was not influenced primarily by the severity of their human and physical consequences but rather by where (what country or region) in the world they occur. He suggested that Western news media prioritized the rest of the world and assigned least importance to disasters occurring in the developing nations. Masmoudi (1978) contended that Western media in general devoted only 20 to 30 percent of news coverage to the developing countries despite the fact that the latter accounted for almost three-quarters of the world's population. Rosenblum (1979) and McPhail (1981) both characterized the amount of West-

ern coverage of the Third World as meager. They argued that lack of extensive reporting was the result of high coverage costs, low worldwide interest, and restrictions on journalists by some Third World governments. In addition, theory developed in Chapter Four of this work suggests that Western media might have assigned low priority to Third World leaders, conditions, and events in order to keep them less well defined, more ambiguous, and, therefore, more available for interpretation and evaluation in terms serving the political and economic interests of economically developed nations. In keeping with Masmoudi's (1978) contention, in the research reported on the following pages, an international radio station's newscasts were considered to be consistent with the claim that they do not define leaders, conditions, and events in the Third World as being as important as leaders, conditions, and events in more economically developed nations if 25 percent or less of its news items concerned Third World countries.

2. *International media fail to cover gains in educational, social, and humanitarian aspects of developing countries.* This specific claim was made by several participants in the original UNESCO study of international communication problems (UNESCO 1979). Analysts asserted that when Western media did pay attention to the developing areas, it was usually only when events or conditions in a nation (such as political instability) appeared to threaten the routine conduct of economic exchanges that were highly profitable for the West (deCosta et al. 1979). Furthermore, corruption, wars, political intrigues, and civil disorders make for exciting stories, while economic and social development is a very slow, and, over short periods, almost imperceptible process (Smith 1980: 9).

Soviet economic involvement in the Third World was not the same as Western capitalist involvement. However, the Soviets did carry on trade throughout much of the Third World. Historically, they made heavy investments in countries such as Afghanistan, Algeria, Angola, Cuba, Ethiopia, and Somalia. Like Western media, Soviet media also may have failed to cover positive social and economic aspects of change in the developing countries. It might be reasoned that Soviet international media defined Third World events as important when the events appeared to threaten investments that they had made in the regions.

In the study described on the following pages, newscasts of an international radio station were considered consistent with the claim that positive developments in the Third World received little attention if 5 percent or less of the items about the Third World concerned processes such as improving literacy rates, national systems of communication, or national or regional health standards. While the 5 percent criterion was in itself arbitrary, it seemed reasonable to argue that if less than one item in twenty about the Third World was about positive aspects of development, then such processes were not being given much consideration.

3. *International media single out the Third World for negative coverage.* Some analysts (Masmoudi 1978; Rosenblum 1979; Giffard 1984) contended that while the categories of news covered by the international media were the same for developed and developing countries, there was more negative news coverage of the less developed countries. They argued that the composite portrait of the developing countries that emerged from the international media depicted them as being relatively more prone to internal conflicts and crises, more likely to be the setting of armed conflict, more likely to be frequent recipients of disaster relief or economic and military aid, and proportionately more often the location of criminal activity. Such negative coverage of Third World countries was consistent with stereotypes, long held by many Americans, about social and political life in the developing countries (Gans 1989: 32). Stereotyped items that correspond to unconscious values and reality judgments are likely to be accepted as facts by Western journalists and reported by them (Tuchman 1972). Social constructions become reified and are reported as news by those adhering to professional practices that supposedly guarantee objectivity and a commitment to telling the truth.

There are at least two reasons to expect that the VOA and Radio Moscow both reported Third World items that were disproportionately negative. Insofar as Western and Soviet media practices were supporting the conflicting interests of the West and the Soviet Union during the time the research reported below was conducted (September 1986), discussion of some unfavorable conditions presented the opportunity for attributing responsibility for the undesirable conditions to a political adversary, thereby discrediting that nation's presence in the developing area. Second, accounts constructed in this manner would tend to discredit Third World nations and suggest their need to depend on more economically developed nations for economic and technological assistance. For purposes of this investigation, newscasts of an international station were considered consistent with the claim that they were singling out the Third World for negative coverage if 50 percent or more of the reported items were classified as negative. While the 50 percent criterion was arbitrary, it indicated, on balance, how much emphasis an international broadcasting organization placed on events such as civilian disturbances rather than on processes such as reducing illiteracy rates.

4. *International media politicize issues and present peripheral materials as substitutes for social, political, and technical information needed by developing countries.* Some international media theorists (Masmoudi 1978; Smith 1980; O'Brien 1984; Stephenson and Gaddy 1984) contended that inter-

national media failed to provide political and economic information that Third World citizens found relevant to their interests. It was claimed that Western definitions of news and newsworthiness precluded providing information facilitating the Third World's development of its own social, cultural, and material resources (UNESCO 1979). Communications having such omissions, it was argued, increased, rather than decreased, the divisions between the information-rich and information-poor countries. The information gap created further inequities in wealth that could be more difficult to overcome than divisions founded on economic exploitation (Smith 1980).

From the standpoint of style, items in newscasts may be classified in a number of ways. For example, there is the "news" itself: the who, what, when, and where of conditions or events having national significance—potentially affecting many lives in important ways in at least one country. As discussed in Chapter Three, audiences tend to adopt a posture of naive realism with respect to most media reports. They tend to accept as nonproblematic a correspondence between objects and events in the world of experience and their symbolic representations as printed or broadcast by the mass media. In the following discussion, *news* refers to reports about political actors, conditions, and events that appear to have at least national significance and that are understood in this manner. In addition to news there is perspective material. This is media content that offers information or background purportedly aiding audience understanding of the news. There is also peripheral material that provides information or background on actors, conditions, or events that apparently lack international or even national significance (see Theberge 1979).

The proportion of Third World items reported in these various styles constituted a fourth dimension for comparing VOA and Radio Moscow newscasts. In essence, the comparison indicated the extent to which each organization provided Third World citizens with information that they were likely to find important and the extent to which it provided commentary or merely discussed peripheral matters. This also suggests the relative extent to which the VOA and Radio Moscow were giving the Third World information that its own domestic media may have been ill-prepared to gather and report, and the extent to which they may have been pursuing other objectives through their newscasts. Newscasts of an international station were considered consistent with the fourth criticism of international media if a minimum of 50 percent of its Third World items were not news. On the other hand, a pattern in which 50 percent or more of its Third World items were classified as news suggests that the station may have been meeting some information needs of developing nations, even if it was doing so incidentally. In addition, it must be remembered that the distinction between providing news and broadcasting propaganda is seldom clear.

5. *International media interpret events in the Third World from an ethnocentric perspective.* A fifth criticism of Western international media concerned the manner in which events in the Third World were reported. Western media, it was claimed, interpret Third World events primarily from the perspective of how such events impact on the West rather than examining the meaning of the events for the citizens of the developing nations. For example, Smith (1980: 9) noted that when a coup took place in Afghanistan in 1978, almost all Western newspapers treated the event as an occasion to inquire, "Is the new leadership pro-Western or pro-Soviet?" long before they wrote about conditions in Afghanistan or the importance of the new regime for its people. Similarly, Western coverage of the collapse of the shah of Iran focused on contracts lost to Western companies and on the loss of Western military bases and tended to ignore the problems suffered by the inhabitants of Iran under the shah's rule.

Perspective on Third World items were the fifth basis for comparing VOA and Radio Moscow newscasts in this chapter. Comparison on this dimension suggested something about the manner in and the extent to which the United States and the Soviet Union were pursuing their own ideological interests through their newscasts. A method of analyzing the perspective of newscast items is described in the procedures section later in this chapter. Newscasts of an international station were consistent with the fifth criticism of international media if a minimum of 50 percent of its Third World items emphasized the activities of the broadcasting nation in the Third World or East-West conflict rather than the Third World nations themselves. A pattern in which 50 percent or more of a station's Third World items focused on developing nations themselves was not, in itself, sufficient to deny that a nation was using its international station's newscasts for its own political-economic purposes. Such a pattern was only one indication that newscasts may have been serving some information needs of Third World nations to which they were transmitted. It is possible for a station to serve some Third World information needs while pursuing its own nation's objectives.

6. *International media attempt to influence political decisions in the Third World by constructing highly positive images of their nations and highly negative images of their political adversaries.* Many, if not most, news items that made up VOA and Radio Moscow newscasts to the Third World were not about the developing nations themselves but about the sponsoring nation's own country and ideological adversaries. If international newscasts can be understood, at least in part, as tools of social, political, and military competition, then one might anticipate that items presented by

a broadcaster concerning its own nation and its nation's allies will be generally favorable, while items about political adversaries will be generally negative in tone.

For purposes of this study, the positive or negative character of newscast items about self (the sponsoring nation) and adversaries was the sixth dimension for comparing VOA and Radio Moscow newscasts to the Third World. The comparison indicated the extent to which the United States and the Soviet Union may have been using their newscasts to influence evaluations of themselves and their adversaries, thereby attempting to influence an important component of political decision making in developing nations. Newscasts of an international station were considered consistent with the claim that they were serving as a means of social, political, and military competition if a minimum of 50 percent of the items dealing with the broadcasting nation and its allies were positive and a minimum of 50 percent of items dealing with its adversaries were negative. The specific procedures for evaluating international newscasts are outlined below.

Procedures

Comparison were made of VOA and Radio Moscow newscasts in Spanish transmitted to Latin America and their newscasts in English beamed to Africa. One top-of-the-hour newscast was monitored, recorded, and transcribed for each service each day for a seven-day period extending from September 20 through September 26, 1986. Recordings were made as close to the same hour for each service as broadcasting schedules, equipment, and receiving conditions permitted. However, due to different newscast times, which take into account world time differences, Africa Service newscasts were monitored three hours earlier than the others. The Spanish broadcasts were translated into English. The selection of the particular seven-day period was made solely on the basis of practical considerations, such as available time and receiving conditions. During the period, events reported most often by the international radio stations that were monitored included: meetings between U.S. Secretary of State George Schultz and Soviet Foreign Minister Eduard Shevardnadze, the related cases of accused Soviet spy Gennady Zakharov and American journalist Nicholas Daniloff, who was charged with espionage by the Soviet Union, Israeli military activity along its boarder with Lebanon, military activity in Togo following an attack by a military force entering from Ghana, and developments in the continuing Iran-Iraq War.

It was also important to view the newscasts of the VOA and Radio Moscow in a broad comparative perspective. For example, it might have been found that VOA newscasts tended to present more Third World items than the newscasts of Radio Moscow. However, some conclusions that might have been drawn from such an isolated finding would be misleading. It might also have been the case that Third World coverage in VOA newscasts was significantly less than the attention given Third World items in the newscasts of other major international broadcasting organizations. To provide some context for understanding the VOA–Radio Moscow comparisons, same-day newscasts in the English-language World Services of three additional stations were monitored, recorded, and transcribed. The three included a Western station (the BBC), the station of a nation with a nonmarket economy (Radio Beijing), and the station of a politically neutral state (Swiss Radio International).

Four Purdue University students served as coders for the study. They were trained at three sessions during which the coding system was explained, and practice using the coding categories was provided by having them code several newscasts prepared for that purpose. Forty-nine newscasts were recorded for the study. These contained a total of 583 news items. Each item was coded for its nation-subject location. The classification of countries as Western, Soviet Bloc, Third World, or Other followed the classification scheme used by the World Bank (1984). Western nations corresponded to those listed as nations with industrialized market economies ($N = 19$); Soviet Bloc nations were those classified as Eastern European nonmarket economies ($N = 9$); Third World nations were those classified as low-income and low-middle-income economies ($N = 71$); while the remaining category was composed of nations classified as upper-middle-income ($N = 27$) or high-income oil exporters ($N = 5$).

The classification of a large number of nations (seventy-one) as Third World provided a greater pool of newscast items that could be examined in relation to the six claims than would have been possible with a more restrictive definition. To add further to the number of reports that could be analyzed as Third World items, those mentioning a Third World nation were automatically classified as such, no matter what the nature of the event. For example, the BBC item (September 24, 1986): "France is sending troops to Togo following an attempt to overthrow its president" was not coded as an item about France, but rather as an item about Togo, and therefore as a Third World item.

Nations also were classified as Allies or as Adversaries from the Cold War perspective of the broadcasting nations. For the VOA, Allies were nineteen Western nations and Adversaries were the nine Soviet Bloc countries. For Radio Moscow the pattern was reversed. Other and Third World nations were not classified as Allies or Adversaries. Allies and Adversaries were not specified for the three stations used for comparative purposes. Rather, nations simply were coded as Self, Third World, or Other in their newscasts.

Six news categories were utilized: (1) *foreign affairs*: including all trans-actions, ongoing or anticipated, between nations; (2) *domestic political and economic affairs*, such as items dealing with elections, social programs, presentations of policy intent, and business news occurring within each of the categories of nations; (3) *domestic disorder*:made up of items dealing with crime, corruption, rampant inflation, and challenges to established political authority occurring within each of the categories of nations; (4) *arts, sciences, and education*; (5) *sports and human interest*; and (6) *natural disasters*. Average intercoder reliability on news item topics was 86 per-cent.

Broadcast items concerning Third World nations also were coded ac-cording to their perspective. Three categories were employed. If dis-cussion of the subject matter contained no reference of any sort to the broadcasting nation or its allies or adversaries, the item was coded *na-tional*. If the discussion contained reference to the broadcasting nation, but not to its allies or adversaries, the item was coded *domestic*. If dis-cussion contained reference to the broadcasting nation's adversaries, the item was coded *West–Soviet Bloc conflict*. The purpose of such coding was to reveal the extent to which items discussing events in the Third World or the activities of Third World leaders were treated as Third World news rather than as stories emphasizing (and possibly justifying) involvement of the broadcasting nation in the event or as stories em-phasizing (and possibly criticizing) the involvement of the broadcasting nation's adversaries in the event. Average intercoder reliability on the focus of Third World news was 73 percent.

The method relied on to classify item style derived from a study per-taining to coverage of nuclear energy by nightly newscasts of U.S. tele-vision networks (Theberge 1979). In that categorization five styles were identified, the last two being combinations of the first three: news, per-spective, peripheral material, news/perspective, and news/peripheral. The category system was shown to have considerable analytic utility for comparing the newscasts of several international broadcasting organi-zations (Trice and Nimmo 1985). Average intercoder reliability on style of items in this study was 88 percent.

Finally, items were coded as being positive, negative, or neutral. Sim-ply put, an item's positive, negative, or neutral quality refers to whether the content is "good news," "bad news," or "balanced." Characteristics of good news include reports of problem solving or events that are pleasant, constructive, favorable, cooperative, or helping. Examples of good news include items reporting increases in a nation's literacy rate or per capita productivity or improvements in the nation's transportation or communications infrastructures. Characteristics of bad news include events that are unpleasant, obstructive, troubling, or dangerous. Ex-amples of bad news include items reporting armed conflict, corruption, natural disaster, or other disorders within a nation. The study used the scale developed by Haskins and Miller (1984) for classifying items according to positive or negative quality. The Trice and Nimmo (1985) study also demonstrated this measure to be useful in comparing newscasts such as those of the VOA and Radio Moscow. Average intercoder reliability on the positive or negative quality of newscast items for the present study was 86 percent.

Findings

Table 1 provides an overview of the contents of each of the international broadcasting organizations' newscasts. The patterns common to all stations included their emphasis on foreign affairs (accounting for 50.5 to 88.0 percent of their total number of items), their relative lack of emphasis on domestic political and economic matters (six of the seven stations devoted between 12.1 and 18.9 percent of their items to this class of topics), and, with the noteworthy exception of the two Radio Moscow services, their almost total lack of items dealing with the arts, science, education, sports, human interest, and natural disasters. (The absence of natural disaster items, unlike the other items, can be explained fully in terms of the failure of major events of this type to occur during the week the newscasts were monitored.)

One pattern clearly distinguished the VOA and Radio Moscow newscasts from those of the three stations used for comparative purposes. The amount of coverage given the Third World by the two VOA and the two Radio Moscow services ranged from 11.9 to 23.0 percent, while the coverage given the Third World by the BBC, Radio Beijing, and Swiss Radio International ranged from 32.5 to 41.8 percent. These percentages are particularly interesting given the generous operational definition of Third World items and in light of the fact that the VOA and Radio Moscow newscasts were transmitted on services targeted to the Third World, while the other newscasts were transmitted on world services.

Three broadcasting organizations had particularly distinctive emphases. Radio Moscow devoted about half its items to its own affairs and the affairs of its Cold War allies. The VOA services devoted less than one-third of their items to this topical category, and the three comparison stations were in the 12.2–18.1 percent range. Radio Beijing newscasts were unusual in their heavy emphasis on foreign affairs (88 percent of items) and their attention to the Third World nations (41.8 percent of items concerned the Third World).

Third, and of importance for this study, the VOA services were distinguished by the fact that they devoted half (in Spanish to Latin America) or more (64.4 percent, Africa Service) of their Third World items to

Table 1
Station, Classification of Nation in Which Reported Item Occurs, and Topic of Item (in percent)

Station	Topics	Self and Allies	Adversaries	Other	Third World	Total
Voice of America	Foreign affairs	18.8	3.8	27.5	6.2	56.3
(Africa Service)	Domestic poli. &					
(N = 80)	econ.	5.0	7.5	1.2		13.7
	Domestic disorder	5.0		13.8	11.2	30.0
	Arts, science, ed.					
	Sports, human int.					
	Natural disaster					
	Total	28.8	11.3	42.5	17.4	100.0
Radio Moscow	Foreign affairs	19.4	12.0	16.7	9.3	57.4
(Africa Service)	Domestic poli. &					
(N = 108)	econ.	3.7	5.6	0.9	2.8	13.0
	Domestic disorder			0.9	0.9	1.8
	Arts, science, ed.	19.4	2.8			22.2
	Sports, human int.	5.6				5.6
	Natural disaster					
	Total	48.1	20.4	18.5	13.0	100.0
Voice of America	Foreign affairs	21.8	13.8	21.8	10.3	67.7
(Spanish to Latin	Domestic poli. &					
America)	econ.	9.2	1.2	2.3	1.2	13.9
(N = 87)	Domestic disorder	1.2		5.7	11.5	18.4
	Arts, science, ed.					
	Sports, human int.					
	Natural disaster					
	Total	32.2	15.0	29.8	23.0	100.1
Radio Moscow	Foreign affairs	17.8	12.9	8.9	10.9	50.5
(Spanish to Latin	Domestic poli. &					
America)	econ.	13.9	3.0	1.0	1.0	18.9
(N = 101)	Domestic disorder		6.9	2.0		8.9
	Arts, science, ed.	19.8				19.8
	Sports, human int.	2.0				2.0
	Natural disaster					
	Total	53.5	22.8	11.9	11.9	100.1
BBC	Foreign affairs	3.0		43.9	12.1	59.0
(World Service)	Domestic, poli. &					
(N = 66)	econ.	9.1			3.0	12.1
	Domestic disorder	3.0			16.7	19.7
	Arts, science, ed.					
	Sports, human int.	3.0			3.0	6.0
	Natural disaster				3.0	3.0
	Total	18.1		43.9	37.8	99.8
Radio Beijing	Foreign affairs	16.4		41.8	29.8	88.0
(World Service)	Domestic poli. &					
(N = 67)	econ.					
	Domestic disorder				7.5	7.5
	Arts, science, ed.					
	Sports, human int.				4.5	4.5
	Natural disaster					
	Total	16.4		41.8	41.8	100.0
Swiss Radio	Foreign affairs	5.4		47.3	23.0	75.7
International	Domestic poli. &					
(World Service)	econ.	2.7		5.4	5.4	13.5
(N = 74)	Domestic disorder				2.7	2.7
	Arts, science, ed.	2.7		2.7	1.4	6.8
	Sports, human int.	1.4				1.4
	Natural disaster					
	Total	12.2		55.4	32.5	100.1

Table 2
Station, Classification of Nation in Which Reported Item Occurs, and
Positive or Negative Quality of Item (in percent)

Station	Quality of Items	Self and Allies	Adversaries	Other	Third World	Total
Voice of America	Positive	21.7	0	32.4	14.3	22.5
(Africa Service)	Neutral	52.2	55.5	2.9	42.9	30.0
	Negative	26.1	44.4	64.7	42.9	47.5
	N =	23	9	34	14	80
Radio Moscow	Positive	76.9	9.0	28.6	30.8	48.1
(Africa Service)	Neutral	23.1	0	38.1	23.1	21.3
	Negative	0	91.0	33.3	46.1	30.6
	N =	52	22	21	13	108
Voice of America	Positive	25.0	15.4	23.1	25.0	23.0
(Spanish to Latin	Neutral	60.7	53.8	19.2	20.0	37.9
America)	Negative	14.3	30.8	57.7	55.0	39.1
	N =	28	13	26	20	87
Radio Moscow	Positive	72.2	13.0	25.0	16.7	46.5
(Spanish to Latin	Neutral	27.8	8.7	33.3	33.3	24.8
America)	Negative	0	78.3	41.7	50.0	28.7
	N =	54	23	12	12	101
BBC	Positive	8.3		24.1	20.0	19.7
(World Service)	Neutral	58.3		24.1	20.0	28.8
	Negative	33.3		51.7	60.0	51.5
	N =	12		29	25	66
Radio Beijing	Positive	63.6		21.4	28.6	31.3
(World Service)	Neutral	36.4		46.4	35.7	40.3
	Negative	0		32.1	35.7	28.3
	N =	11		28	28	67
Swiss Radio	Positive	33.3		17.1	16.7	18.9
Intnl. (World	Neutral	66.7		39.0	29.2	39.2
Service)	Negative	0		43.9	54.2	41.9
	N =	9		41	24	74

domestic disorder. Only the BBC, the other Western station, had a similar emphasis (44.2 percent). Corresponding figures for the other stations were: Radio Moscow Africa Service, 6.9 percent; Radio Moscow Spanish to Latin America, zero; Radio Beijing, 17.7 percent; and Swiss Radio International, 8.3 percent. The following items illustrate the type of Third World items that are often reported on the VOA services:

In Ecuador, a confrontation has developed between the executive and legislative branches of government over a grant of amnesty to an Ecuadoran general and a former mayor. The dispute is the latest to emerge since opposition parties gained control of the Ecuadoran legislature during parliamentary elections last June. The assembly has also been questioning President Leon Febres-Cordero's finance minister and is considering bringing him to trial for mismanagement. (Voice of America, Spanish to Latin America, September 23, 1986)

Table 3
Station, Classification of Nation in Which Reported Item Occurs, and Style of Item (in percent)

Station	Style of Item	Self and Allies	Adversary	Other	Third World	Total
Voice of America (Africa Service)	News	82.6	77.8	61.8	85.7	73.8
	Perspective			2.9	7.1	2.5
	Peripheral	4.3		5.9		3.6
	News/Perspective	8.7	22.2	26.5	7.1	17.5
	News/Peripheral	4.3		2.9		2.5
	N =	23	9	34	14	80
Radio Moscow (Africa Service)	News	21.2	18.2	47.6	15.4	25.0
	Perspective	5.8	50.0	4.8	7.7	14.8
	Peripheral	30.8	4.5			15.7
	News/Perspective	28.8	27.3	47.6	76.9	38.0
	News/Peripheral	13.4				6.5
	N =	52	22	21	13	108
Voice of America (Spanish to Latin America)	News	78.6	69.2	73.1	80.0	75.9
	Perspective			11.5		3.4
	Peripheral					
	News/Perspective	17.8	30.8	11.5	20.0	18.4
	News/Peripheral	3.6		3.9		2.3
	N =	28	13	26	30	87

Table 3 (continued)

Radio Moscow (Spanish to Latin America)	News	31.5	30.4	33.3	25.0	30.7
	Perspective	9.3	43.5	8.3	8.3	16.8
	Peripheral	38.9				20.8
	News/Perspective	14.8	26.1	50.0	66.7	27.7
	News/Peripheral	5.6		8.3		4.0
	N =	54	23	12	12	101
BBC (World Service)	News	91.7		72.4	88.0	81.8
	Perspective			3.4		1.5
	Peripheral	8.3			4.0	3.0
	News/Perspective			24.1	8.0	13.6
	News/Peripheral					
	N =	12		29	25	66
Radio Beijing (World Service)	News		63.6	85.7	89.3	83.5
	Perspective					
	Peripheral					
	News/Perspective		36.4	14.3		12.0
	News/Peripheral				10.7	4.5
	N =		11	28	28	67
Swiss Radio International (World Service)	News		77.8	78.8	79.2	78.4
	Perspective				4.2	1.4
	Peripheral		11.1			1.4
	News/Perspective			19.5	16.7	16.2
	News/Peripheral		11.1	2.4		2.7
	N =		9	41	24	74

The Peruvian government is investigating the deaths of 13 peasants under mysterious circumstances last weekend in Southern Peru. Police initially said they killed the peasants in anti-guerrilla operations in the Andean region, but opposition politicians and some witnesses say the peasants were members of two families who were attending a birthday party when the killings took place. Amid a public outcry, the interior minister says he has formed a special commission to investigate. (Voice of America, Spanish to Latin America, September 26, 1986)

The percentage figures in Table 2 reveal some major differences among the overall proportions of positive and negative items presented by the broadcasting organizations. Almost half the items of the Radio Moscow services items were coded positive (Radio Moscow Africa Service, 48.1; Radio Moscow in Spanish to Latin America, 46.5 percent). This was more than twice the percentage of positive items presented by each of the other stations, with the exception of Radio Beijing (31.3 percent). The Radio Moscow Services and Radio Beijing also had very similar and comparatively low percentages of negative items (Radio Moscow Africa Service, 30.6; Radio Moscow to Latin America, 28.7; Radio Beijing, 28.3 percent). By contrast, overall, the VOA Services, the BBC, and Swiss Radio International each had less than one-fourth of its items coded as positive and approximately two-fifths of its items coded as negative (VOA Africa Service, 47.5; VOA in Spanish to Latin America, 39.1; BBC, 51.5; Swiss Radio International, 41.9 percent).

Particularly important patterns, common to all the stations, concern the relative proportion of positive and negative Third World items presented by each. Not a single station presented as much as a third of its Third World items as positive, and no station presented more positive than negative Third World items. With the exception of Radio Beijing, the proportion of Third World items that were negative presented by all the stations ranged from 42.9 to 60.0 percent.

Data in Table 3 suggest that, with the obvious exception of the Radio Moscow Services, the international broadcasting organizations devoted about three-fourths of their newscast items to so-called hard news; "news" accounted for from 78.8 to 81.8 percent of their total number of items. Contrary to what might be expected, the Radio Moscow Services devoted a rather large percentage of their non-news items to peripheral matters. For example, the Radio Moscow Africa Service newscasts of September 31, 1986, presented fifteen items. The last five of these concerned a festival of Bulgarian culture opening in Moscow, an international scientific conference on climate and human health being held in Leningrad, proposals for a new Moscow subway line, the Bolshoi Ballet, and the World Chess Championship matches.

Items presented in perspective and news/perspective styles appeared relatively frequently in the newscasts of four services: VOA Africa Ser-

Table 4
Station and Perspective on Third World Items (in percent)

Station	N	National	Domestic	West-Soviet Bloc Conflict
Voice of America (Africa Service)	14	64.3	14.3	21.4
Radio Moscow (Africa Service)	13	7.7	15.4	76.9
Voice of America (Spanish to Latin America)	20	60.0	30.0	10.0
Radio Moscow (Spanish to Latin America)	12	8.3	8.3	83.3
BBC (World Service)	25	96.0	0	4.0
Radio Beijing (World Service)	28	89.3	10.7	0
Swiss Radio Intnl. (World Service)	24	79.2	12.5	14.3

vice, 20.0; VOA Spanish to Latin America, 21.8; BBC, 15.1; and Swiss Radio International, 17.7 percent. Radio Beijing was unusual in the remarkably small proportion of its items presented in these styles (4.5 percent). At the other extreme, the Radio Moscow Africa Service presented over half its items in these styles (52.8 percent), and its Spanish Service to Latin America also was comparatively quite high (44.5 percent). The majority of items presented in perspective style by both Radio Moscow services were items concerning Soviet adversaries (68.8 percent, Radio Moscow Africa Service; 58.9 percent, Radio Moscow Spanish to Latin America).

The data in Table 4 show sharp differences among the broadcasters in their manner of treating Third World items. Three patterns emerged: a "Radio Moscow pattern," in which the vast majority (76.9 percent and 83.3 percent for the two services) of Third World items were treated as East-West conflict; a "comparative station pattern," in which such interpretation of Third World items was rare (BBC, 4.9 percent; Radio Beijing, 0 percent; and Swiss Radio International, 14.3 percent); and a VOA pattern falling in between, but much closer to the comparison station pattern (21.4 percent and 10.0 percent for the two services). The Radio Moscow pattern is significant enough to merit illustration.

The General Secretary of the Soviet Communist Party, Mikhail Gorbachev, has received in the Kremlin President Didier Ratsiraka of Madagascar. The two leaders spoke of the favorable prospects for the development of relations between their countries and the ruling parties. After an exchange of opinions on international issues, they expressed the conviction that the problems of development, the elimination of poverty and backwardness, were inseparable from stopping the arms race and disarmament. Mikhail Gorbachev and Didier Ratsiraka denounced the "Star Wars" plans. They stressed that the implementation of these plans would increase manyfold the threat of the self-destruction of modern civilization. The two leaders spoke for speedily proclaiming the Indian Ocean a zone of peace. Mikhail Gorbachev confirmed the determination of the Soviet Union to continue giving all-around support to the struggle of newly free countries for political and economic security. (Radio Moscow, Africa Service, September 24, 1986)

The president of Angola, Jose Eduardo dos Santos, has accused the Western powers, led by the United States, of continuing attempts to destabilize the frontline states in the south of Africa. The Angolan president also denounced the continued occupation of Namibia by racist South Africa. (Radio Moscow, Africa Service, September 22, 1986)

Data concerning the positive and negative character of items that a station broadcasts about its own country, its allies, and its adversaries are presented in Table 2. The data show that the two Radio Moscow services were alone in presenting more than two-thirds of such items as positive: Radio Moscow Africa Service, 76.9; and Radio Moscow in Spanish to Latin America, 72.2 percent. The following illustrates such items:

The agreement reached at the [Stockholm Conference on European Security and Disarmament in Europe] is a major contribution to strengthening peace and preventing war in Europe and outside it, and in improving East-West relations. The news analysts say the success was largely promoted by the constructive approach of the socialist countries. (Radio Moscow, Africa Service, September 21, 1986)

At the 41st U.N General Assembly, the foreign minister of Laos described the unilateral moratorium on nuclear explosions as convincing evidence the USSR wanted to save world peace. (Radio Moscow, Africa Service, September 24, 1986)

Finally, the Radio Moscow services were distinctive in the extent of their treatment of adversaries. The VOA services did not refrain from presenting negative items about the Soviet Bloc nations during the period of this study. For example, the VOA questioned the veracity of Soviet media and also questioned the Soviet Union's concern for nuclear safety, as these items illustrate:

The Soviet Union has announced major restructuring of its foreign trade operations, abandoning the Foreign Trade Ministry's monopoly on commerce with other countries. A decree carried by the government-run Soviet news media says, beginning January first, more than 20 ministries and departments will have the right to operate in foreign markets. Western correspondents in Moscow say full control will not be abandoned. They note the creation of a foreign economic commission headed by a deputy premier to oversee trade and guarantee state interests. (Voice of America, Africa Service, September 22, 1986)

Within the next few days the Chernobyl nuclear power plant in the Ukraine will resume part of its energy production. The opening comes 5 months after an explosion destroyed one of its reactors, killing 31 people and spreading radiation across Europe. There are still some problems in and near that station. (Voice of America, Africa Service, September 23, 1986)

More than 44 percent of VOA Africa Service items about adversaries of the United States were negative, while the figure for the Spanish Service to Latin America was 30.8 percent. However, these percentages seem low when compared to the corresponding 91.0 percent of Radio Moscow's Africa Service and the 78.3 percent of its Spanish Service to Latin America. The two following items illustrate the content of items concerning Western nations that regularly appeared in Radio Moscow newscasts to the Third World.

On the average, every minute, one rural employee loses his job in the Common Market Countries. There are some 17 million unemployed now in the EEC countries, and the figure continues to grow. (Radio Moscow, Africa Service, September 20, 1986)

Mexico and its coastal waters are subjected to radioactive contamination as a result of the nuclear tests conducted by the United States. A statement has been made by Manuel deLasco Suarez, the President of the Mexican Branch of International Physicians for the Prevention of Nuclear War. (Radio Moscow, Spanish to Latin America, September 25, 1986)

Additional patterns common to all stations as well as patterns that are exhibited by only one broadcaster might be identified using the data in the four tables. Those that were discussed and illustrated were directly related to claims asserted by several analysts who were critical of Western

communications to and about the Third World. In addition, the particular patterns that were discussed were selected to reveal possible verbal
strategies employed by the VOA and Radio Moscow in the period toward
the end of the Cold War. More generally, they were selected to provide
some insight into the ways in which international radio broadcasting
has been used to serve the interests of nations that transmit to the Third
World.

Discussion of the Case Study

Analysts who were critical of international communications to and
about the Third World made a number of claims concerning the message
content of Western international media. The first claim was that Western
international media do not define conditions and events occurring in
the Third World as being as important as the conditions and events
occurring in more economically developed nations. Hence, Western media tend to devote little coverage to the developing nations. In keeping
with suggestions outlined in the literature, it was decided that a station
was ignoring the Third World if one-quarter or less of its newscast items
concerned the developing nations. Both Voice of America and Radio
Moscow Services, all of which were targeted to areas of the Third World,
failed to devote more than 25 percent of their news items to these nations. Hence, there is some support for the claim that international news
media—at least major international radio broadcasting stations—tended
to ignore the Third World. However, the data in this study suggest that
critics of the world information order missed the mark in placing sole
blame on Western media for inattention to the low-income nations. Each
of the Radio Moscow Services devoted less than one-fourth of its news
items to the Third World. On the other hand, a major Western station,
the BBC, discussed Third World affairs rather frequently. (Data in Table
1 show that 37.8 percent of BBC news items concerned Third World
nations.) Therefore, at least in terms of international radio newscasts in
the late 1980s, the two major superpowers tended to ignore the Third
World, but other nations, including at least one major Western country,
did not.

Another contention of some analysts of international communication
was that Western media tended to ignore processes involving positive
social development in the Third Word. A station that devoted only 5
percent or less of its items about the Third World to processes such as
improving literacy rates or upgrading regional health standards and the
like was considered to be giving little attention to positive processes of
Third World development. Data in Table 1 suggested that the VOA
services and the BBC gave little consideration to matters of development
within the Third World. However, data in Table 1 also show that no

international radio stations in this study emphasized domestic political, social, and economic matters, including conditions of their own political economies. The claim that the international news media tend to ignore Third World development was true in the case of international radio broadcasting, but only trivially so during the survey period. Furthermore, Third World development received no less attention from the Western Services than it did from Radio Moscow Services or Radio Beijing.

Did news of the Third World, reported in the international media, focus on coups and corruption rather than on positive social, economic, and political development? A station that devoted half or more of its Third World news items, in late September 1986, to domestic disorder was defined as exhibiting such a pattern. Here Voice of America Services stands out. The BBC pattern did not meet the 50 percent criterion for emphasis on domestic disorder, but its pattern was close. The data, then, were consistent with the view that Western media, in this case Western international broadcasting organizations, focused on domestic disorder when transmitting to and discussing the Third World.

Even when Third World items are discussed by the international media, they can be treated in such a way as to direct attention to political and economic relationships outside the developing areas. Statements about leaders, conditions, or events in the Third World can be endowed with meanings that are intended to serve the political, economic, or cultural interests of those who control a particular news medium rather than the information needs of Third World nations. A fourth claim made by some analysts of international communication was that Western media politicize issues as a substitute for factual information needed by developing nations. Newscasts of an international station were considered consistent with this view if 50 percent or more of its Third World items were other than hard news. Data in Table 3 suggest that the vast majority of Third World items presented by the VOA services could be classified as news. Such data do not support the view that Western media substituted commentary for information in their communications to and about the developing nations. On the other hand, the data do suggest that the Radio Moscow services did present more than half of their Third World items in styles other than news. Hence, the fourth claim, while not applying to VOA newscasts, did apply to the newscasts of the Radio Moscow services.

A fifth claim of some analysis of international communication was that Western media view Third World events from the perspective of how such events affect the West rather than analyzing the meaning that the events might have for the citizens of the developing nations. Newscasts of a station were considered consistent with this claim if 50 percent or more of its Third World items emphasized the activities of the broadcasting nation in the Third World or East-West conflict rather than the Third World nations themselves. Data in Table 3 clearly show a pattern in which the Radio Moscow services presented the vast majority of its Third World items as East-West conflicts, while the other stations did not do so. Like the fourth claim, the fifth claim did not apply to VOA newscasts but did apply to the newscasts of the Radio Moscow services.

Finally, some analysts contended that Western international media attempt to influence political decision making in the Third World by constructing highly positive images of their nations and highly negative images of their political adversaries. Newscasts of an international station were considered consistent with the sixth contention if 50 percent or more of its items dealing with the broadcasting nation and its allies were positive *and* 50 percent or more of its items dealing with its adversaries were negative. Data in Table 2 suggest that the VOA did not refrain from presenting positive images of the United States and negative images of the Soviet Union and its allies, although the frequency with which the services did this fell short of the 50 percent criterion. Data in Table 2 also suggest that the two Radio Moscow Services presented over two-thirds of their news items about the Soviet Union and its allies in positive fashion and over three-fourths of its news items about the United States and its allies negatively. It appears that the Soviet Union was more involved in manipulating the self and adversary images it broadcasts to the Third World than was the United States.

MEDIA IMPERIALISM IN A MORE AMBIGUOUS CONTEXT OF WORLD POLITICS

This study, conducted in late September 1986, identified some of the similarities and differences in the content of VOA and Radio Moscow newscasts which competed for the attention of citizens in developing nations at a time when the United States and the Soviet Union unambiguously defined one another as political, military, economic, and ideological rivals. In so doing, it demonstrated that newscasts symbolically constructed conditions and events in ways reflecting the interests of the broadcasting nations. There is nothing new in this, for, as we have seen, the history of IRB is the history of organizations serving their sponsoring nations.

The contents and apparent aims of VOA and Radio Moscow newscasts to the Third World were viewed from the perspectives of six claims that have been made by some analysts who are critical of the structure of international communications. Consistent with several of the claims, it was found that VOA newscasts paid relatively little attention to Third World nations, said virtually nothing about matters of development, emphasized disorder within the Third World to a great extent, and generally presented a substantial number of Third World newscast items that were negative.

However, many of the Radio Moscow newscast patterns that were identified during the period of study were also in line with the objections presented in literature critical of Western international media. The Soviet stations also failed to say much about the Third World or about ongoing social and economic development within it. Unlike the United States, the former Soviet Union did not emphasize disorder in the regions. However, it did tend to treat Third World items in a way suggesting a view of the Third World in a context of East-West conflict rather than as various nations with their own social, economic, and political difficulties as well as at least some of their own developmental successes.

Taken together, the findings offer only limited support for those who explained the structure and operation of international communications in terms of theoretical constructs such as media imperialism, cultural domination, and electronic colonialism. Findings also suggest that, at least in the mid to late 1980s, Soviet international media, as well as the international media of the West, worked to promote their own particular forms of social, political, and economic organizations.

IRB undoubtedly did, and does, provide Third World leaders and citizens with considerable information about world affairs. During the Cold War it also provided information about the divergent positions of the West and the Socialist nations. However, it is doubtful that it has contributed much to understanding the developing nations, encouraging cooperation between East and West for solving problems of development, or promoting world peace. In this sense, the political performance of IRB probably was neither more nor less disappointing than that of films, television programs, magazines, newspapers, and other cultural materials that are sent to the Third World from more economically developed nations.

Since 1986 the world information order has changed appreciably. Throughout the Third World, private communication conglomerates have grown and become more interconnected nationally and internationally. The distinction between foreign and national media ownership, control, and content has become blurred (Fox 1988: 30). Furthermore, the international flow of communications is no longer unidirectional from north to south. For example, some Latin American television companies have now set up distribution organizations and television networks for the large Spanish-speaking audiences in the United States and Western Europe. In the West, the penetration of cable and the emergence of other distribution technologies, such as videocassette recorders and low-power television stations (and, in the near future, multichannel multipoint distribution services and direct broadcast satellites) are eroding the audience share held by over-the-air broadcasters and may open new markets for media materials produced in the Third World (Mueller 1989: 4). In this increasingly complex context of international communication, the ways in which Third World populations will continue to include IRB as part of the media systems they construct for themselves and the extent to which they will continue to depend on IRB as a major provider of truth about world politics remain to be seen.

It is not only the context of IRB to the Third World that is changing. The content of VOA and Radio Moscow newscasts to the Third World undoubtedly are changing as well. Recent content analyses of two major American news media, *Newsweek* and the *Christian Science Monitor*, indicate that long-enduring adversary stereotypes of the Soviet Union are being replaced by considerably less negative images. For example, accounts of the former Soviet Union showed no clear focus on long-standing favorite topics such as repression, State Security Committee (KGB) activities, dissidents, and Jewish emigration. Similarly, recent content analyses of two major Soviet news media, *Novoye Vremya* and *Izvestia*, revealed little of the old tendency to depict the United States as the land of drug addiction, unemployment, and crime and poverty, ruled by a government pursuing an international policy of neocolonialism (Richter 1991; Lukosinunas 1991). It seems likely that the changes in the domestic media in the United States and Russia will also be found in the newscasts of the VOA and Radio Moscow. It is clear that IRB to the Third World is entering a new era in which newscasts cannot be understood well through the use of theoretical constructs associated with the Cold War era.

David Martin, Pentagon reporter for the *Wall Street Journal,* recently wrote that developments in the relations between the United States and nations of the former Soviet Bloc will be defined by Western media as the world's most important news for the foreseeable future. As a consequence, he anticipated a significant reduction in Western coverage of the Third World. He commented that:

Most of the stories we do about the Third World are done in the context of proxy superpower confrontation—Afghanistan, Angola, Cambodia, Nicaragua. Without those confrontations, I think reporting interest will quickly dwindle (except where—Panama for instance—American lives are at stake). However, this will be offset by more reporting on the Soviet Union, as Western journalists continue to gain access to what used to be off-limits. (Dennis, Gerbner, and Zassoursky 1991: 143)

Should this come about, several of the criticisms of Western media reviewed in this chapter will no doubt be expressed with renewed vigor.

Chapter Five

A Case Study of Broadcasting Counterpropaganda: South Africa's Use of International Radio Broadcasting

As we have seen, from its inception, a major use that governments have made of IRB is to counter the critical messages of political adversaries. For example, Lenin used shortwave radio in 1918 to debate claims made by foreign newspapers about conditions in Russian (Paulu 1974). In 1933, Germany initiated anticommunist broadcasts over its Deutschlandsender, touching off a radio war with Russia that lasted until 1939, when the German-Soviet Friendship Treaty was signed (Browne 1982: 225). During the Vietnam War, the International Communication Agency of the United States labored to convince the world that America had selfishly intervened to install a democratic regime in Vietnam (Parenti 1986: 176). Today, some portion of the mass communication of most governments is devoted to countering criticism from both domestic and foreign sources. Such activity is consistent with the view of Habermas (1975: 12) that in the modern world, claims of normative validity must be justified in an increasingly explicit way.

In modern nations with competitive, multiparty systems, domestic criticism of the actions and policies of those who govern comes from a variety of sources including opposition parties, organizations related to social movements, interest groups of various sorts, and, occasionally, in periods of elite dissensus, the mass media. Historically, domestic criticism of government has been less common in modern, single-party states. Some domestic criticism of the governments of nations with such party systems does emerge from intraparty conflict and from dissident groups, particularly those that have attracted the attention of the international media. However, in late 1989, domestic criticism of single-party states increased dramatically in China and Eastern Europe. It finally found wide expression throughout the former Soviet Union in August 1991 in response to an attempted coup aimed at replacing the government and policies of Mikhail Gorbachev.

In the world arena, criticism of governments and regimes originates from several sources which include the governments of foreign nations, dissident groups in exile, prominent individuals who are exiled, and international organizations such as the United Nations, the World Council of Churches, and Amnesty International. This chapter concerns government use of IRB to respond to symbolic attacks emanating from such sources. It draws on the discussion of varieties of propaganda (introduced in Chapter Three) to identify the strategies that can be employed by a contemporary government in an effort to nullify the possible negative effects of international criticism.

COUNTERPROPAGANDA

Because there has been a tremendous increase in exposure to the electronic mass media throughout all nations, it is increasingly difficult to maintain a country in isolation from ideas and information that are common to the rest of the world (Bogart 1976: xxiii). A major consequence of broadcasting propaganda is that the use of international radio virtually compels responses from governments that are subject to political criticism. Today it is unlikely that any government will be willing to leave uncontested the ability of political competitors to define major political leaders, conditions, and events for the world community. No government is likely to passively accept the loss of domestic and international influence entailed in failing to construct and effectively communicate symbolic realities that can offset the politically damaging images disseminated by its critics.

Every channel of communication has some effects on the structure and content of the messages it conveys. In the case of electronic media such as IRB, one of the effects is particularly relevant: Electronic communications are instantaneous. When an event occurs, electronic media make possible its immediate reporting. When a government is criticized, electronic media provides that government with the opportunity for instant response.

Due to time constraints, reports or responses cannot always be constructed with great care. Hastily produced framing of politically significant conditions or events can provide political adversaries with the opportunities for counterpropaganda. To cite an event discussed earlier, in September 1983, a South Korean airliner was shot down by Soviet interceptor planes after intruding inside Soviet airspace. The reaction of U.S. media was instantaneous and unrestrained, referring to the act with terms such as "barbaric," "savage," and "inhuman" and suggesting that the Soviet Union was tougher, more brutal, and less civilized than the rest of the world (Parenti 1986: 156–160). Such broadcast reactions presented the Soviets with not only an opportunity to construct carefully worded rebuttals that appeared to be factually based, but also an opportunity to accuse the United States of clandestine spy activities throughout the world; to recount incidents of civilian airliner destruction in Angola, Cuba, Israel, and India in which the CIA was purported to be implicated; and to argue that the occurrence was being used cynically by the Reagan administration to mobilize support for the MX missile and an increased arms budget (Edelman 1988: 70; Herman and Chomsky 1988: 33).

Failure to immediately report any major domestic occurrence that is known independently by those outside a nation also can provide the nation's competitors with an opportunity for counterpropaganda. For example, only after Sweden detected increases in radioactivity, two days after the April 1986 Chernobyl nuclear accident, did the Soviet government acknowledge that an accident had occurred. Throughout Europe, harsh criticism was directed at the Soviet government for failing to provide full and prompt information about the radioactivity spreading over Europe or even warn its own citizens in the affected areas. In addition, Western media used the situation as an opportunity to point out the lack of free and independent news media in the Soviet Union (Hachten 1987: 26).

In this chapter, counterpropaganda is understood as sets of messages that deliberately are intended by their sender to nullify or turn to the sender's perceived advantage the political effects of the communications of the sender's critics. The effects are those that the sender anticipates and defines as both politically significant and undesirable. In any given case, the distinction between propaganda and counterpropaganda may be unclear. Often it is difficult to determine whether a particular media item represents a direct response to some assertion of a political critic or adversary. Kenneth Boulding (1961) was among the first theorists to elaborate the view that political behavior is a response to political images that are shaped in a complex process of transmission and feedback involving various communication networks. Messages transmitted by the international broadcasting organization of any nation can find almost immediate responses from other interested governments and organizations. The process of message construction, transmission, reaction, and defense is continuous. The positive messages that a government transmits conveying its national self-image are intended, in part, to counteract malevolent images of the government advanced by critics, competitors, and adversaries. Defensive strategies can affect positive self-image construction, and many of these strategies can be classified as counterpropaganda.

Determination that particular media content constitutes counterpropaganda is most easily made in cases where specific empirical claims (claims that are verifiable or falsifiable by methods that are conventionally accepted more-or-less universally) are asserted by the media of one nation and are explicitly denied by the media of another nation. In this case, the response (discussed in Chapter Three as contradicting assertions, a category of factual propaganda) represents the least ambiguous form of counterpropaganda. In the face of purportedly factual claims that appear to be damaging to a government, potentially the most effective strategy of response is the presentation of compelling evidence that an adversary is not telling the truth. Such a presentation destroys the adversary's ability to further wage a war of words and may even raise doubts about the adversary's actual strength. Hitler's minister of propaganda, Joseph Goebbels, understood well the power of propaganda but apparently failed to appreciate the risk of the potentially even greater power of counterpropaganda. Developments in communication technology, such as satellites capable of photographing everything from missiles in Cuba and the nuclear disaster in Chernobyl to troop movements in the Persian Gulf and the former Soviet Union have vastly increased the risks associated with presenting claims that can be effectively denied. Contradicting assertions can take the form of bureaucratic counterpropaganda in which seemingly factual official reports are issued in response to verbal attacks. The difference between bureaucratic propaganda and bureaucratic counterpropaganda is that the latter represents a response to a direct challenge to organizational (in the case of IRB-national) integrity.

A second, relatively clear form of counterpropaganda involves a form of linguistic propaganda—borrowing conceptual justifications. In the face of foreign criticism of a government's international actions, the use of conceptual justifications borrowed from the critic can serve as an effective response. As Thomas Franck and Edward Weisband (1972) demonstrated, a government's use of a set of principles to justify its actions commits that government to acknowledge the legitimacy of the principles even when they are evoked by an adversary. Failure to grant such recognition introduces unpredictability and instability in international relations unwanted by any involved nation.

Strategies of counterpropaganda such as presenting contradicting assertions and using borrowed conceptual justifications are not always available. A critic's claims can be accompanied by enough purported evidence to undermine the credibility of efforts at denial and make difficult efforts to identify, organize, and characterize the criticized actions or policies in a way that effectively legitimizes them. A critic can create circumstances in which denial or alternative constructions of reality are experienced by an audience as "mere propaganda." A government's critics also can fail to provide a serviceable set of legitimating principles. Governments, therefore, must employ other strategies for responding to criticism.

A third approach consists in the counterattack. This involves a form of factual propaganda—accusing assertions. The strategy can promote a negative evaluation of the motives and actions of the critic and suggest that the criticism is both cynical and hypocritical. Successfully impugning the integrity of a source of communication can reduce the effectiveness of criticism coming from the source. The Soviet response to U.S. commentary on the downing of the 1983 Korean airliner (cited earlier), is one example.

Reorienting counterpropaganda is another variant of factual counterpropaganda. The strategy involves providing information that is intended to establish a new cognitive context for evaluating criticism. For example, Herman and Chomsky (1988: 87–142) pointed out that American media characterized the 1984 election in Nicaragua as a farce. However, that criticism is likely to be reevaluated in light of information about the favorable conditions under which the Nicaraguan election was held, in contrast to the highly questionable conditions under which elections were held in El Salvador in 1982 and 1984 and in Guatemala in 1984–1985 (elections that the U.S. government and the American media nevertheless supported).

The varieties of counterpropaganda discussed thus far are issue-specific. They represent reactions to claims made by critics about a particular act, condition, policy, event, or series of events. Other forms of counterpropaganda represent reactions to more diffuse charges made by political critics or adversaries. The accusation that a nation used chemical or biological weapons in a military encounter calls for a denial of the specific claims that were reported as facts. The accusation that a nation is insensitive to human rights or is militarily adventurous calls for the construction and presentation of a national image inconsistent with the labeling. The distinction between issue-specific and what will be termed thematic counterpropaganda is not hard and fast. However, it does clarify how manifestly nonpolitical material can be employed as a form of counterpropaganda.

Even the most cursory glance at the programming schedules of the major international broadcasting organizations reveals that a substantial amount of broadcast time is devoted to the transmission of materials such a music, sporting events, verbal travelogues, cultural affairs, business, and features purporting to depict daily life in the nation. Although lacking obvious political content, numerous analysts have contended that such cultural materials can effectively promote particular values and national images that serve political and economic interests (Cherry 1978; Hedeboro 1982; Lee 1980; McPhail 1981; Morley 1990; Nordenstreng and

Schiller 1979; Rosenblum 1979; Schiller, 1976; Smith 1980; Tunstall 1977). Benevolence-malevolence is a common cognitive dimension of international images attributed to nations (Scott 1965). A likely reason for allocating time to materials lacking obvious political intent is that they can cultivate a more benevolent image of a nation. Such materials do not evoke the resistance aroused by assertions that deal explicitly with political events, conditions, policies, principles, or other potentially controversial matters (Allport and Simpson 1946; Janis and Smith 1965; Nimmo and Combs 1980).

The governments that most often outrage their citizens or force unwelcome changes in their behavior plainly have the greatest need to employ reassuring symbols (Edelman 1964). It is such governments that are the most likely to be active producers of both propaganda and counterpropaganda. For example, for decades the government of the Republic of South Africa clearly has been among the most active counterpropaganda producing nations. Analysis of South Africa's IRB should reveal not only how that nation has responded to what has been termed "the ultimate public relations challenge" (Venter 1988: 3), but also should illustrate counterpropaganda strategies available to all governments in their IRB. More generally, the study reported below is intended as an exploration of the political ends that can be served by all broadcast materials, even those that are not manifestly political.

THE ULTIMATE PUBLIC RELATIONS CHALLENGE OF RADIO RSA, THE VOICE OF SOUTH AFRICA

The regime of the Republic of South Africa long has been the object of worldwide criticism, particularly since 1948 when the National party came to power, extending and formally institutionalizing the policies of apartheid and harshly suppressing the political and economic rights of nonwhites. Criticisms have come from nations as politically diverse as the former Soviet Union and the United States as well as from other African nations. Verbal attacks have been launched by a wide variety of international political organizations such as the Organization of African Unity and the United Nations, by international religious bodies such as the All African Council of Churches and the World Council of Churches, and by numerous international labor organizations and sporting groups (Dugard 1980; Gerhart 1978; Leatt, Kneifel, and Nurnberger 1986; Tatum 1987).

The South African government long has made full use of the media of mass communication to present its perspective on South African social, economic, and political affairs to both domestic and foreign audiences. Within South Africa, most events and ideological debates are filtered through the mass media in such a way that accounts tend to support existing social inequalities (Gerhart 1978; Hachten and Giffard 1984; Jowett and O'Donnell 1986; Pollak 1981).

South Africa initiated its international radio service—Radio RSA, the Voice of South Africa—in 1966. Radio RSA is the external service of the South African Broadcasting Corporation (SABC), which, since 1981, has been a section of the South African government's Department of Foreign Affairs and Information. The SABC has no formal mechanism for ensuring equal or even proportionate broadcasting time for all South Africa's political parties. Historically, SABC newscasts have equated the interests of South Africa with the interests of the National party. The SABC has justified its progovernment stance on the grounds that English and black media were giving their audiences false constructions of reality and that, if the world knew the truth, South Africa's critics would give apartheid a fair hearing (Tomaselli, Tomaselli, and Muller 1989: 87–91).

In 1988, when the study reported in this chapter was conducted, Radio RSA was on the air 208 hours a week in eleven languages. Its target areas were Africa, Latin America, East and West Germany, Austria, Switzerland, the Netherlands, France, the Middle East, the United Kingdom, Ireland, and North America (South African Broadcasting Corporation 1988). Audience research conducted by other international broadcasting organizations showed that while Radio RSA did not appear to have substantial audiences in Western Europe or North America, its programs reached almost as many listeners as did those of the VOA and the BBC in parts of the Third World, and it outstripped both these stations in eastern Africa and much of southern Africa (Browne 1982). In part because of widespread illiteracy, there are only about 125 daily newspapers in all Africa, compared with more than 1,770 in the United States. In Africa, as elsewhere in the Third World, radio serves as a chief source of information (Hachten 1987). This suggests that Radio RSA was an important carrier of the messages of the South African government. The materials broadcast by Radio RSA's Africa Services may have differed in some respects from those broadcast by its North America Service. However, it seems unlikely that the international broadcasting organization's most basic propaganda and counterpropaganda messages differed significantly from one service to another because inconsistencies could easily be monitored and reported worldwide by critics of the South African regime.

The administration of Radio RSA has always been well aware that its target audiences are likely to be skeptical of much of its broadcast material. Fanus Venter, head of Radio RSA, characterized the mission of the station as the ultimate public relations challenge. According to Venter, the main objective of the station has been to foster understanding of South Africa's unique situation in the world and to counteract the untruths and half-truths about the nation that have been spread world-wide (Venter 1988). To this end, the SABC claimed that Radio RSA presented balanced and objective information that enabled its audiences to make a more accurate assessment of South African affairs against a background of what it described as inaccurate and often one-sided coverage given events in South Africa by foreign media (South African Broadcast Corporation 1982). Much of this so-called balanced and objective information constitutes Radio RSA's counterpropaganda.

Procedures

Radio RSA's nightly broadcasts to North America were monitored from February 6 through March 13, 1988. This particular period later proved to be one of considerable political significance in South African history. On February 24, the South African government banned political activity by 17 opposition groups, including the nation's largest anti-apartheid coalition, the African National Congress (ANC), and the largest black labor federation, the Congress of South African Trade Unions, in the most sweeping crackdown in a decade. International response to this action prompted the South African government to initiate vigorous counter-propaganda activity.

From February 6 through March 5, Radio RSA broadcast one hour nightly to North America on three frequencies. From March 6 through March 13, Radio RSA increased its broadcast time to two hours on the same frequencies. In all, forty-five hours of broadcasts were recorded. This provided a considerable amount of material for analysis.

Each hour of Radio RSA broadcasting began with nine minutes of news consisting of nine or ten items. Items tended to deal almost exclusively with conditions and events in South Africa itself or with conditions and events in southern African states. News always was followed by a three-minute "Editorial Comment" which discussed official policies of the South African government. The labeling of this three-minute program segment, differentiating it from the news, clearly suggested that the news that preceded it had consisted of a purely factual recounting of occurrences of importance in southern Africa. When a time is designated for editorials, the implicit message is that what has gone before and what follows is fundamentally different in terms of values and opinions (Altheide and Snow 1980).

The remaining programming for each hour consisted of "Africa To-day—News and Views of the African Continent." This segment of programming, employing a newsmagazine format, generally contained four or five items, each running several minutes, and two weekly features, each running thirteen to sixteen minutes. Many of the shorter items were indistinguishable from the type of material that appeared in the

"Editorial Comment" segment. The regular weekly features included a program on South African authors, a shortwave hobbyist program, "Touring RSA: Travel Impressions of South Africa," and "Our Wild Heritage: A Weekly Look at Conservation and Environmental Matters on the African Subcontinent."

Four students served as coders. Three classes of items were used in the study: "news," "editorials," and "features." The study analyzed a total of 774 items. Individual items in all classes were categorized according to their primary focus: South African domestic affairs (including government activities and policies, economy, natural environment, culture, and social structure–race relations), 51.0 percent; relations of South Africa with other African nations and organizations (including political and economic relations, cultural exchanges, and military engagements), 6.7 percent; relations of South Africa with non-African nations and with world organizations, 12.0 percent; domestic and foreign affairs of other African nations and activities of African organizations, 27.0 percent; and domestic and foreign affairs of non-African nations and activities of world organizations, 1.2 percent. A residual category was used for items such as sports and shortwave hobbyist features that could not be located in any of the five categories: 2.1 percent. An item was assigned to a primary focus category only if at least three of the four coders so classified it.

Coders were instructed to write one, or at most two, summary sentences for each item. (In the case of news items, coders usually took this sentence from the presentation of news highlights, a portion of programming not included in the analysis.) Each coder provided an average of 1,165 summary sentences. Each of these summary sentences was typed on an individual index card.

Coders were given a pack of their summary sentence cards, divided into the primary focus categories. Working within each primary focus category, coders were instructed to sort the cards by placing them into five piles or less, with each pile expressing a common idea, set of related ideas, or theme. Coders were then instructed to write a paragraph of no more than four sentences that expressed the central idea of the cards in each pile.

The procedure generated 92 brief summary paragraphs. The summary paragraphs were typed, producing an eleven-page document, a copy of which was given to each coder. Each summary paragraph was assigned a number. Coders then met to determine collectively which summary paragraphs seemed to them to express a common idea, set of related ideas, or theme. Two or more summary paragraphs were recorded as expressing a common theme only if at least three of the four coders agreed that they did so.

The decision rule was adopted that a set of summary paragraphs, the members of which had been coded as interrelated, would be considered a major theme of Radio RSA if the set contained at least eight members. Six sets of summary paragraphs met this criterion. These are reported as the six major themes discussed in this chapter. The number of summary paragraphs subsumed under each of the six themes was: Theme 1 = 19, Theme 2 = 11, Theme 3 = 8, Theme 4 = 8, Theme 5 = 9, and Theme 6 = 10. These frequencies do not necessarily reflect the relative amount of time Radio RSA devoted to the presentation of each theme. Moreover, the themes do not represent mutually exclusive sets of logically interrelated statements. Rather, they represent clusters of ideas that were perceived as being interrelated.

Findings: Thematic Counterpropaganda

As noted, analysis of the forty-five hours of broadcasts suggested that much of South Africa's counterpropaganda focused on the presentation of six major themes. The themes constitute counterpropaganda in the sense that they can be understood as sets of messages that are intended by their sender to nullify or turn to a perceived advantage the political effects of the communications of political adversaries.

Theme 1. South Africa is an unusually complex, modern society with a pro-Western government, a vital capitalist economy, vast natural resources, and a rich cultural life with ties to Western Europe. While the nation faces serious continuing problems of race, exclusive focus on the single aspect of South African society by the media of other countries has produced a highly distorted and misleading international image of the nation.

The majority of Radio RSA's programming appeared to be devoted to transmitting this most general message. It was carried primarily by feature programming rather than by items in the context of formal news broadcasts. Features on the presentation of Shakespearean plays in Afrikaans (February 6, 1988); the theater of protest in South Africa (February 6, 1988); the Natural History Museum in Cape Town (February 15, 1988); efforts by South African scientists to reintroduce extinct species (March 12, 1988); South Africa's businesswoman of the year (March 12, 1988); and the possible creation of additional funds for social reform by the privatization of state utilities and other companies (March 9, 1988) all depicted a nation going about its cultural, scientific, and economic life in a manner not unlike other Western societies.

Theme 2. South Africa is wantonly and hypocritically singled out as a nation that oppresses its people. The government of South Africa is committed to democratic development. To this end, it is working to promote economic advancement, literacy, order, and stability, all of which are social preconditions for the maintenance of political liberties.

Such apparent abridgments of democracy as occur should be viewed in that light, and in fact, they are consonant with the practices of other democratic states.

This theme became particularly prominent after the February 24, 1988, banning of seventeen opposition groups. It was stated explicitly in speeches by various government officials who were quoted at length in newscasts on the days immediately following the banning.

The second theme also was expressed in a wide variety of other contexts. For example, in an "Editorial Comment" segment, Simon Jenkins, a noted British writer and regular columnist for the *London Sunday Times* was quoted as having written that:

The past week saw media attention being paid to the violence in Northern Ireland, Israeli soldiers beating Palestinians, [and] the reporting of uprisings in the Soviet Union as well as the news of the restrictions placed on organizations in South Africa . . . [I was] shocked by the complexity of the problems in Israel and South Africa, many of which were inherited from British policy decisions. [I was] impressed, however, by the efforts being made to overcome these problems. [I do] not believe that either Tel Aviv or Pretoria takes any more delight in increasing the permanent emergency powers than does the British government in extending its own increasingly permanent emergency powers. (March 1, 1988)

The theme even was incorporated in a feature on acquired immune deficiency syndrome (AIDS), which pointed out that all nations, including Western democracies, must occasionally face the difficult issue of forming public policy in circumstances under which the strict maintenance of individual rights might compromise the general welfare of society.

One of the main dilemmas of the epidemic will be political: where to balance between harsh public measures to combat the scourge, and the democratic rights of the infected individual. The first clarion calls of the coming moral battle have already been heard from the United States of America, where some politicians have demanded compulsory blood testing and the quarantine of AIDS carriers to protect society as a whole. In West Germany, also, the CSU [Christian Social Union] party wants compulsory registration of carriers and protection of the health. (February 10, 1988)

Theme 3. South Africa has undertaken major programs to improve black-white relations, particularly through increasing black participation in the management of the South African economy.

This theme was expressed in numerous interviews with South African business leaders. For example, the director of the International Executive Service of South Africa discussed a program to develop small, black-owned businesses in Soweto (March 9, 1988) and the director of South Africa's Urban Foundation described how the South African business community has tried to respond to the social needs of black South Africans (February 19, 1988).

In addition to such interviews, the main strategy for expressing this theme seemed to be the presentation of studies that purportedly documented the economic advances of black South Africans. For example:

Contrary to much international criticism that blacks in South Africa lack opportunities, a recent survey shows that increasing numbers of black businessmen are reaching the top in the executive field with local companies. [Voice of Trevor Woodburn, head of the Woodburn-Mann consulting organization which conducted the survey] "I was absolutely shocked to find that we, in fact, have placed far more blacks at the senior executive levels than most of the consultants around the world—in countries like Britain, Australia, Canada, for example, or even Italy or Germany." (March 12, 1988)

Theme 4. South Africa maintains a policy of peaceful coexistence and helpfulness toward the other nations of Africa.

Given that South Africa's domestic social policies are criticized worldwide, it would seem important for the South African government to promote a positive image of its conduct of international affairs. This is a difficult task. In 1988 South Africa provided support for opposition groups in Angola—(the Union for the Total Independence of Angola, UNITA) and in Mozambique (the Mozambique National Resistance, Renamo). South Africa continued its long-term military conflict with the South West Africa People's Organization (SWAPO) for control over South West Africa/Namibia. South Africa also had hostile relations with Zimbabwe, which provided sanctuaries for paramilitary groups with ties to the African National Congress (ANC), the major black organization opposing white domination in South Africa.

Regular, top-of-the-hour newscasts were the chief carriers of messages designed to counter objections to South Africa's relations with other southern African nations. In the newscasts, items frequently appeared which claimed that many nations, in addition to South Africa, supported UNITA and Renamo, and that these organizations merited international support because they combatted communism and terrorism on the African subcontinent. The following items serve as examples.

The South African forces went into Angola towards the end of last year in order to stage a preempting strike against the terrorist group SWAPO. The objective of this strike was to prevent SWAPO terror gangs from infiltrating into Southwest Africa in large numbers on missions of murder. This objective was achieved successfully. Thereafter South African forces were compelled to take limited action against communist troops who had intervened in the battle between the UNITA Liberation Movement and the Angolan army. (February 18, 1988)

The South African Minister of Defense has denied an article appearing in *Paris Match* on the nature of South African involvement in Angola. [He noted that] South Africa's limited support for UNITA was being granted in South Africa's own interest and in the interest of the subcontinent of which it is a part. (March 12, 1988)

Regarding Mozambique's remarks about South African support to the Renamo movement, Mr. [Pik] Botha said Mozambique had recently informed the Bavarian premier that Renamo's main support came from France, Portugal, Brazil and other countries. (February 19, 1988)

Angola had accused ten African countries of interfering in its internal affairs by giving financial and diplomatic support to the UNITA movement. (March 9, 1988)

Items expressing South Africa's positive relationships with other African nations took the form of presumably factual claims presented in the newsmagazine format segment of programming. Examples included the following:

A spokesman for the South African Department of Foreign Affairs said the positive areas of cooperation between South Africa and Mozambique are often overlooked by the international community. A group of diplomats had been invited so that they could be shown an aspect of the cooperation that existed. The spokesman said it was significant that representatives of countries such as Canada and Australia, which have been so vociferous in their criticisms of South Africa, had failed to use the opportunity to see the true state of affairs. (March 5, 1988)

South African presence in Central Africa has been criticized by the Nigerian government, according to two articles in the Johannesburg press yesterday. But South Africa's aid to development of agriculture in Equatorial Guinea will achieve wider acceptance of the fact that South Africa, with its economic strength and depth of agricultural and technical know-how, is well placed to contribute significantly to development in Africa. (February 10, 1988)

Theme 5. Efforts by foreign states to influence South Africa's domestic policies through the imposition of negative economic sanctions are both futile and counterproductive. South Africa's economy is fundamentally sound. A slide backward into recession, unemployment and falling real income would worsen social problems. The nation's social-political difficulties are complex and can be solved best by its own people.

The theme that international economic sanctions fail to achieve their

manifest goal was expressed frequently in a variety of ways. In programming segments labeled editorial, efforts were made to raise doubts
about the meaning of reports, issued by critics of South Africa, on the
performance of the South African economy. Numerous items were presented that suggested the vitality of the economy. For example:

Some rather dated figures crawled out of the woodwork in Johannesburg this
week, released apparently by the American Commerce Department. They deal
with the first nine months of last year and confirm what everyone has been
saying for months—that there has been a reduction in South African–American
trade. What has not been stated is the extent to which the slack has been taken
up by other countries. It is true that as South Africa becomes more sanctions-
aware, and builds up its sanctions immunity, it is becoming more difficult to
report openly on trade statistics and trade performance. Eventually one will find
little information revealed in the official statistics, so that even the figures now
released by the American sources probably ignore the laundering effects—a
process that simply means selling through Asian countries. In addition, much
of South Africa's major exports, such as gold, is sold on the open market any-
way. And there is no telling when and in what form it will end up in those countries that claim to be reducing their trade with South Africa. (March 12, 1988)

The governor of the South African Reserve Bank says the country's economy
underwent a remarkable change for the better last year . . . [and] there have been
welcome increases in almost all of South Africa's economic indicators. A higher
growth rate of about 3 percent and a lower inflation rate of about 14 percent are
expected this year. The upswing in the economy is also expected to result in a
decreased current account surplus. (February 10, 1988)

The following item explicitly expressed the theme that negative economic sanctions are counterproductive:

The London branch of the Washington-based International Freedom Foundation
has issued a publication that questions whether massive disruption of the South
African economy is either in the interest of, or supported by, the blacks in South
Africa. Entitled *Understanding Sanctions*, it analyzes opinions held by black
South Africans and finds that opposition to sanctions encompasses all sectors,
including trade unionists, church and tribal leaders, and the ordinary black
population. It says disinvestment hurts no one except those too poor to do
anything about it, and that means the vast majority of the black population of
South Africa. The publication concluded that for positive reform to accelerate,
the West had to take moral courage and positive action in the form of investment
in South Africa. (February 19, 1988)

Theme 6. Political and economic instability is widespread across southern Africa. The chief sources of such problems are tribalism, incompetence, crime, corruption, and, most important, foreign interference.

South Africa deserves Western support because of its potential as a major stabilizing force on the subcontinent.

With the assertion of this theme, South African counterpropaganda came full circle. It moved from the defensive position that criticisms of South Africa's domestic and foreign policies are based, for the most part, on misunderstanding and hypocrisy, to the offensive position that criticism and negative sanctions should be replaced by various forms of support for South Africa from the West.

To pursue this offensive strategy, it was first necessary to establish that factors other than the activities of South Africa itself were responsible for the region's political and economic problems. This objective was approached in two ways. First, numerous items appeared in the top-of-the-hour newscasts that dealt with lack of cooperation, incompetence, and corruption in other African nations and even in Africa's international organizations. For example:

Zairian businessmen and traders have been warned to respect the rules of the country's economic reform program. . . . Zaire's inflation rate increased to over 100 percent in the past year. (March 11, 1988)

The Zambian government has continued its crackdown on suspected black marketeers. . . . The government blames them for shortages of maize meal, bread and cooking oil. (March 9, 1988)

Allegations of corruption within the secretariat of the OAU were contained in an annual report of the auditor general. It accused several senior officials of the OAU [Organization of African Unity] of dishonesty, incompetence and negligence in their management of the finances of the organization. (February 29, 1988)

In addition to such items, analyses by various authorities were presented in the context of the newsmagazine programming. For example:

The chief executive of a large South African industrial group[,] . . . Mr. Peter Whitten, has called on the First World to do away with subsidizing food production. . . . He said such subsidization has been one of the major causes of poverty in Third World countries. European and American farmers were encouraged to produce huge surpluses which were then dumped on other markets at prices far below the cost of production. Mr. Whitten said this meant that Third World farmers could not compete in the one area where most Third World countries would be able to end foreign exchange. (March 12, 1988)

The position that the Republic of South Africa contributed to such stability as there was in southern Africa rested on many of the same items presented in support of Theme 4, which expressed South Africa's helpfulness toward the other nations of the continent. Additional items also were presented that expressed South Africa's importance to the overall economy of Africa. For example:

A large marble complex is to be developed in Namibia by the Johannesburg-based Apex Group. (March 1, 1988)

Negotiations are underway between a South African chemical company, AECI, Ltd., and the Botswana government regarding the development of a giant plant for the production of soda ash in Botswana. (March 5, 1988)

Trade between South Africa and the rest of the continent has increased steadily, amounting to more than 3,000 million dollars last year. (February 10, 1988)

The South African Minister of Foreign Affairs, Mr. Pik Botha, says it is time that South Africa asserts itself as the regional power of southern Africa. In an interview with Radio RSA in Cape Town, Mr. Botha said the international community should take note of the fact that South Africa was the stabilizing factor in southern Africa. This was simply a statement of fact, and it did not mean that South Africa was on the warpath or that it wanted to be aggressive or arrogant. (March 5, 1988)

A "news commentary" segment concluded: "Investments, not sanctions, is the only way in which Europe [can] contribute towards a peaceful resolution of southern Africa's problems. South Africa needs assistance in its struggle for stability, not avoidance or neglect" (March 12, 1988).

Two more specific reasons also were advanced to counter arguments for negative sanctions. First, South Africa fights to eliminate communism from the subcontinent. For example: "[In Angola] we are committed on one side of a civil conflict where the Soviet Union and the Cubans are committed on the other" (February 27, 1988). Second, increasing investment in the Third World can encourage the development of new markets for Western commodities: "A study published in Washington by the Overseas Development Council says only strong growth in the Third World can attract enough American goods to solve the United States' own problem, and such growth, in turn, requires more United States help (February 29, 1988).

There might have been broad themes developed in the counterpropaganda of Radio RSA in addition to the six identified above. These might have been located through a more formal content analysis of the recorded material or through an examination of a larger sample of material gathered over a longer period of time. Nevertheless, the themes that were identified do appear to be consistent and mutually supporting. They also responded to criticisms that seem to be the ones most often directed at the South African government: racism, lack of democracy, and aggressive policies toward other African states. Finally, they responded to the negative economic sanctions applied by several Western nations.

Radio RSA's presentation of thematic counterpropaganda probably should not be seen entirely as the product of a carefully planned and integrated strategy. Unreflective use of typifications, such as seeing black rule as synonymous with chaos, violence, and impoverishment, undoubtedly played some role, as did following organizational practices such as depending almost exclusively on government ministers and officials for information. However, in the case of the SABC, organizational practices do appear to be aimed explicitly at producing material supporting the government. For example, an SABC employee who once was in charge of its Durban office commented:

They [the news department] used to say "Can't you find someone to interview who will always be our sort of contact—he will have sympathetic views aligning himself with government." This was something that was told to me all the time. I was the eyes and ears of the SABC in Natal. This directive would come from the Senior News Editor. . . . He would try to get you to do things that would automatically make the person who is talking in favor of the policy of the day. (Quoted in Tomaselli, Tomaselli, and Muller 1989: 88)

The reality of South Africa as a modern, productive society with strong cultural ties to the West, working to achieve greater participation for all its citizens in national, political, and economic life through gradual reform, was constructed in a piecemeal fashion. Items depicting day-to-day life in South Africa, music, literature, art, business, and flora and fauna all carried Radio RSA's most important message: Contrary to the propaganda about South Africa published and broadcast by the international media, and despite admitted difficulties, South Africa is a vital, progressive nation with much to admire and is deserving of support from the West.

Findings: Issue-Specific Counterpropaganda

In addition to the six general themes, Radio RSA also broadcast issues-specific counterpropaganda. During the February and March 1988 programming, aspects of two events, one continuing and one date-specific, received considerable attention: ongoing military conflict with Angola and the banning of seventeen antiapartheid organizations on February 24.

On several occasions Radio RSA presented assertions that directly contradicted claims made by a foreign government. For example:

The South African Defense Force has denied that its forces used chemical weapons in Angola. A spokesman for the media liaison division of the South African Defence Force was commenting on a claim by the Angolan Ambassador to France, who had issued a statement in Paris accusing South Africa of using poison gas against government troops in a battle for the strategic town of Cuito Cuanavale. The spokesman said that it was predictable that Angola would accuse South Africa of using chemical weapons. He said this was especially so after the Defense Force had already confirmed that a South African team of medical experts had been invited by the UNITA movement to investigate the use of this kind of substance by Angola (February 10, 1988).

Such a response, which couples denial with counteraccusation, can promote negative evaluations of the motives and actions of foreign governments which are the sources of criticism. Using this technique, Radio RSA also discussed government corruption in several of the states of southern Africa and pointed out that the United States and Western European nations were dumping agricultural surplus in Africa with severe consequences for African farmers.

Reorienting assertions also were broadcast, providing a new cognitive context for understanding South Africa's prohibition of seventeen antiapartheid groups. Radio RSA reminded listeners that the South African government was not alone in establishing emergency powers, Israel and Britain recently had also taken such action. Similarly, listeners were informed that South Africa was not the sole supporter of the Renamo movement; France, Portugal, and Brazil also were major contributors, and a report on AIDS suggested that the United States and West Germany, as well as South Africa, had politicians who were willing to restrict the rights of some citizens for what they believe is in the interest of public well-being.

Radio RSA also made frequent use of bureaucratic counterpropaganda in its monitored broadcasts. In partial response to criticisms of the limited opportunities for blacks in South Africa, it reported results of a survey indicating that far more blacks have been placed at the senior executive level in South Africa consulting firms than have been placed in comparable positions in most of the Western nations. In response to claims made by many nations about the effectiveness of economic sanctions imposed by the world community, Radio RSA presented numerous statistical reports reflecting favorably on the performance of the South African economy. Frequent detailed reports on the military success of the South African Defense Force in Angola also can be placed in this category of counterpropaganda.

Radio RSA employed two different forms of linguistic counterpropaganda. Each involved the use of legitimating symbols also used by critics of the South African government. Newscasts referred to the government's economic and political policies toward its various racial groups as "democratic development." This particular rationalizing phrase was employed numerous times during the forty-five hours of programming that were monitored. "Democratic development" appears to have replaced the phrase "separate development" which long had been used by the government to refer to its policies. The latter phrase became incorporated in the newscasts of the government's critics, who assigned to it strongly negative connotations (Leatt, Kneifel, and Nurnberger 1986; Magubane 1979).

Radio RSA also made extensive use of conceptual justifications. In its newscasts, Radio RSA commonly portrayed South Africa as staunchly anticommunist (Browne 1987). Numerous RSA reports either specifically mentioned or suggested Communist involvement in southern Africa. For example:

The massive incursions of foreign troops from Communist countries have caused and continue to cause destabilization found today in Angola and elsewhere in southern Africa. (February 18, 1988)

Mr. Botha says Mozambique would have to prove that it had rid itself of foreign ideologies before it qualified to take part [in a conference of leaders of southern African states]. (February 19, 1988)

Two speeches by South Africa's minister of foreign affairs (March 5, 1988, and March 9, 1988) emphasized that the government of his nation was the major source of political and economic stability in its region of influence and the only provider of resistance to the encroachment of international communism—an ideology alien to the region. Such statements were presented as justification for the military actions of South Africa across the subcontinent. The justification used concepts employed at that time by the United States government to legitimize its involvement in Central America. The rhetorical strategy made it difficult for the United States to criticize South African policies toward Angola, Namibia, and Mozambique.

Discussion of the Case Study

Unlike most other international broadcast organizations, the primary raison d'être of Radio RSA appears to be to counteract international criticism. The organization has played an important role in the effort of the regime of the Republic of South Africa to establish a legitimate place for itself in the world political community. The way in which any government establishes its legitimacy, both domestically and internationally, is through an efficacious social construction (Boulding 1961; Lyman and Scott 1975). Politics itself involves competition among groups to establish hegemony of their construction of social reality (Edelman 1988). In this sense, Radio RSA is involved in a political struggle with the media of other nations. It is an ongoing struggle involving attacks, defenses, and counterattacks: propaganda and counterpropaganda.

Radio RSA presented several themes that provided a positive image of the nation and responded to specific allegations of misconduct. Its strategies of response included presenting accounts of events in terms favorable to the South African government within the news format that had consequences for legitimating the accounts, issuing assertions that contradicted the claims of adversaries, verbally counterattacking, providing information that might serve as a new cognitive context for understanding and evaluating government policies, describing official reports that promoted the interests of the South African government, and using language that rationalized actions and provided conceptual justification for policies. The presentation of manifestly nonpolitical materials, such as discussion of literature, science, and the arts, also can be seen as another means by which the government of the Republic of South Africa responded to its often malevolent image offered by the media of other nations.

The varieties of counterpropaganda used by Radio RSA undoubtedly are employed by the international broadcasting organizations of other nations as well. Further research might explore the ways in which other stations make use of these strategies of reality construction in their efforts to legitimize their nation's policies and positions in the world political economy and the structure of international military competition. Additional audience research might examine the relative effectiveness of the various forms of counterpropaganda. Such research would represent a context for again asking William James's question: Under what circumstances do we think things are real?

BROADCASTING COUNTERPROPAGANDA IN A RAPIDLY CHANGING SOUTH AFRICA

Radio RSA's programming at the time of the study probably provided as clear an example of broadcasting counterpropaganda as can be found in the recent history of IRB. Social and political conditions in South Africa have changed considerably since early 1988; so, too, has the focus of Radio RSA's activities. These changes raise some questions, not only about the future of Radio RSA in particular, but also some general questions about how processes of broadcasting counter-propaganda are subject to change.

Only four months after the monitoring reported above had been completed, some 2 million South African black workers staged a massive strike to protest not only the banning of the seventeen antiapartheid groups but also new labor laws that the government had imposed. Pik W. Botha, who had been head of the government for a decade, resigned and was replaced by F. W. deKlerk. In 1990 the government lifted its ban on the ANC and released its leader Nelson Mandela, who had been imprisoned for more than 27 years. In 1991, the South African parliament took a major step toward dismantling apartheid by repealing one of its cornerstones, the Population Regulation Act, which had required all South African newborns to be classified by race.

The deKlerk government has begun eliminating some of the legal framework for discrimination. However, South Africa remains open to considerable criticism from the international community. For example, blacks still lack the right to vote. The ANC claims that South Africa still has nearly 1,000 political prisoners. While nonwhites are now permitted to live on and own land anywhere they want, deKlerk rejected a proposal that would have allowed more than 3 million nonwhites who were forcibly removed from land, homes, and businesses under apartheid to seek compensation. Whites continue to be provided with larger pensions than blacks, and the government still spends four times as much to educate a white child as it does to educate a black child.

In 1990, Radio RSA also underwent major changes. Its transmissions were reduced to 154 hours a week in seven languages: English, Swahili, French, Lozi, Portuguese, Chichewa and Tsonga. The station discontinued broadcasting outside Africa, adopting a motto that reflected its new focus: "Africa speaks to Africa." The reason given by the SABC for discontinuing Radio RSA's worldwide services was stated vaguely as "new priorities in a reduced budget" (South African Broadcasting Corporation 1990: 5).

The most effective means for legitimating government policies at a time when they are shifting and have highly uncertain outcomes is not clear. The limiting of Radio RSA's shortwave services may be an adaptive strategy for broadcasting propaganda and counterpropaganda under these conditions. The policy of attempting to respond to every new criticism that emerges as political, economic, and social conditions change, and doing so to a traditionally antagonistic world audience, would not appear to be promising. An apparently more viable approach would be to systematically construct, through diverse programming, a broad image of Africa in which the Republic of South Africa plays a new, competitive, and peaceful (yet dominant) role on the subcontinent. Such a view, transmitted to a more limited audience, would emphasize the new progressive nature of the Republic of South Africa as it finally finds its proper place among Africa's nations.

The Radio RSA English Service schedule for September–December 1991 described programs in a manner consistent with the suggestion. A variety of programs, including "Africa South," "Talking Point," "This is South Africa," and "Business Opportunities" are described collectively as presenting "the voices and events that are changing the face of the subcontinent." On "Science and Technology," South Africa is depicted as "a leading nation in scientific and technological research which is of benefit not only to our country, but to the whole of Africa." Similarly, the emphasis of "Sport RSA" is described as follows: "In the past South Africa has suffered from isolation from the international sporting scene, but with the emergence of the new South Africa these barriers are being removed. We have many world-class sportsmen and women who are beginning to take their rightful place throughout the world."

In the future, more subtle forms of propaganda and counterpropaganda are likely to be broadcast by Radio RSA. With some initial dismantling of apartheid, efforts are likely to be made to construct an image of the new South Africa that supports the development of considerably less antagonistic and more profitable social, political, and economic relations with the rest of Africa. It seems probable that the government of the Republic of South Africa, like the government of Russia, will continue for some time to invest considerable resources in an effort to establish a new symbolic identity. The involvement of these governments in the process of broadcasting propaganda and counterpropaganda, is likely to accelerate. At the very least, it will be in the organizational interests of the international media of these nations, particularly their international radio stations, if this happens.

Chapter Six

Broadcasting Propaganda: A Research Agenda

By the last decade of the twentieth century, colonial empires had collapsed, the government of the United States had learned that it had neither the influence nor the power to impose its political and economic will everywhere in the world, apartheid was being dismantled, the communist hegemony in Eastern Europe had ended, the Cold War had been declared over, and the Soviet Union had disintegrated. Perhaps this will now mean a changing role for propaganda and counterpropaganda in international affairs. What are these new roles, and how might they involve IRB? What important questions remain about broadcasting propaganda that will facilitate understanding the process if it continues in a vastly changed international political environment? Addressing these questions is the task of this chapter.

THE END OF PROPAGANDA?

Sometime in the early to mid-1950s, several influential political analysts began writing about the "end of ideology" in Western industrialized nations. One of the most widely discussed statements of this thesis (Bell 1960) claimed that a rough consensus had emerged among Western intellectuals on political issues: the acceptance of the welfare state, the desirability of decentralized power, and a system of mixed economy and political pluralism. A similar thesis (Lipset 1981: 442–443) argued that workers had achieved industrial and political citizenship, conservatives had accepted the welfare state, and the democratic left had recognized that an increase in overall state power carried with it more dangers to freedom than solutions for economic problems. According to this formulation, political conflict between left and right had become a relatively inconsequential debate over degrees of government ownership and economic planning. A subsequent statement of the "end of ideology" thesis (Bell and Aiken 1968) contended that all large-scale societies, both capitalist like the United States and socialist like the Soviet Union, were faced with similar complex problems of political and economic administration. Such problems were seen as too complex for solutions that were presented in utopian schemes. They could be dealt with efficiently and effectively only one by one in a piecemeal and pragmatic fashion by bureaucratically appropriate managers and technically appropriate experts.

In a manner analogous to the end of ideology thesis, it might be argued that today we are witnessing, or are about to witness, the end of propaganda. Colonial empires of the sort once ruled by Great Britain and the Netherlands are gone; first fascism and then communism collapsed; racial oppression is no longer accepted anywhere in the world, and the limits of superpower status have been demonstrated. Today, throughout the world, a rough concensus is emerging on the desirability of freedom of expression, media systems immune from government censorship, democratic rule, and mixed economies. Without empires to integrate, major international military actions to support, alien ideologies to oppose, or cold wars to fight, it is conceivable that international broadcasting organizations might go out of business. The VOA, RFE/RL, the BBC, Radio Moscow, and other organizations might become casualties of peace.

There are reasons to question such a thesis. The argument may mistake a passing historical moment for an entire future. While the age of empires may be over, the exploitation of Third World labor, raw materials, and markets by more economically developed nations continues. Powerful nations are likely to continue to employ the means of international communication to legitimate (and therefore make more stable, predictable, and secure) profitable transactions with their unequal partners.

The United States and Russia continue to possess massive destructive capabilities, and race relations in South Africa are far from resolved; outcomes in both situations are uncertain. In addition, new crises akin to the Hungarian uprising, Suez, the Bay of Pigs, the invasion of Czechoslovakia, and the military incursion into Kuwait can always emerge. The Middle East and Eastern Europe remain likely venues for such events.

Unresolved issues always remain and new propaganda opportunities certainly will emerge for all nations. For example, the VOA referred to the Gulf War as having furthered continuing U.S. efforts to open Asian markets: "President Bush says he will work to open markets for U.S. products in South Korea and Japan during his coming trip to Asia.

Speaking at an electronics plant in Mississippi, Mr. Bush said the United States has gained new respect and credibility around the world since the Gulf War." (Voice of America, December 3, 1991)

Similarly, the VOA immediately used the formal dissolution of the Soviet Union to launch this symbolic attack against a long-time adversary:

Now that the Soviet Union is dead and communism appears to have been discredited, President Bush sees a bleak future for Cuban leader Fidel Castro. Mr. Bush tells reporters he sees what he calls a pretty pessimistic prospect for Fidel Castro in the wake of the collapse of Soviet communist rule. He calls the road ahead for the Cuban leader a dead end with no hope [voice of George Bush] "because it is so hard to be the only one who still thinks that communism is a good idea—and that's what he thinks—he is hurting his own people, and the republics will be—if not cutting him off entirely—cutting him back considerably." The President says Mr. Castro should brighten the future for Cubans by letting them have the same kinds of freedoms the people in the former Soviet republics now enjoy. (Voice of America, December 26, 1991)

New issues heightening international tensions such as environmental concerns, access to scarce and industrially necessary minerals, or intensifying economic competition with increasingly powerful nations also can develop and will call for some management through symbolic means. All these conditions will continue to prompt governments to disseminate factual, bureaucratic, linguistic, and sociological propaganda through all channels of international communication, including IRB. Propaganda has not become obsolete.

SOME TOPICS FOR RESEARCH

Ever since its invention, IRB has been used in the pursuit of major political objectives. It has supported empires, wars, ideologies, and economic interests. Today, throughout the world, governments continue to invest considerable resources in their international broadcasting organizations. Today, millions continue to depend on IRB for their understanding of world affairs, often including political situations in their own nations. Despite all this, IRB has been paid scant attention by sociologists, political scientists, and communication researchers. There are several possible explanations for this oversight, some personal and some professional.

Most social scientists live in Western nations in which there is an apparent abundance of alternative domestic sources of political information that are generally assumed to be independent of direct government manipulation and control. Hence, they seldom rely personally on foreign news and political information sources. At least in the United

States, very few individuals, including social scientists, have had any contact with IRB, except perhaps indirectly via rebroadcasts on domestic stations of BBC programming. Furthermore, IRB still carries some stigma, which was inherited for the most part from earlier decades. Reference to IRB still can bring to mind Gobbels's Deutschlandsender promoting the Nazi campaign in the early 1940s, the covert funding of Radio Free Europe by the CIA in the 1950s and 1960s, or, perhaps, Radio Moscow's presentation of the Russian invasion of Afghanistan or the Chernbyl nuclear disaster. Such images do little to attract scholars to study this medium of international communication.

Political scientists and sociologists may have a more theoretical reason for ignoring not only IRB specifically, but, more generally, the role of the mass media in modern political life. An aspect of the history of sociology in the United States bears on this point: "Sociology in America, since its very first years as a new and untested discipline, . . . recognized the significance of mass communication in analyses of contemporary society" (Wright 1986: 23). Extensive empirical research on politically relevant media content was first seen in the classic series on voting behavior (Lazarsfeld, Berelson, and Gaudet 1944; Berelson, Lazarsfeld, and McPhee 1954; Campbell, Gurin, and Miller 1954; Campbell et al. 1960). However, these studies generally concluded that the direct political effects of the mass media were limited almost exclusively to reinforcing existing orientations and, to a minor degree, to mobilizing those with relatively little political interests. Many of the successors of these studies reached a similar general conclusion that the mass media have little direct political effect (Klapper 1960).

In part, as a reaction to the voting studies, many political scientists and sociologists took the position illustrated by the assertion that "shifts in the distribution of power and wealth within French society [account] for the French Revolution [rather than Jean-Jacques] Rousseau's writings or [George-Jacques] Danton's agitations [or the argument that] the women's movement was a predictable consequence of the pill, the dishwasher and the need for female labor after World War II" rather than a response to altered perceptions prompted by the torrent of feminist rhetoric of the 1960s (Simons and Mechling 1981: 421).

More recent research on the political role of the media has moved beyond what Nimmo and Swanson aptly termed the "voter persuasion paradigm" (1990: 7–47). Almost all the research conducted during the period of the classic voting studies "focused on the effects of content without recognition that the content was created within a social system" (Ball-Rokeach and Cantor 1986: 13).

It is now widely recognized that by focusing on changes that media might promote in the political behavior of individuals (such as voting for a Republican rather than a Democratic candidate), researchers overlooked the cumulative long-term effects of media content on maintaining or challenging the legitimacy of a given political economic order. "Narrowing the focus of communication research to effects on individuals and treating mass communication as yet another form of personal stimulus . . . [deprived the] research [of] relevance for precisely those topics central to sociological interest" (Wright 1986: 30–31).

The social construction of reality perspective reminds us that the social meanings assigned to political actors, events, conditions, processes, and structures influence both individual and social evaluations of and behavioral predispositions toward these objects. Schutz (1932), Berger and Luckmann (1966), and Goffman (1974) provided the theoretical foundation for recognizing that all evaluation and social action takes place within some scheme of interpretation that provides an understanding of relevant social objects. This understanding influences the probability that the objects will be evaluated in a certain way and the related probability that particular courses of action will be taken toward the objects. Media system dependency theory reminds us that the mass media assign the specific meanings to social objects and events that serve as the basis for the individual and shared response of members of mass publics toward these objects. In virtually all modern societies, people routinely turn to the mass media for their understanding of political affairs ranging from domestic, institutionalized events such as voting to disruptive domestic events such as coups to wars between foreign nations.

The research agenda for furthering understanding of propaganda broadcast by international radio stations that is proposed on the following pages is guided, for the most part, by broad suggestions derived from the perspectives of the social construction of reality and media system dependency. However, in the course of discussion, ideas from additional, promising theoretical approaches also will be identified. Four areas for research will be considered: the contents of international radio broadcasts, international broadcasting organizations as complex organizations, IRB audiences, and the effects of IRB.

The Contents of International Radio Broadcasts

For purposes of systematically studying the propaganda contents of IRB it is useful to set up three categories. First, there are official political materials, including statements of official government policies, formal speeches and statements of public officials, presentations of official government views on particular political matters (official editorial statements), and announcements of the contents of official government reports (bureaucratic propaganda). Second, there is news, including programs explicitly labeled "the news" as well as accounts of political and economic affairs presented in other formats such as "news magazines" or within programs purportedly depicting daily life in the broadcasting country. Third, there is manifestly nonpolitical programming, including popular culture, classical music and literature, verbal travelogues, sporting news and events, features on environmental matters, and so on.

A major formal responsibility of all government-sponsored international radio stations is to announce the official policies of their governments. For purposes of systematically generating research questions on broadcasting propaganda, policy announcements can be approached as a form of broadcasting linguistic propaganda. The following are questions for empirical research on this topic: Under what set of social, political, and economic conditions, both domestic and international, will a government tend to select one particular set of available rationalizing terms over another? Does a government's choice of particular rationalizing terms change over time in response to changes in such conditions as the state of its domestic economy, the stability of its domestic political institutions, or the state of its relations with other particular governments? Are there any identifiable terms that a government selects to redefine and use in the service of its announced policies? If there are, does the particular choice reflect a degree of existing international consensus on broad political values such as "representative democracy" or "human rights"? Does a government tend to employ a particular conceptual justification borrowed from a present or former political adversary? If so, what have been the implications of this usage for stabilizing relations between the nations in light of various policy announcements?

Excerpts from formal speeches of presidents, prime ministers, and other high-ranking government officials are often heard on IRB. There is a vast literature on rhetoric, extending from works written in ancient Greece to contemporary empirical studies conducted throughout the world. The focus is on the theory and practice of all argumentation that aims to secure the persuasion and conviction of audiences in political matters (see Burke 1962). Contexts in which such argumentation occurs include courts, legislatures, political campaigns, social movements, and public ceremonies. Present scholarly concern with this subject matter is often legitimated on historical grounds. The most influential rhetorics, the classical theories of ancient Greece and Rome, were political in nature. "All major writers—Isocrates, Aristotle, Cicero, Quintilian— thought that politics was the principal locus for rhetorical thought and communication, and therefore designed their theories for use by political agents" (Bitzer 1981: 227).

A review and bibliography of recent political communication research (Johnston 1990: 329–389) identifies dozens of theoretically and methodologically diverse studies conducted in the 1980s that explored how reality was constructed by politicians' use of rhetorical strategies. The literature can serve as a foundation for exploring the following questions about the formal speeches and statements of officials broadcast on international radio stations. How do the themes and messages in the broadcast rhetoric of a given political leader define a particular situation for an international audience? Do international radio stations tend to select for broadcasting segments of official's speeches that emphasize particular themes or metaphors in order to construct a political reality and unite an audience in their belief in that reality? Do international broadcasting organizations employ more-or-less distinctive rhetorical styles in their newscasts that reflect those of their political leaders? If so, how do these distinctive rhetoric qualities influence the character of the political reality they construct?

Statements of official editorial opinion broadcast by Western international radio stations, like editorials published in most Western newspapers and newsmagazines, are clearly labeled as such and are presented separately from news. As David Altheide and Robert Snow (1980) observed, this format suggests to audiences that there is a sharp distinction to be made between news and editorials and that what they read or listen to in the news is factual material that is appropriate to approach from the perspective of naive realism.

The distinction between news and editorial statements is not so clearly made by media outside the industrialized West. In Third World nations and other nations with nonmarket economies, news is defined, at least in part, as information that serves state interests and advances goals and policies established by government (Hachten 1987: 23–24; Head 1985: 308–311; Siebert, Peterson, and Schramm 1956). Given this difference between Western and other conceptions of news, the relationship between presenting official editorial positions and presenting news would appear to be problematic for Western international radio stations in a way that it is not problematic for other stations. Research might investigate these questions. Within a specific time frame or for a specific event, will non-Western international stations tend to broadcast a greater proportion of their news that is consistent with the expressed official position of their governments than will Western stations? Are there systematic differences between the reactions of Western and non-Western governments to their international broadcasting organizations on any occasions on which their news presentations contain material that runs counter to their expressed positions? Answers to these questions will indicate the amount of sovereignty actually enjoyed by any international broadcasting organization. In particular, data would show how Western international broadcasting organizations behave at the "uncomfortable intersection of journalism and diplomacy" (Alexandre 1988: 61).

Another class of official political materials, government reports, contains the clearest examples of bureaucratic propaganda as identified by

Altheide and Johnson (1980). Such reports are prepared by a government to maintain its legitimacy and the legitimacy of its actions. Future comparative research might scrutinize the methods and editing processes used by various government agencies in different nations in their preparation of official reports intended for national and international audiences. Data from such research would reveal the structure and operation of any collusive nets existing within the government agencies and the linkage of such nets to international broadcasting organizations which might, in turn, have their own collusive nets working to ensure the worldwide broadcasting of the reports. Additional research might explore the tenability of the hypothesis that "widely reported criticism of official policy increases the defensiveness of policy makers and their obliviousness to inconsistent facts" (Edelman 1988: 96).

Empirical studies of news, the second major category of IRB contents, were presented in Chapters Four and Five. Further research might continue the analysis of IRB news, both domestic and international, as factual, bureaucratic, linguistic, and sociological propaganda. The social construction of reality perspective suggests the importance of exploring newscast uses of typifications, the process of reification in the news, the development and use of frames in the presentation of news, and the manner in which news bestows both cognitive validity and normative legitimacy upon a political-economic order.

Methodologically, empirical studies of the contents of IRB newscasts now can make use of computer-augmented content analysis, the capabilities of which are continually increasing as a result of enhancements in hardware and software technologies. Machine-readable data have been available since equipment was developed to interface shortwave receivers with computer-printer systems. Computer content analyses, ranging from those of presidential speeches (Hart 1984, 1987) to the actual application of computer augmentation in the coding of IRB content and the statistical analysis of key-words-in-context (Frederick 1986), indicate the considerable potential of this approach.

Perhaps the most interesting and theoretically and methodogically challenging area for research on broadcasting propaganda concerns the manifestly nonpolitical contents of international radio programming. As demonstrated in Chapter Five, the functions of such content extend beyond its ability to attract audiences and maintain their attention for subsequent exposure to official political materials and news. However, the political use of nonpolitical programming on IRB has yet to be investigated empirically in any systematic manner.

Throughout history, numerous forms of expression such as novels, plays, films, music and songs, and paintings and posters have been used to convey persuasive political messages (see Jowett and O'Donnell 1986: 38–62). How such materials might work to produce intended political effects such as deference to constituted authority, patriotism or ideological allegiance, is only vaguely understood. Future research might investigate the use of manifestly nonpolitical materials in a nation's sociological propaganda and (as illustrated in the case study of Radio RSA in the preceding chapter) its use as thematic counterpropaganda.

There are some suggestions dealing with specific uses of some manifestly nonpolitical materials of the kind that are presented on IRB. For example, with respect to "human interest stories," Edelman observed that "stories about heroic actions of ordinary people and the disasters from which they suffer similarly erase structural conditions from notice, even when they divert attention from the rest of the political spectacle. Heroic, pathetic and purient stores . . . help prevent more revealing news from disturbing ideologies" (1988: 99). With regard to sports news, Real (1989: 222–249) identified a number of political functions performed by media coverage of the Olympics. For example, he argued that in 1980 and 1984, media coverage of the Olympic boycotts were microcosms of conflicting Cold War ideologies and rhetorical posturing. Soviet coverage tended to picture the United States as an imperialistic force pressuring allies around the world to follow a U.S. party line. American media accounts portrayed the United States as accepting its responsibility as "leader of the free world" to boycott Moscow's "showcase Olympics" in protest against Soviet aggression in Afghanistan. During the Cold War, Real concluded: "Media often used[d] plot lines, character portrayals, terminology, settings, stylistic emphasis and other devices that subtly reinforce[d] the "Cold War" even when the subject matter [was] supposedly apolitical as in sports events and action adventure stories" (1989: 211). Parenti (1992: 53–55) noted that ideological subtext often is present in domestic U.S. media sports coverage. For example, he observed that in their reporting of the 1985 World Series, media attended to the remark of Kansas City Manager Dick Houser that "we think we did it the American way, with hard work" (p. 54). Future research on broadcasting propaganda might identify similar but less obvious themes in information and entertainment programming on IRB.

International Broadcasting Organizations as Complex Organizations

In terms of their formal structures, daily work output, far-flung network of news bureaus, semiautonomous language services, number of employees, and budgets, major international broadcasting organizations are large and complex. For example, in 1990, the VOA maintained offices of the director, external affairs, policy, administration, programs, engineering and technical operations, and personnel, and each office had its own substructure. The station produced 170 hours of programming daily—a blend of central and language service contributions. It maintained twenty-five news bureaus from Abidjan and Amman to Vienna and Warsaw, and operated forty-three language services. The VOA had approximately 2,500 employees and an operating budget of approximately $170 million for salary and expenses and construction obligations of approximately $68 million (VOA 1990).

Such size and complexity indicates that international broadcasting organizations are potentially rich contexts for empirical research on such traditional sociological topics as the dynamics of work roles and role sets; inter- and intra-organizational coordination, cooperation, and conflict; organizational decision making and management performance; organization ideology; organizational stability and adaptation; organizational goals and environment; innovation within the organization, and so on. The research on international broadcasting organizations as organizations (identified below) would bear most directly on the process of broadcasting propaganda.

A fundamental feature of any broadcasting organization is that "its most important problem is to engineer its own survival and to find some point at which it can make bargains of style and content with the civil power. Of its many products the most important is itself" (Smith 1973: 72). This is certainly true of all international broadcasting organizations because their resources are controlled by a civil power. Such resource control is an essential feature of their environments as organizations, no matter what statutory guarantees or buffering structures have been established to preempt or evade direct government intervention in their operations.

One of the most basic research questions to pose with respect to any international broadcasting organization concerns the actual manner in which it has negotiated, and historically renegotiated, its autonomy from direct governmental supervision and control, as well as the outcomes of the negotiations. Such negotiation processes and their consequences can differ significantly from the publicly visible formal norms which, in principle, define the relationship between a government and its broadcasting station. When, historically, an international broadcasting organization has experienced considerable constraint to reproduce official constructions of political reality in its broadcasts, active and meaningful (as opposed to purely symbolic) negotiations between the international broadcasting organization and its sponsoring government may cease. Those who direct the organization may become much more concerned with the management of the technical enterprises they direct than they are seriously concerned with the truth of the claims about political, economic, and social affairs that they broadcast. The extent to which such a perspective typifies management of various international broadcasting organizations is a question for future comparative research.

The political culture within which an international broadcasting organization is situated is likely to support certain types of linkage between the organization and government, certain types of organizational structures, and certain organizational goals, while making alternatives to each of those less probable. Some Marxist theorists (Althusser 1971; Poulantzas 1975) have argued that Western media in general are best understood as ideological state apparatuses promoting the survival of capitalism. From this perspective, the high value accorded unlimited rights to international communication, which is found in the political culture of all Western industrial nations, is a rationalization that facilitates the pursuit of this goal. More specifically, it is argued that the major supporters of the free flow of information across international borders are governments responding to pressure from multinational corporations, ranging from American Express to Xerox, to protect and extend their interests. Linkage of media to government, the structure of media organizations, and the appointment of personnel to key roles within these organizations all serve dominant economic interests.

Such critical views of international broadcasting embody claims that merit empirical inquiry. For example, studies might be undertaken to investigate ways in which multinational corporations may have sought to influence the operations of various organizations such as the BBC, VOA, or RFE/RL. Other research might investigate the extent to which ideological orthodoxy and political connections rather than technical competence determine job placement within various broadcasting organizations, and with what consequences. The broadcasting organizations of one-party states, such as Radio Beijing or Radio Havana Cuba, would appear to be appropriate, though difficult, settings in which to conduct this line of inquiry. Similar and also difficult questions could be raised within the contexts of Western organizations. For example, to what extent do the ideological proclivities of a particular administration influence the roles that will be assigned at various VOA language services to political dissidents from nations at which its broadcasts are targeted?

Additional research might consider the relation between the degree of organizational autonomy formally accorded an international broadcasting organization by a state and a range of hypothesized dependent variables such as the perceptions of listeners in other nations of the organization's credibility as a source of political information (as a news source rather than as a source of propaganda) or the frequency with which the operation of the organization becomes a topic of domestic political controversy.

The research literature on news organizations can serve as a rich source of additional hypotheses on broadcasting propaganda by international radio. For example, studies by Bennett (1983), Schudson (1978), and

Tuchman (1978) revealed the standardization and routinization of the process by which news is constructed. These qualities, necessitated by the volume of material that is available to be defined as newsworthy, and the immediacy with which accounts must be produced, often encourage reliance on the use of typifications and conventional frames. Research might investigate the extent to which the ease of typifying an event and presenting it in the context of a well-established frame influences the prominence given news about it and the resources that are devoted to its coverage.

IRB Audiences

Broadcaster assumptions about the characteristics of their audiences are important influences on the materials they transmit. Those assumptions, however, often are not entirely based on the result of systematic audience research. Rather, "the institution itself defines those characteristics of the audience which are important to it and therefore broadcasters tend to see their audiences through a haze of professional and institutional assumptions" (Smith 1973: iii). Future research might inquire into the nature of the assumptions made by particular international broadcasting organizations and the ways in which such assumptions affect the legitimations they offer.

While it is difficult for an international station to obtain extensive information about its audiences throughout the world (particularly those living in a politically antagonistic or economically competitive nation), major international broadcasting organizations do make some effort to determine who is listening to them and why. The methods they employ include the use, in Western nations, of sample surveys conducted by independent market or opinion research companies, extensive and intensive interviews of travelers from the audience countries to Western Europe and the United States, analysis of listener mail and of the reactions of foreign media to the contents of their transmissions, the use of listener panels made up of people whose substantial knowledge of the target audience gives them insights into probable reactions to given broadcast material, the use of computer simulations of audiences, and the use of anecdotal material, such as comments of refugees or reports of their country's diplomatic corps (British Broadcasting Corporation 1983: 62–63, 1989: 74–76; Board for International Broadcasting 1983: 16–22; Browne 1982: 318–338).

Reasons for listening to IRB, the ways in which the received materials are understood and evaluated, and the uses to which ideas presented in the broadcasts are put are likely to vary from nation to nation. As media system dependency theory points out, audiences use media-derived material to understand trends, the world of their everyday experience, and the realm beyond their limit of experience, and also to orient their actions and interactions with others (DeFleur and Ball-Rokeach 1989: 302–327). Extensive research has been conducted on the motives, cognitive and evaluative processes, and communication patterns of various domestic media audiences. However, theoretical approaches that have been developed on the basis of such empirical studies have never been applied to international broadcasting. News research guided by several of these approaches has the potential for producing insights into such topics as the ways in which citizens of one nation or class of nations tend to understand world politics, national differences in citizen attitudes toward and use of political information derived from foreign sources, and national differences in patterns of diffusion of political information. Antecedents of the motives underlying the use of the political contents of international broadcasts might also be investigated. Factors to be considered would include normative influences that are socially imposed by various, sometimes competing, agents of political socialization; socially distributed life chances such as frequency of social contacts through work settings or social organizations; and the subjective adjustment or reaction of audience members to their situations, indexed through such variables as partisanship, feelings of political efficacy, and political trust.

The approach to audiences that emphasizes their active role in political communication encourages the review and subsequent incorporation in empirical research of theory dealing with problematic aspects of the ways in which people deconstruct political messages and then reconstruct them in order to make the messages personally meaningful. Research on IRB audiences might utilize an interactionist perspective, such as that of Nimmo (1978), which understands political meaning as created and accomplished in a process of social interaction and negotiation, or a symbolist view, such as that of Combs (1980), which sees political meaning as produced through the invocation or selection of trans-situational, usually culturally embedded, structures.

All broadcasting organizations have some interest not only in the audiences that they reach directly, but also in those that they reach indirectly via interpersonal communication networks. New research might be undertaken to explore various features of the diffusion of political materials transmitted by IRB. Such studies could draw on the extensive body of literature dealing with the diffusion of rumors and information about news events and campaign messages as well as broad suggestions derived from studies in epidemiology, cybernetics, and sociometry.

The Effects of IRB

Most of the original empirical studies of media have been commissioned by broadcasting, political, advertising, and marketing organizations interested in learning what kinds of materials and techniques of presentation would produce certain effects such as voting or purchasing (Lazarsfeld and Stanton 1944/1979; McPhail 1981: 75). In the political realm, studies of the mass media as agents of political socialization, voting studies, and research on the social distribution of political information all exemplified this approach, which involves a microlevel, linear, one-time analysis (Kraus and Davis 1976: 249–262). Although informative, such studies also were limited since they typically failed to consider the historical, cultural, and institutional contexts within which the political communication occurred (Noell-Neumann 1959). This limitation particularly restricts the ability of such research to provide insights into IRB, which is part of a complex network of international communication, the characteristics of which influence its content and the cognitive context in which it is received, and hence, its potential effects (Davison 1965: 13–26). Such studies also failed to explore the ways in which the understanding of a communication could be enriched by questioning such basic societal characteristics as the differential distribution of power and access to the media, conflicts of interest in media power centers, and the ideological support of society's power structure in the context of mass media messages (Schiller 1976). While (as noted earlier), research on media effects has moved well beyond the voter persuasion paradigm, numerous basic questions remain unanswered. The effects of IRB, in particular, remain almost totally unexplored.

McQuail (1983: 180–182) developed the typology of media effects used below in order to organize a number of suggestions for future research on the political effects of IRB. The suggestions take into account the criticisms of much of the earlier research on media effects.

Individual Response. Research concerns the process by which individuals change or resist change in responding to IRB messages that are designed to influence their attitudes, beliefs, or behavior. Research might draw on media system dependency theory which specifies the conditions under which people will rely on mass media to help them understand aspects of their environment and indicate appropriate courses for their action. Recent political history provides conditions that might still be investigated. For example, how did Poles respond to RFE feature programming in Polish devoted to Polish domestic affairs such as the development of the Solidarity Labor Movement? Their response took on political significance when RFE initially informed them that protests in their nation were widespread and not limited to Gdansk, as their own domestic media had reported.

Media Campaign. Research concerns the effectiveness of authoritatively sponsored programming used to achieve a persuasive or informational purpose with a chosen population. A sample question for research would be, how are various African audiences now responding to Radio

RSA's efforts to legitimize the process by which the South African government is disassembling apartheid?

Individual Reaction. Research concerns unplanned or unpredictable consequences of exposure of a person to a media stimulus. For example, in times of armed conflict is it more advantageous for an international broadcasting organization to discuss candidly its nation's military defeats in an effort to gain credibility and consequently increase its own influence, or to downplay military defeats in an effort to promote an image of military power and military victory? The experiences of the BBC during World War II and the experiences of the VOA during the Vietnam War suggest quite different answers.

Collection Action. Research concerns some of the same individual effects that are experienced simultaneously by many people, leading to collective action, usually of an unregulated and noninstitutional kind. For example, under what social conditions will the use of intimidation through international broadcasts be effective? Here, the experiences of German broadcasters just before and in the early years of World War II might be compared with those of certain contemporary clandestine stations in Eastern Europe and the Middle East.

Diffusion in Development. Research concerns the planned diffusion of innovation for purposes of long-term development. For example, to what extent has the penetration of Western broadcasts into Sub-Saharan Africa promoted the adoption of social forms and personal behavior consistent with capitalism and the political institutions and prescriptions that predominate in Western industrial nations?

Knowledge Distribution. Research concerns the consequences of media activity in the sphere of news and information for the distribution of political beliefs among social groups, the variable awareness of events, and the priorities assigned to political occurrences. In particular, research might draw on the agenda-setting approach originally developed by McCombs and Shaw (1972). Studies could investigate the extent to which the importance attributed by an international broadcasting organization to a political event influences the importance assigned to that event by the target audiences, particularly audiences in nations whose domestic media assign the same event a very different priority.

Socialization. Research concerns the informal contributions of media to the learning and adoption of established norms, values, and expectations of behavior in given social roles and situations. For example, what, if any, subtle, politically relevant effects has a given international broadcasting organization's manifestly nonpolitical programming had on various audiences? The hypothesis that cultural programming that is free of any obvious political content can have implicit political significance by establishing links with an audience who would distrust, reject, or perhaps be bored by material that touched directly on political issues or events could be explored in such a setting. The topic is particularly important in light of the fact that approximately 70 percent of international broadcasts involve programming other than news presentations. Even more complex questions might be asked about the impact of manifestly nonpolitical programming by the VOA in particular. Throughout the world, American media products in the form of entertainment are immensely popular. American films and television programs contain depictions of class, race, and gender relations in the United States that sometime may reinforce and other times may contradict the political reality of the nation as constructed and offered to the world by the VOA (see Parenti 1992). Research might investigate the relative frequency of such support and contradiction and the impact this had had on the image of the United States held by VOA audiences.

Social Control. Research concerns the ways in which the media tend to propagate a conformity to an established order and to reaffirm the legitimacy of existing authority. Much IRB activity is not aimed at supporting an established political-economic order. Rather, it is subversive (Hale 1975: xivi). It can undermine any government's claim to a monopoly on the source of news and information. One example of a question for research concerns the political influence of IRB in the Republic of South Africa, a nation with strict state control of all media, which receives political criticism in one form or another from a large number of international broadcasting organizations.

Reality Definition. Research concerns cognitive effects resulting from the systematic tendency of the media to construct a rather distinctive reality. For example, does persistent exposure to the programming of an international broadcasting organization lead to the adoption of its view of world politics? Research also might follow Noell-Neumann's suggestion that media coverage that predicts trends in public opinion can actually create such trends or serve as a catalyst for them (Noell-Neumann 1974, 1977, 1983).

Institutional Change. Research concerns the results of unplanned adaptations by existing institutions to developments in the media. For example, how have Western transmissions to the Third World that explicitly promote and supposedly embody the political values of objectivity and independent adjudication, influenced the political information-gathering, interpretation, and presentation process of Third World domestic and international media?

Further Considerations

Many additional questions for research on broadcasting propaganda via IRB can be raised. Those identified above were chosen to indicate the broad range of subjects available for future investigation. While previous chapters have drawn largely on the social construction of reality perspective and on media system dependency theory, an effort was made to present examples of topics that might be explored using additional theoretical orientations currently being employed by researchers in political communication. The specific examples that were presented suggested that critical theory might provide some insights into international broadcasting organizations as organizations. The analysis of political languages and other message-centered theories can provide some basis for analyzing the contents of broadcasts. Questions about audiences might be approached from any number of general theoretical orientations such as diffusion of information theory. The political effects of broadcasts might be considered from a number of perspectives including agenda setting theory.

Empirical research on many of the proposed questions faces practical difficulties in addition to those already noted. No multinational corporation is likely to readily admit that it attempted to influence the activities of a Western international broadcasting organization whose manifest purpose is to provide reliable political information to the world—particularly to the citizens of nations who are denied access to such information by their own governments. Probably few Western broadcasters would be willing to state that they were appointed to their positions on grounds other than professional competence or to discuss openly the ways in which government officials attempt to shape certain news presentations. Undoubtedly international broadcasting organizations under direct government control would be reluctant to facilitate research that they believed they could not manipulate for their own ends. There are no data for international broadcasting equivalent to the overnight ratings used by U.S. broadcasters to indicate the impact of their programming. Difficulties, however, are not impossibilities. The history of social research provide countless examples of overcoming just such obstacles. There is no reason to assume that the supply of ingenuity and resourcefulness has been depleted.

MARCONI'S DREAM RECONSIDERED

Has Marconi's invention been used to reduce the misperception of one nation by another and thereby decrease the likelihood of international conflicts? Has his device helped encourage mutual understanding, trust, and peace among people and among nations? The apparently obvious answer to both of these questions is a resounding "no." The history of IRB shows shortwave radio serving mercantile colonialism, bolstering various revolutionary and counterrevolutionary movements, supporting nations at war, carrying forward a Cold War, serving oppressive regimes, and participating in a world system of media imperialism. The analysis of IRB content shows that the medium of communication offers materials that can be understood as factual, bureaucratic, linguistic, and sociological propaganda as well as issue-specific and thematic counterpropaganda. Broadcast contents typify and reify events and social structures, offering constructions of political realities that operate as legitimations for actions, processes, and structures. In all this, the notion of making the truth available to the world at large through the medium of IRB seems thoroughly discredited.

To some extent, the claim that Marconi's dream was not, and cannot be, realized is misleading. IRB history certainly indicates that it was not. However, if news is more realistically understood, and if the sharp distinction between news and propaganda is abandoned, along with other commonly understood distinctions such as that between news and editorials and between political and non-political materials (information and entertainment), the contribution of IRB to international understanding might be appreciated.

As we saw in Chapter One, the Netherlands was one of the first nations to develop a domestic radio broadcasting system. The norms of that media system, termed *pillarization*, required stations to devote equal time to programming for each of the country's four major political-religious organizations: Protestant, Catholic, Socialist, and a fourth group that was neither politically nor religiously committed. Dutch citizens could turn on their radios to select from among clearly recognized alternative political perspectives. Within such a media system, it seems likely that audiences would recognize the ambiguous nature of political events, and, therefore, understand that they are subject to alternative symbolic representations. While the less educated as well as the most partisan among them may have tended to ignore, forget, misconstrue, or otherwise reject the media messages of political-religious associations other than their own, may others surely recognized that political, economic, and social affairs generally lend themselves to a variety of perspectives and that the selection of one construction of reality over another usually is just that. They had several alternative political viewpoints available out of which they could construct their own understanding of the Dutch political and social world. In any event, as the result of the explicit norms of their media system, the Dutch would seem to have been less likely to understand media messages to which they attended with the degree of naive realism characteristic of many present-day media audiences.

Much of the same can be said about the readers of America's early colonial presses. As noted in Chapter Three, newspapers within this media system typically were sponsored by political organizations and explicitly presented their perspectives. Because of the nature of their media system, readers of colonial presses also were likely to have had some sense of the constructed nature of political reality offered by the newspapers available to them. Every paper did not simply offer the same news. Readers could sort out the truth for themselves.

Finally, audiences in nations with media systems formally under strict government control, such as the Soviet Union prior to the Gorbachev era, are also likely to understand the constructed nature of news. Mass publics in nations with strictly controlled media systems may have more confidence in their mass media than Western images of the Soviet press long have suggested. However, they also apparently take a cautious approach to accepting what is offered them as news and commonly develop personal strategies for determining how to find out about (and what to believe about) political, social, and economic affairs (see Smith 1976: 344–374). They, too, understand that news and propaganda often cannot easily be differentiated.

In contrast to the Dutch, the colonial Americans, and Soviet citizens, research cited throughout this book has indicated that contemporary Western audiences generally tend to accept the presentation of news by their media system without serious reservations. Occasionally, audiences might question the truth of a particular media account or raise the question of bias. For the most part, however, following the formal conventions of their media, they quickly draw a distinction between news and editorials. They feel reasonably confident that propaganda or, in the popular parlance, government propaganda, is rarely incorporated in routine media content and that, when it is, they usually can immediately identify it. This set of shared perceptions is associated with the size, complexity, and apparent diversity of the media systems of the West and with the systems' formal commitment to norms of balance and objectivity.

Citizens of Western industrial nations, particularly Americans, listen less frequently to IRB than do citizens of nations elsewhere in the world. However, Western audiences generally, and particularly those who construct the news for them, would benefit from tuning in. Such benefit would be derived, not by listening to the truth as embodied in the programming of foreign broadcasting organizations, but by confronting constructions of political reality that sometimes can represent credible alternatives to the circumscribed perspectives they routinely hear, read, and, in the case of media workers, produce as unbiased and balanced news.

In his classic study of the "CBS Evening News," "NBC Nightly News," *Newsweek*, and *Time*, Gans (1979) set forth a case for the desirability of what he termed "multiperspectival news." He argued that:

The primary purpose of the news derives from the journalists' function as constructors of nation and society, and as managers of the symbolic arena. The most important purpose of the news, therefore, is to provide the symbolic arena, and the citizenry, with comprehensive and representative images (or constructs) of nations and society. In order to be comprehensive, the news must report nation and society in terms of all known perspectives; in order to be representative, it must enable all sectors of nation and society to place their actors and activities messages—in the symbolic arena. (Gans 1979: 312)

This argument can be extended to address the developing communication needs of the world community. With the enormous changes in Eastern Europe that began in 1989, and with the disintegration of the Soviet Union at the very end of 1991, the structure of international relations became far more uncertain. To increase the promise of a more peaceful future it is important for people everywhere in the world to have access to a symbolic arena in which the perspectives of all nations are available. IRB can provide such an arena.

By listening to the international broadcasting organizations of several nations, citizens anywhere are able to construct for themselves media systems that provide more comprehensive and diverse coverage of national and international political affairs than that provided by their domestic media. News about the politics of dominant states, such as the United States and Japan, can be understood in the light of information about the reactions of the governments of less powerful nations that would be affected by these policies. News about international programs, such as foreign aid and assistance programs of dominant states or the relief programs of international agencies, can be understood in light of information about how they have worked out in practice, specifying both their intended and unintended consequences. IRB can provide listeners everywhere, particularly in dominant states, information about how citizens of less powerful nations view themselves, and how they view the actions of dominant states as well. By tuning to IRB, listeners the world over may be able to locate news that is particularly relevant to them.

Political reality constructed by individuals incorporating IRB into their own media systems in the ways suggested would be truly multiperspectival. If Marconi's device is used in this way, while it carries propaganda, it nevertheless might well encourage some mutual understanding, cooperation, and peace among citizens throughout the world.

References

Abshire, David M. *International Broadcasting: A New Dimension of Western Diplomacy*. Beverly Hills, CA: Sage, 1976.

Adams, William C. "Whose Lives Count? TV Coverage of Natural Disasters." *Journal of Communication* 36: (1986): 113–122.

———. ed. *Television Coverage of the 1980 Presidential Campaign*. Lexington, MA: D. C. Health, 1984.

Adoni, Hanna, and Sherrill Mane. "Media and the Social Construction of Reality: Toward an Integration of Theory and Research." *Communication Research* 11 (1984): 323–340.

Alexandre, Laurien. *The Voice of America: From Detente to the Reagan Doctrine*. Norwood, NJ: Ablex, 1988.

Alexeyeva, Ludmilla. *U.S. Broadcasting to the Soviet Union*. New York: Helsinki Watch Committee, 1986.

Allport, Floyd H., and M. H. Simpson. "Broadcasting to a Foreign Country: What Appeals Work and Why." *Journal of Social Psychology* 23 (1946): 217–224.

Altheide, David L., and John M. Johnson. *Bureaucratic Propaganda*. Boston: Allyn and Bacon, 1980.

Altheide, David L., and Robert P. Snow. *Media Logic*. Beverly Hills, CA: Sage, 1980.

Althusser, Louis. "Ideology and Ideological State Apparatuses." In Louis Althusser, ed., *Lenin and Philosophy and Other Essays*, pp. 127–186. New York: Monthly Review Press, 1971.

Aronson, James. *The Press and the Cold War*. Boston: Beacon Press, 1973.

Arterton, F. Christopher. *Media Politics: The News Strategies of Political Campaigns*. Lexington, MA: D. C. Heath, 1984.

Balfour, Micheal Leonard Graham. *Propaganda in War, 1939–1945: Organizations, Policies and Publics in Britain and Germany*. Boston: Routledge and Kegan Paul, 1979.

Ball-Rokeach, Sandra J., and Muriel G. Cantor, eds. *Media, Audience and Social Structure*. Newbury Park, CA: Sage, 1986.

Barghoorn, Frederick C. *Soviet Foreign Propaganda*. Princeton, NJ: Princeton University Press, 1964.

Barker, Elisabeth. *The Cold War*. London: Wayland, 1972.

Bell, Daniel. *The End of Ideology*. New York: Free Press, 1960.

———, and Henry David Aiken. "Ideology—A Debate." In Chaim I. Waxman, ed., *The End of Ideology Debate*, pp. 259–280. New York: Simon and Schuster, 1968.

Bellah, Robert N. *The Broken Covenant: American Civil Religion in Time of Trial*. New York: Seabury Press, 1975.

Bennett, W. Lance. *News, the Politics of Illusion*. New York: Longman, 1983.

Berelson, Bernard, Paul Lazarsfeld, and William McPhee. *Voting*. Chicago: University of Chicago Press, 1954.

Berger, Peter, and Thomas Luckmann. *The Social Construction of Reality*. New York: Doubleday, 1966.

Bitzer, Lloyd F. "Political Rhetoric." In Dan D. Nimmo and Keith R. Sanders, eds., *Handbook of Political Communication*, pp. 225–248. Beverly Hills, CA: Sage, 1981.

Board for International Broadcasting. *1985 Annual Report*. Washington, DC: Board for International Broadcasting, 1985.

Bogart, Leo. *Premises for Propaganda: The United States Information Agency's Assumptions in the Cold War*. New York: Free Press, 1976.

Boorstein, Daniel J., and Brooks M. Kelley. *A History of the United States*. Lexington, MA: Ginn, 1986.

Boulding, Kenneth. *The Image*. Ann Arbor: University of Michigan Press, 1961.

Braestrup, Peter. *Big Story: How the American Press and Television Reported and Interpreted the Crisis of Tet 1968 in Vietnam and Washington*. Garden City, NY: Anchor/Doubleday, 1978.

Bramsted, Ernest Kohn. *Goebbels and National Socialist Propaganda, 1925–1945*. East Lansing: Michigan State University Press, 1965.

Briggs, Asa. *A History of Broadcasting in the United Kingdom*, vol. 1. London: Oxford University Press, 1961.

———. *The BBC: The First Fifty Years*. New York: Oxford University Press, 1985.

British Broadcasting Corporation. *BBC Annual Report and Handbook 1983*. London: British Broadcasting Corporation, 1983.

———. *BBC Annual Report and Accounts 1989–90*. London: British Broadcasting Corporation, 1990.

Browne, Donald R. *International Radio Broadcasting: The Limits of the Limitless Medium*. New York: Praeger, 1982.

———. "The International Newsroom: A Study of Practices at the Voice of America, BBC and Deutsche Welle." *Journal of Broadcasting* 27 (1983): 205–231.

———. "Something New Out of Africa? South African International Radio's Presentation of Africa to Listeners in North America." *Journal of African Studies* 14 (1987): 17–24.

Burke, Kenneth. *A Grammar of Motives and a Rhetoric of Motives*. Cleveland, OH: World Publishing, 1962.

Burns, Tom. *The BBC: Public Institution and Private World*. New York: Oxford University Press, 1977.

Campbell, Angus, Philip Converse, Warren Miller, and Donald Stokes. *The American Voter*. New York: John Wiley, 1960.

Campbell, Angus, Gerald Gurin, and Warren Miller. *The Voter Decides*. Evanston, IL: Row, Peterson, 1954.

Carsten, Francis L. *The Rise of Fascism*. Berkeley: University of California Press, 1969.

Cherry, Colin. *World Communication: Threat or Promise?* rev. ed. New York: Wiley, 1978.

Childs, Harwood L., and John B. Whitton, eds. *Propaganda by Short Wave*. Princeton, NJ: Princeton University Press, 1942.

Chomsky, Noam. *Toward a New Cold War*. New York: Pantheon, 1982.

Cohen, Akiba, Hanna Adoni, and Charles Bantz. *Social Conflict and Television News*. Newbury Park, CA: Sage, 1990.

Combs, James E. *Dimensions of Political Drama*. Santa Monica, CA: Goodyear, 1980.

Council on Foreign Relations Annual. *The United States in World Affairs*. New York: Harper, 1950; 1951; 1952.

Crossman, R.II.S. "Supplementary Essay." In Daniel Lerner, ed., *Sykewar: Psychological Warfare Against Germany: D-Day to VE-Day*. Cornwall, NY: Cornwall Press, 1949.

Davison, W. Phillips. *International Political Communication*. New York: Praeger, 1965.

de Costa, Alcino, Yehia Aboubakr, Pran Chopra, and Fernando Reyes Matta. "News Values and Principles: A Cross-National Communication." *Reports of Papers on Mass Communication No. 85*. Paris: UNESCO, 1979.

DeFleur, Melvin L., and Sandra Ball-Rokeach. *Theories of Mass Communication*. 5th ed. New York: Longman, 1989.

Dennis, Everett, George Gerbner, and Yassen N. Zassoursky, eds. *Beyond the Cold War: Soviet and American Media Images*. Newbury Park, CA: Sage, 1991.

Denver, D. T., and J. M. Bochel. "The Political Socialization of Activists in the British Communist Party." *British Journal of Political Science* 3 (1973): 53–72.

Deutsche Welle. *DW Handbuch für Internationalen Kurzwellenrundfunk*. Berlin: Verlag Volker Spiess, 1982.

Dugard, C.J.R. "Political Options for South Africa and Implications for the West." In R. I. Rotberg and J. Barratt, eds., *Conflict and Compromise in South Africa*, pp. 17–30. Lexington, MA: D. C. Heath, 1980.

Dunlap, Orrin E. *Marconi: The Man and His Wireless*. New York: Macmillan, 1937.

Edelman, Murray. *The Symbolic Uses of Politics*. Urbana: University of Illinois Press, 1964.

———. *Constructing the Political Spectacle*. Chicago: University of Chicago Press, 1988.

Elder, Charles D., and Roger W. Cobb. *The Political Use of Symbols*. New York: Longman, 1983.

Ellul, Jacques. *Propaganda: The Formation of Men's Attitudes*. New York: Knopf, 1966.

Entman, Robert M. *Democracy without Citizens: Media and the Decay of American Politics*. New York: Oxford University Press, 1989.

Epstein, Edward J. *News from Nowhere*. New York: Random House, 1973.

———. *Between Fact and Fiction*. New York: Vintage, 1975.

Ettinger, Harold. *The Axis on the Air*. New York: Bobbs-Merrill, 1943.

Fisher, Heinz-Dietrich, and John E. Merrill. *International and Intercultural Communication*. New York: Hastings House, 1976.

Fishman, Mark. *Manufacturing the News*. Austin: University of Texas Press, 1980.

Fleming, Deena Frank. *The Cold War and Its Origins*. London: George Allen and Unwin, 1961.

Fox, Elizabeth, ed. *Media and Politics in Latin America: The Struggle for Democracy*. Newbury Park, CA: Sage, 1988.

Franck, Thomas M., and Edward Weisband. *Word Politics: Verbal Strategy among the Superpowers*. New York: Oxford University Press, 1972.

Frederick, Howard H. *Cuban-American Radio Wars: Ideology in International Telecommunications*. Norwood, NJ: Ablex, 1986.

Freed, Kenneth. "Hard-to-Find Radio Baghdad Tells Iraq's Side." *Los Angeles Times*, 26 January 1991, p. A3.

Gannett News Service. "Salvos of Propaganda Accompany Conflict." News Service Release, 3 February 1991.

Gans, Herbert J. *Deciding What's News*. New York: Random House, 1979.

Gendzier, Irene L. "Notes toward a Reading of the Passing of Traditional Society." *Review of Middle East Studies* 3 (1978): 32–47.

George, A. L. *Propaganda Analysis: A Study of Inference Made from Nazi Propaganda in World War II*. Evanston, IL: Row, Peterson, 1959.

Gerbner, George, and Marsha Siefert, eds. *World Communications: A Handbook*. New York: Longman, 1984.

Gerhart, Gail M. *Black Power in South Africa*. Berkeley: University of California Press, 1978.

Giffard, C. Anthony. "Developed and Developing Nation News in U.S. Wire Service Files to Asia." *Journalism Quarterly* 61 (1984): 14–19.

Gitlin, Todd. *The Whole World is Watching*. Berkeley: University of California Press, 1980.

Glascow University Media Group. *Bad News*. London: Routledge and Kegan Paul, 1976.

———. *More Bad News*. London: Routledge and Kegan Paul, 1980.

———. *War and Peace News*. Philadelphia: Open University Press, 1985.

Goffman, Erving. *Frame Analysis: An Essay on the Organization of Experience*. New York: Harper and Row, 1974.

Graber, Doris A. *Mass Media and American Politics*. 2d ed. Washington, DC: CQ Press, 1984a.

———. *Processing the News*. New York: Longman, 1984b.

Grandin, Thomas. *The Political Uses of Radio*. 1939. Reprint, New York: Arno Press Reprint, 1971.

Graves, Harold N., Jr. "Propaganda in the Air: Princeton Listening Center Covers the War." *Princeton University Library Chronicle* 2 (1941): 91–96.

Greenfield, Meg. "Whose Side Are We On?" *Newsweek*, 3 September 1990, p. 76.

Grzybowski, Kazimierez. "Propaganda and the Soviet Concept of World Public Order." In Clark C. Havinghurst, ed., *International Control of Propaganda*, pp. 41–67. Dobbs Ferry, NY: Oceana, 1967.

Guback, Thomas. *The International Film Industry*. Bloomington: Indiana University Press, 1969.

Guimaraes, Cesar, and Roberto Amaral. "Brazilian Television: A Rapid Conversion to the New Order." In E. Fox, ed., *Media and Politics in Latin America: The Struggle for Democracy*, pp. 125–137. Newbury Park, CA: Sage, 1988.

Habermas, Jurgen. *Legitimation Crisis*. Boston: Beacon Press, 1975.

Hachten, William A. *The World News Prism*. Ames: Iowa State University Press, 1987.

———. and C. A. Giffard. *The Press and Apartheid: Repression and Propaganda in South Africa*. Madison: University of Wisconsin Press, 1984.

Hale, Julian. *Radio Power: Propaganda and International Broadcasting*. Philadelphia: Temple University Press, 1975.

Hallin, Daniel C. *The "Uncensored War": The Media and Vietnam*. New York: Oxford University Press, 1986a.

———. "We Keep America on Top of the World." In Todd Gitlin, ed. *Watching Television*, pp. 9–41. New York: Pantheon, 1986b.

Hart, Roderick P. *Verbal Style and the Presidency: A Computer-Based Analysis*. New York: Academic Press, 1984.

———. *The Sound of Leadership: Political Communication in the Modern Age*. Chicago: University of Chicago Press, 1987.

Haskins, Jack B., and Mark Miller. "The Effects of Bad News and Good News on a Newspaper's Image." *Journalism Quarterly* 61 (1984): 3–31.

Head, Sydney W. *World Broadcasting Systems: A Comparative Analysis*. Belmont, CA: Wadsworth, 1985.

Hedeboro, Goran. *Communication and Social Change in Developing Nations: A Critical View*. Ames: Iowa State University Press, 1982.

Heil, Alan, and Barbara Schiele. "The Voice Past, VOA, the U.S.S.R. and Communist Europe." In K.R.M. Short, ed., *Western Broadcasting over the Iron Curtain*, pp. 98–112. New York: St. Martin's Press, 1986.

Henderson, Caspar. "The Filtered War." *New Statesman and Society*, April 5 (1991): 16–18.

Herman, Edward S., and Noam Chomsky. *Manufacturing Consent: The Political Economy of the Mass Media*. New York: Pantheon Books, 1988.

Hertsgaard, Mark. *On Bended Knee: The Press and the Reagan Presidency*. New York: Schocken Books, 1989.

Hirschburg, Peter, Don Dillman, and Sandra Ball-Rokeach. "Media System Dependency Theory: Responses to the Eruption of Mount St. Helens." In Sandra J. Ball-Rokeach and Muriel G. Cantor, eds., *Media, Audience and Social Structure*, pp. 117–126. Newbury Park, CA: Sage, 1986.

Holston, Mark H. "The Falkland/Malvinas War: British and Argentine Reporting of the South Atlantic Conflict." Paper presented at the Thirty-Seventh Annual Conference of the International Communication Association, Montreal, Canada, May 22, 1987.

Horowitz, David. *The Free World Colossus: A Critique of American Foreign Policy in the Cold War*. London: MacGibbon and Kee, 1965.

Inkeles, Alex. "The Soviet Attack on the Voice of America: A Case Study in Propaganda Warfare." *American Slavic and Eastern European Review* 12 (1953): 319–320.

Janis, Irving L., and M. Brewster Smith. "Effects of Education and Persuasion on National and International Images." In H. C. Kelman, ed., *International Behavior: A Social Psychological Analysis*, pp. 190–232. New York: Holt, Rinehart and Winston, 1965.

Johnston, Anne. "Trends in Political Communication Research—A Review and Bibliography." In David L. Swanson, and Dan Nimmo, eds., *New Directions in Political Communication*, pp. 329–362. Newbury Pack, CA: Sage 1990.

Joslyn, Richard. *Mass Media and Elections*. Reading, MA: Addison-Wesley, 1984.

Jowett, Garth S., and Victoria O'Donnell. *Propaganda and Persuasion*. Newbury Park, CA: Sage, 1986.

Kaftanov, S. V. *Radio and Television in the U.S.S.R.* Washington, DC: Joint Publication Research Service, 1961.

Kecskemeti, Paul. "The Soviet Approach to International Political Communication." *Public Opinion Quarterly* 20 (1956): 299–307.

Kirsch, Botho. "Deutsche Welle's Russian Service, 1962–1985." In K.R.M. Short, ed., *Western Broadcasting over the Iron Curtain*, pp. 158–171. New York: St. Martin's Press, 1986.

Klapper, Joseph T. *The Effects of Mass Communication*. New York: Free Press, 1960.

————, and Leo Lowenthal. "The Contribution of Opinion Research to the Evaluation of Psychological Warfare." *Public Opinions Quarterly* 15 (1951–1952): 651–662.

Kneitel, Tom. "Secrets of Propaganda Broadcasting." *Popular Communication* 4 (1982): 8–20.

Kraus, Sidney, and Dennis Davis. *The Effects of Mass Communication on Political Behavior*. University Park: PA. Pennsylvania State University Press, 1976.

Kris, Ernst, and Hans Speier. *German Radio Propaganda*. New York: Oxford University Press, 1944.

Lang, Kurt, and Gladys Lang. *The Battle for Public Opinion: The President, the Press and the Polls during Watergate*. New York: Columbia University Press, 1983.

Larson, Arthur. "The Present Status of Propaganda in International Law." In Clark C. Havinghurt, ed., *International Control of Propaganda*, pp. 1–13. Dobbs Ferry, NY: Oceana, 1967.

Lazarsfeld, Paul, Bernard Berelson, and Hazel Gaudet. *The People's Choice*. New York: Duell, Sloan and Pearce, 1944.

Lazarsfeld, Paul, and Frank N. Stanton. *Radio Research: 1942–1943*. 1944. Repr. ed. New York: Arno Press, 1979.

Leatt, James, Theo Kneifel, and Klaus Nurnberger. *Contending Ideologies in South Africa*. Cape Town, South Africa: David Philip, 1986.

Lee, Chin-Chuan. *Media Imperialism Reconsidered*. Beverly Hills, CA: Sage, 1980.

Lee, Martin, and Norman Solomon. *Unreliable Sources*. New York: Lyle Stuart, 1991.

LeFeber, Walter. *America, Russia and the Cold War*. New York: Wiley, 1976.

Lenin, Vladimir I. *What Is to Be Done?* 1902. Translated by S. V. Utechin and P. Utechin. Oxford: Clarendon Press, 1963.

Lerner, Daniel. *The Passing of Traditional Society: Modernizing the Middle East*. Glencoe, IL: Free Press, 1958.

Lindblom, Charles. *Politics and Markets*. New York: Basic Books, 1977.

Linski, Martin, ed. *Television and the Presidential Elections: Self-Interest and the Public-Interest*. Lexington, MA: D. C. Heath, 1983.

Linz, Juan J. "Some Notes toward a Comparative Study of Fascism in Sociological Historical Perspective." In W. Laqueur, ed., *Fascism: A Reader's Guide*, pp. 3–121. Berkeley: University of California Press, 1976.

Lipset, Seymour Martin. *Political Man: The Social Base of Politics*. Baltimore, MD: Johns Hopkins University Press, 1981.

Lisann, Maury. *Broadcasting to the Soviet Union*. New York: Praeger, 1975.

Lukosiunas, Marius Aleksas. "Enemy, Friend or Competitor? A Content Analysis of the *Christian Science Monitor* and *Izvestia*." In E. E. Dennis, G. Gerbner, and Y. N. Zassoursky, eds., *Beyond the Cold War: Soviet and American Media Images*, pp. 100–110. Newbury Park, CA: Sage, 1991.

Lyman, Stanford M., and Marvin B. Scott. *The Drama of Social Reality*. New York: Oxford University Press, 1975.

McClelland, David C. *The Achieving Society*. Princeton, NJ: Van Nostrand, 1961.

McCombs, Maxwell E., and Donald L. Shaw. "The Agenda-Setting Function of the Mass Media." *Public Opinion Quarterly* 36 (1972): 176–187.

MacDonald, C. A. "Radio Bari: Italian Wireless Propaganda in the Middle East and British Countermeasures, 1934–1938." *Middle East Studies* 13 (1977): 195–207.

McPhail, Thomas L. *Electronic Colonialism: The Future of International Broadcasting and Communication*. Beverly Hills, CA: Sage, 1981.

McQuail, Denis. *Toward a Sociology of Mass Communication*. London: Collier McMillan, 1969.

———. *Mass Communication Theory*. Beverly Hills, CA: Sage, 1983.

Magubane, Bernard M. *The Political Economy of Race and Class in South Africa*. New York: Monthly Review Press, 1979.

Manoff, Robert Karl, and Michael Schudson, eds. *Reading the News*. New York: Pantheon Books, 1986.

Margolin, Leo J. *Paper Bullets: A Brief Story of Psychological Warfare in World War II*. New York: Froben Press, 1946.

Martin, L. John. *International Propaganda: Its Legal and Diplomatic Control*. Minneapolis: University of Minnesota Press, 1958.

Masmoudi, Mustapha. "The New World Information Order." Document 21, UNESCO International Commission for the Study of Social Problems. Paris: UNESCO, 1978.

Mattelart, Armand. *Multinational Corporations and the Control of Culture: The Ideological Apparatuses of Imperialism*. Atlantic Highlands, NJ: Harvester Press, 1979.

Meyrowitz, Joshua. *No Sense of Place: The Impact of Electronic Media on Social Behavior*. New York: Oxford University Press, 1985.

Mickelson, Sig. *America's Other Voice: The Story of Radio Free Europe and Radio Liberty*. New York: Praeger, 1983.

Mills, C. Wright. *White Collar*. New York: Oxford University Press, 1951.

Mitchell, Malcolm G. *Propaganda Polls and Public Opinion*. Englewood Cliffs, NJ: Prentice-Hall, 1970.

Molotch, Harvey, David Protess, and Margaret Gordon. *The Media Policy Connection: Ecologies of News*. Evanston, IL: Northwestern University, Center for Urban Affairs and Policy Research, Occasional Paper, 1983.

Morley, David. "The Construction of Everyday Life: Political Communication and Domestic Media." In D. L. Swanson and D. Nimmo, eds., *New Directions in Political Communication*, pp. 123–146. Newbury Park, CA: Sage, 1990.

Mueller, Claus. *The Politics of Communication*. New York: Oxford University Press, 1973.

———. *Third World Television Access to U.S. Media*. New York: Friedrich Naumann Foundation, 1989.

Murty, B. S. *Propaganda and World Public Order*. New Haven, CT: Yale University Press, 1968.

National Public Radio. *War of Words*. Washington, DC: National Public Radio Education Services, 1982. Audio Cassette.

Nimmo, Dan. D. *Political Communication and Public Opinion in America*. Santa Monica, CA: Goodyear, 1978.

Nimmo, Dan D. and James E. Combs. *Subliminal Politics*. Englewood Cliffs, NJ: Prentice-Hall, 1980.

———. *Mediated Political Realities*. New York: Longman, 1983.

Nimmo, Dan D. and David L. Swanson. "The Field of Political Communication: Beyond the Voter Persuasion Paradigm." In David L. Swanson and Dan D. Nimmo, eds., *New Directions in Political Communication*, pp. 7–47. Newbury Park, CA: Sage, 1990.

Noell-Neumann, Elisabeth. "Mass Communication Media and Public Opinion." *Journalism Quarterly* 36 (1959): 401–410.

———. "The Spiral of Silence: A Theory of Public Opinion." *Journal of Communication* 24 (1974): 43–51.

———. "Turbulences in the Climate of Opinion: Methodological Application of the Spiral of Science Theory." *Public Opinion Quarterly*. 41 (1977): 143–158.

———. *The Spiral of Silence*. Chicago: University of Chicago Press, 1983.

Nordenstreng, Kaarle, and Herbert Schiller. *National Sovereignty and International Communication*. Norwood, NJ: Ablex, 1979.

O'Brien, Rita Cruise. "The Political Economy of Information: A North-South Perspective." In G. Gerbner and M. Seifert, eds. *World Communications: A Handbook*, pp. 37–44. New York: Longman, 1984.

Parenti, Michael. *Inventing Reality: The Politics of the Mass Media*. New York: St. Martin's Press, 1986.

———. *Make-Believe Media: The Politics of Entertainment*. New York: St. Martin's Press, 1992.

Paulu, Burton. *Radio and Television Broadcasting in Eastern Europe*. Minneapolis: University of Minnesota Press, 1974.

————. *Television and Radio in the United Kingdom*. Minneapolis: University of Minnesota Press, 1981.

Pohle, Heinz. *Der Rundfunk als Instrument der Politik: Zur Geschichte des deutschen Rundfunks von 1923–38*. Hamburg: Verlag Hans Bredow Institut, 1955.

Pollak, Richard. *Up against Apartheid: The Role and Plight of the Press in South Africa*. Carbondale: Southern Illinois University Press, 1981.

Poulantzas, Nicos. *Classes in Contemporary Society*. London: New Left Books, 1975.

Presidential Study Commission on International Broadcasting. *The Right to Know*. Washington, DC: U.S. Government Printing Office, 1973.

Public Opinion Quarterly. *Special Issue on International Communication Research*, ed. Leo Lowenthal, 16 (1952).

Pye, Lucien W. *Communication and Political Development*. Princeton, NJ: Princeton University Press, 1963.

Qualter, Terence H. *Opinion Control in the Democracies*. New York: St. Martin's Press, 1985.

Radio Nederland Wereldomroep. *Media Wars: Propaganda Past and Present*. Hilversum, the Netherlands: Radio Nederland Transcription Service, 1982.

Real, Michael R. *Super Media: A Cultural Studies Approach*. Newbury Park, CA: Sage, 1989.

Rhodes, Anthony. *Propaganda, the Art of Persuasion: World War II*. 2 vol. ed. New York: Chelsea House, 1983.

Richter, Andrei G. "Enemy Turned Partner: A Content Analysis of Newsweek and Novoye Vremya." In E. E. Dennis, G. Gerbner, and Y. N. Zassoursky, eds. *Beyond the Cold War: Soviet and American Media Images*, pp. 91–99. Newbury Park, CA: Sage, 1991.

Robinson, Michael J., and Margaret A. Sheehan. *Over the Wire and on TV: CBS and UPI in Campaign '80*. New York: Russel Sage Foundation, 1983.

Romano, Carlin. "The Grisly Truth About Bare Facts." In Robert K. Manhoff and Michael Schudson, eds., *Reading the News*, pp. 38–78. New York: Pantheon, 1986.

Rosenblum, Mort. "The Western Wire Services and the Third World." In P. C. Horton, ed., *The Third World and Press Freedom*, pp. 104–126. New York: Praeger, 1978.

————. *Coups and Earthquakes: Reporting the Third World for America*. New York: Harper and Row, 1979.

Ryo, Namik Awa. "Japanese Overseas Broadcasting." In K.R.M. Short, ed., *Film and Propaganda in World War II*, pp. 219–333. Knoxville, TN: University of Tennessee Press, 1983.

Saerchinger, Cesar. "Propaganda Poisons European Air." *Broadcasting* 15 (1938): 131–158.

Samarajiwa, Rohan. "The History of the New World Information Order." *Journal of Communication* 34 (1984): 110–113.

Schiller, Herbert J. *Communication and Cultural Domination*. White Plains, NY: International Arts and Science Press, 1976.

Schramm, Wilbur. *Mass Media and National Development*. Stanford, CA: Stanford University Press, 1964.

Schudson, Michael. *Discovering the News*. New York: Basic Books, 1978.

————. *The News Media and the Democratic Process.* New York: Aspen Institute for Humanistic Studies, 1983.

————. "Deadlines, Datelines and History." In Robert Manhoff and Michael Schudson, eds., *Reading the News*, pp. 79–108. New York: Pantheon, 1986.

Schutz, Alfred. *The Phenomemology of the Social World.* 1932. Repr. Evanston, IL: Northwestern University Press, 1967.

————. *Collected Papers I: The Problem of Social Reality.* The Hague: Marinus Nijhoff, 1962.

Scott, William A. "Psychological and Social Correlates of International Images." In H. C. Kelman, ed., *International Behavior: A Social-Psychological Analysis*, pp. 70–103. New York: Holt, Rinehart and Winston, 1965.

Shay, Robert Paul. *British Rearmament in the Thirties: Politics and Profits.* Princeton, NJ: Princeton University Press, 1977.

Short, K.R.M. *Film and Radio Propaganda in World War II.* Knoxville: University of Tennessee Press, 1983.

————, ed. *Western Broadcasting over the Iron Curtain.* New York: St. Martin's Press, 1986.

Siebert, Fred, Theodore Peterson, and Wilbur Schramm. *Four Theories of the Press.* Urbana: University of Illinois Press, 1956.

Sigal, Leon V. *Reporters and Officials: The Organization of Politics and Newsmaking.* Lexington, MA: D. C. Heath, 1973.

Simons, Herbert W., and Elizabeth W. Mechling. "The Rhetoric of Political Movements." In Dan D. Nimmo and Keith R. Sanders, eds., *Handbook of Political Communication*, pp. 417–444. Beverly Hills, CA: Sage, 1981.

Smith, Anthony. *The Shadow in the Cave: The Broadcaster, His Audience and the State.* Urbana: University of Illinois Press, 1973.

————. *The Geopolitics of Information: How Western Culture Dominates the World.* New York: Oxford University Press, 1980.

Smith, Hedrick. *The Russians.* New York: Quadrangle Books, 1976.

Soley, Lawrence C. *Radio Warfare: O.S.S. and C.I.A. Subversive Propaganda.* New York: Praeger, 1989.

————, and John S. Nichols. *Clandestine Radio Broadcasting: A Study of Revolutionary and Counterrevolutionary Electronic Communication.* New York: Praeger, 1987.

Soloski, John. "News Reporting and Professionalism: Some Constraints on the Reporting of the News." *Media, Culture and Society* 11 (1989): 207–228.

South African Broadcasting Corporation [SABC]. *Forty-Sixth Annual Report of the South African Broadcasting Corporation.* Johannesburg, South Africa: SABC, 1982.

————. *RSA Calling: Programme Magazine of the External Radio Service of the South African Broadcasting Corporation.* Johannesburg, South Africa: SABC, 1988.

————. *Our Corporation—1990: Annual Review to Staff.* Johannesburg, South Africa: SABC, 1990.

Speier, Hans, and Margaret Otis. "German Radio Propaganda to France During the Battle of France." In P. Lazarsfeld and F. N. Stanton, eds., *Radio Research: 1942–1943*. 1944. Repr., New York: Arno Press, 1944/1979, pp. 208–247.

Stephenson, Robert L., and G. D. Gaddy. "Bad News and the Third World."

In R. L. Stephenson and D. L. Shaw, eds., *Foreign News and the New World Information Order*, pp. 88–97. Ames: Iowa State University Press, 1984.

Stevenson, Charles L. *Ethics and Language*. New Haven, CT: Yale University Press, 1958.

Summers, Robert E. *America's Weapons of Psychological Warfare*. New York: H. W. Wilson, 1951.

Tatum, L. ed. *South Africa: Challenge and Hope*. New York: Hill and Wang, 1987.

Taylor, A.J.P. *English History: 1914–1945*. New York: Oxford University Press, 1965.

Theberge, Leonard J. *Television Evening News Covers Nuclear Energy*. Washington, DC: Media Institute, 1979.

Tomaselli, Ruth, Keyan Tomaselli, and Johan Muller. *Broadcasting in South Africa*. New York: St. Martin's Press, 1989.

Trice, Jan, and Dan Nimmo. "Exploring the Content of International Broadcast News." Paper presented at the Thirty-fifth Annual Meeting of the International Communication Association, Honolulu, 1985.

Tuchman, Gaye. "Objectivity as Strategic Ritual: An Examination of Newsmen's Notions of Objectivity." *American Journal of Sociology* 77 (1972): 660–670.

———. *Making News: A Study in the Construction of Reality*. New York: Free Press, 1978.

Tunstall, Jeremy. *The Media Are American*. London: Constable, 1977.

United Nations Educational, Scientific, and Cultural Organization. International Commission for the Study of Communication Problems. *Final Report*. Paris: UNESCO, 1979.

United States Information Agency. *VOA Today*. Washington, DC: Office of Audience Relations, Voice of America, 1986.

Van Den Heuvel, Hans H. J. "Broadcasting in the Netherlands." In William E. McCavitt, ed., *Broadcasting Around the World*, pp. 287–298. Blue Ridge Summit, PA: Tab Books, 1981.

Varis, Tapio. *The Impact of Transnational Corporations on Communication*. Tampere, Finland: Tampere Peace Research Institute, 1975.

———. "The International Flow of Television Programs." *Journal of Communication* 34 (1984): 143–152.

Venter, Fanus. "Editorial." *RSA Calling: Programme Magazine of the External Radio Service of the South African Broadcasting Corporation*, p. 3. 1988.

Voice of America [VOA]. *Broadcasting for the 90's*. Washington, DC: VOA, 1990.

Whitaker, Urban G. *Propaganda and International Relations*. San Francisco: Chandler, 1962.

Whitton, John, and Arthur Larson. *Propaganda: Toward Disarmament in the War of Words*. Dobbs Ferry, NY: Oceana, 1964.

Whitton, John B., and John H. Herz. "Radio Propaganda in International Politics." In H. W. Childs and J. B. Whitton, eds., *Propaganda by Short Wave*, pp. 1–48. Princeton, NJ: Princeton University Press, 1942.

"Will We See the Real War?" *Newsweek*, 14 January 1991, p. 19.

World Bank. *World Development Report 1984*. New York: Oxford University Press, 1984.

Wright, Charles R. "Mass Communication Rediscovered: Its Past and Future in American Sociology." In Sandra J. Ball-Rokeach and Muriel G. Cantor, eds., *Media, Audience and Social Structure*, pp. 22–23. Beverly Hills, CA: Sage, 1986.

Yaroshenko, Vladmir. "Broadcasting in Russia." In William E. McCavitt, ed., *Broadcasting around the World*, pp. 52–75. Blue Ridge Summit, PA: Tab Books, 1981.

Zartman, William. "Political Science." In L. Binder, ed., *The Study of the Middle East*, pp. 22–47. New York: Wiley, 1976.

Zassoursky, Yassen and Sergei Losev. "The MacBride Report: A Soviet Analysis." In G. Gerbner and M. Siefert, eds., *World Communications: A Handbook*, pp. 257–260. New York: Longman, 1984.

Zeman, Zbynek A. *Nazi Propaganda*. London: Oxford University Press, 1964.

Author Index

Subject Index

About the Author

PHILO C. WASBURN is Associate Professor of Sociology at Purdue University. A founding member of the American Sociological Association Section on Political Sociology, he is the author of *Political Sociology: Approaches, Concepts, Hypotheses* and the series editor of *Research in Political Sociology*. He has published numerous articles on political socialization and the role of cognition in political life.